Human Resources Management and the Total Quality Imperative

Human Resources Management and the Total Quality Imperative

Carla C. Carter

amacom

American Management Association

New York • Atlanta • Boston • Chicago • Kansas City • San Francisco • Washington, D.C.
Brussels • Toronto • Mexico City • Tokyo

Library of Congress Cataloging-in-Publication Data

Carter, Carla C.
    Human resources management and the total quality imperative /
Carla C. Carter.
        p.   cm.
    Includes bibliographical references and index.
    ISBN 0-8144-5081-4
    1. Personnel management.   2 Total quality management.   I. Title.
    HF5549.C2956   1993
    658.3'14—dc20   93-27964
                                                                         CIP

Printing number

10   9   8   7   6   5   4   3   2   1

This book is dedicated to all of my human resources colleagues across the nation who continuously strive to improve their organizations and develop their people, and to Total Quality champions everywhere.

Contents

Acknowledgments

No book should begin without acknowledging all of the important people who were responsible for it in one way or another. This book is no different. Often, I have felt that I must have led a charmed life in my career. I have had the unusual opportunity to interact with, work with, and learn from some of the best people in this land. Without them, this book would never have been a reality.

First and foremost, I wish to thank Allan Cohen, professor at Babson College in Massachusetts, without whom I would not have taken my career in large-scale change so seriously. Both Allan and his writing partner, David Bradford, professor at Stanford University, have helped me immensely to understand leadership and take steps toward understanding the role of an empowering manager.

I would also like to thank my friend and colleague Bill Werther, professor at the University of Miami, for encouraging me to press on with this book at the same time he lovingly told me my writing needed considerable improvement. Bill stuck by me throughout the book's writing, and his belief and encouragement were instrumental in helping me overcome those dark moments when any author questions why he/she took on the project in the first place.

Another of my early role models was Daryl Conner, president of ODR Inc. in Atlanta. Although our paths cross only occasionally now, he was a key figure in my early learning about large-scale change, and without his teachings, I would not be considered an expert in this field today.

There are currently many important people in my professional life. Perhaps the most important acknowledgment I can make is to Jack Grayson, chairman of the American Productivity & Quality Center in Houston, Texas. Jack encouraged me from the start of this endeavor and offered the support and resources of the Center to me throughout the time I was researching and writing.

I also want to thank Lyell Jennings, president of the APQC Consulting Group, for offering me the opportunity to truly understand how best to implement Total Quality Management so that it works, and to Carl Thor, former president of the APQC, now with The Cumberland Group, for being tenacious in hiring me so that I could expand my knowledge of the TQM process in the first place.

There have been other important people over the two years it took to complete this effort. Adrienne Hickey, my editor at AMACOM, offered me the opportunity in the first place and Jacqueline Laks Gorman and Richard Gatjens assisted me in refining this text.

Jac Fitz-enz and Barbara Jack of the Saratoga Institute were extremely helpful in keeping my knowledge "up-to-the-minute," so that this book could be as timely as possible. Mark Edwards, president of TEAMS in Tempe, Arizona, also kept me up-to-date with his findings in the area of multi-rater feedback systems.

Cheryl Mulvihill, a courageous manager at Amoco Customer Service Center in Iowa, opened the doors of the corporation to me so that I might showcase their unpublished accomplishments in this book. Some of my government clients—Crane Naval Surface Warfare Center in Crane, Indiana, and the Veterans Administration hospitals in Phoenix and Prescott, Arizona—are acknowledged for the creative, successful approaches taken by their people.

John G. Belcher, a productivity and compensation expert in Houston, Texas, made certain that my content in a nonstrength area was correct, even as he was completing his own literary work. And the staff at the American Compensation Association in Scottsdale, Arizona, gave me many initial ideas and leads for this book that proved invaluable.

Of utmost importance to this book was the collaboration and cooperation of certain staff members of the American Productivity & Quality Center. Joy Holland, who heads library services, and Deanna Thompson, her associate, were with me from start through finish. Fred Bobovnyk, my desktop publisher, came through for me as we attempted to provide clear graphics that would express the ideas we were trying to get across.

Finally, I would like to express appreciation to my mother, who encouraged me in my darkest moments, and my husband, for supporting me in a hundred little ways throughout this project. My father also deserves acknowledgment. He taught me that I could be anything I wanted to be through perseverance and confidence.

I would also like to thank all the heroes and heroines across the United States who are implementing TQM and leading the way. My work and life have been personally enriched by many of them and are given hope and faith by all of them.

Without all these people, and certainly some others that I am sure I forgot, I would not have had the knowledge, the understanding, or the willpower to have accomplished this work.

Human Resources Management and the Total Quality Imperative

Chapter 1
Introduction to Total Quality

Total Quality Management, or TQM, is a system of management that involves all people in an organization delivering products and services that meet or exceed customer requirements. It is a preventive, proactive approach to doing business. As such, it reflects strategic leadership, common sense, data-driven approaches to problem solving and decision making, employee involvement, and sound management practice. Its basic philosophy is that the customer is the driver of the business, suppliers are joint partners, and leaders exist to ensure that the entire organization and all its people are positioned and empowered to meet competitive demand.

TQM embraces the concept of the internal customer, and in doing so, it distinguishes itself from past efforts that address improvement aimed only at the organization's external customer. "If you don't serve the customer, you serve someone who does" is a current principle of customer service experts. TQM respects this credo and uses it to ensure the alignment of the entire organization to quick response to customer needs and wants as a key component of the business strategy.

This alignment is not all that different from the cultures inherent in progressive, responsive human resources functions that have focused themselves outward toward all the other organizational departments as their customers. Truly, the most successful human resources departments in recent history are seen as key players in facilitating the business strategies that further a company's competitive advantage. Depending on the corporation's size and sophistication, these strategies can be as simple as hiring people of exceptional talent or as complex as restructuring the entire organization.

Certainly, some key business strategies are not anchored in what would be called human resources efforts, but no business strategy can be achieved without the dedicated commitment of employees. This fact alone supports the human resources function of the organization as a key player in the game.

Why This Book?

Strategies that align the organization toward meeting or exceeding customer requirements appear to be the critical factor in the success of both the company and each internal function. This book shows how human resources professionals can actively support and even champion these strategies, thereby contributing to and being recognized as true leaders of their institutions. The premise of this book is that Total Quality Management is essential to the health and well-being of any enterprise and, if not already embraced, must be championed at once. The purpose of this book is to convince HR professionals to take up the gauntlet and lead the transformation of their companies and departments to institutionalize TQM as a way of life.

While more and more HR departments have become partners in the development of their organizations' strategies, too many remain in the background as receivers of the TQM implementation plan. As one of my esteemed colleagues, Bill Werther, chairman of the department of executive management at the University of Miami, says, "Either the HR function contributes to corporate strategy or it too becomes unneeded overhead." Howard V. Knicely, vice-president of HR, communications, and information for TRW in Cleveland and winner of the 1992 Society for Human Resource Management's Award of Professional Excellence, agrees. Within the first six months of his arrival at TRW, Knicely had developed a long-term strategic plan that focused the human resources function squarely on the business. "What we did to position the HR function as an integral part of the business began to pay off because . . . the function is positioned to really support those things that are critical to making our businesses more competitive," he states.[1] In this time of flatter organizational structures, world-class quality, and empowered teams that virtually supervise themselves, these strong statements could be precursors of the level of influence the HR function will wield in the future.

If HR is to play a key role in corporate strategy, it must not mistake involvement for, say, creating new gain-sharing or team recognition programs in response to the board's or president's request for "contribution." HR must be a part of the decision-making team that *forges* new strategic initiatives. And TQM is a strategic initiative that is essential in today's competitive world. George Fisher, chairman and CEO of Motorola, told the Economic Club of Phoenix, where the company employs more than 20,000 people, that "we must set our sights on truly being the number one nation in the world in terms of the quality of goods and services we provide."[2] Motorola's TQM program has saved the corporation $3 billion and enabled it to regain or improve market share.

The commonly reported results of top TQM companies show that market share, competitive standing, customer satisfaction, and employee satisfaction all increase with successful Total Quality efforts. Likewise, cost and time to market are reduced. These are key barometers of success in today's world. The head of HR should be leading the call to implement such a strategy, not making it a priority because of others' direction.

Although this book focuses on the role of HR in U.S. organizations, there is much here that can be transferred to companies practicing in other countries as well. It is my hope that *Human Resources Management and the Total Quality Imperative* will be used as a guide to advance both the skills and standing of the HR field around the world at the same time it develops increasing support by human resources professionals for the Total Quality movement.

Before moving into the human resources role in quality initiatives, it may be wise to give a brief overview of the history of Total Quality for those who desire a historical perspective. HR professionals who are already familiar with TQM will want to skim this section and focus instead on the discussion under "The History of HR as a Champion for Employee Involvement," where this book's more specific components are outlined.

The Origins of Total Quality

Quality historically has been defined as reliability, serviceability, maintainability, or conformance to requirements. These definitions focused on the product and were used primarily in manufacturing environments, where outputs were clear and could be counted, measured, and inspected. Once the product was manufactured, quality control was completed, and that was the end of it. Products not meeting specs were sent to be reworked or designated as scrap.

In the late nineteenth century, one worker (or a small number of workers) took responsibility for the manufacture of the entire product. When U.S. companies moved into the assembly line orientation to work prior to World War I, many people began performing similar tasks and then moving the product along to another area, which performed the next step in the process. These work units operated as autonomous entities, seldom treating each other as customers and suppliers. Instead, foremen or inspectors became responsible for checking the quality of the product. As the assembly line became the norm, this organizational design flourished, and even service industry companies adopted structures that resembled functional "silos."

As the United States faced the tremendous mass production requirements of World War II, efficiencies were necessary, and sampling techniques and statistical quality control methods began to be used. Quality control continued to be focused on the shop floor, and products were treated like "burnt toast"—meaning the bad parts were scraped off so they could eventually be "buttered." This worked because of the lack of global competition, and, until 1965, little changed.

It was after World War II that some U.S. experts went to Japan. There, W. Edwards Deming and Joseph Juran found fertile ground for their theories and beliefs about quality. Japan embraced long-term strategy toward high-quality production, and a nation known for cheap, consumable products grew to world-class levels of performance in automobiles, electronics, and even banking. Figure 1-1 shows the quality movement's key players from World War I through the 1990s.

The Shift to Total Quality in the United States

Not until the late 1970s and early 1980s did U.S. companies begin to reconsider their reliance on inspection and question whether they were truly utilizing their work force effectively. During the period, efforts were made to integrate Japanese management techniques with successful U.S. practices, but the swell of world competition necessitated more than a programmatic response. Total Quality came to the forefront as a comprehensive management strategy and system. CEOs of some of the country's largest corporations began the shift that led to an enhanced way of looking at the bottom line: through the eyes of the customer, with a wider definition of quality as the yardstick.

Before anyone gets the idea that the word *productivity* is dated and no longer relevant, defining it as "input-output effectiveness and optimization" clearly makes productivity an integral component of a Total Quality system. The word *system* connotes wholeness, the entirety of the organization. While there are some world-class standards established that remain technically oriented, such as ISO 9000, more and more U.S. institutions are defining Total Quality in the terms used by the Malcolm Baldrige National Quality Award, which is administered by the Secretary of Commerce and designed to promote U.S. organizations' quality achievements. The Baldrige definition of quality includes critical success factors crossing the entire system, from leadership to people utilization

Figure 1-1. The quality movement's family tree.

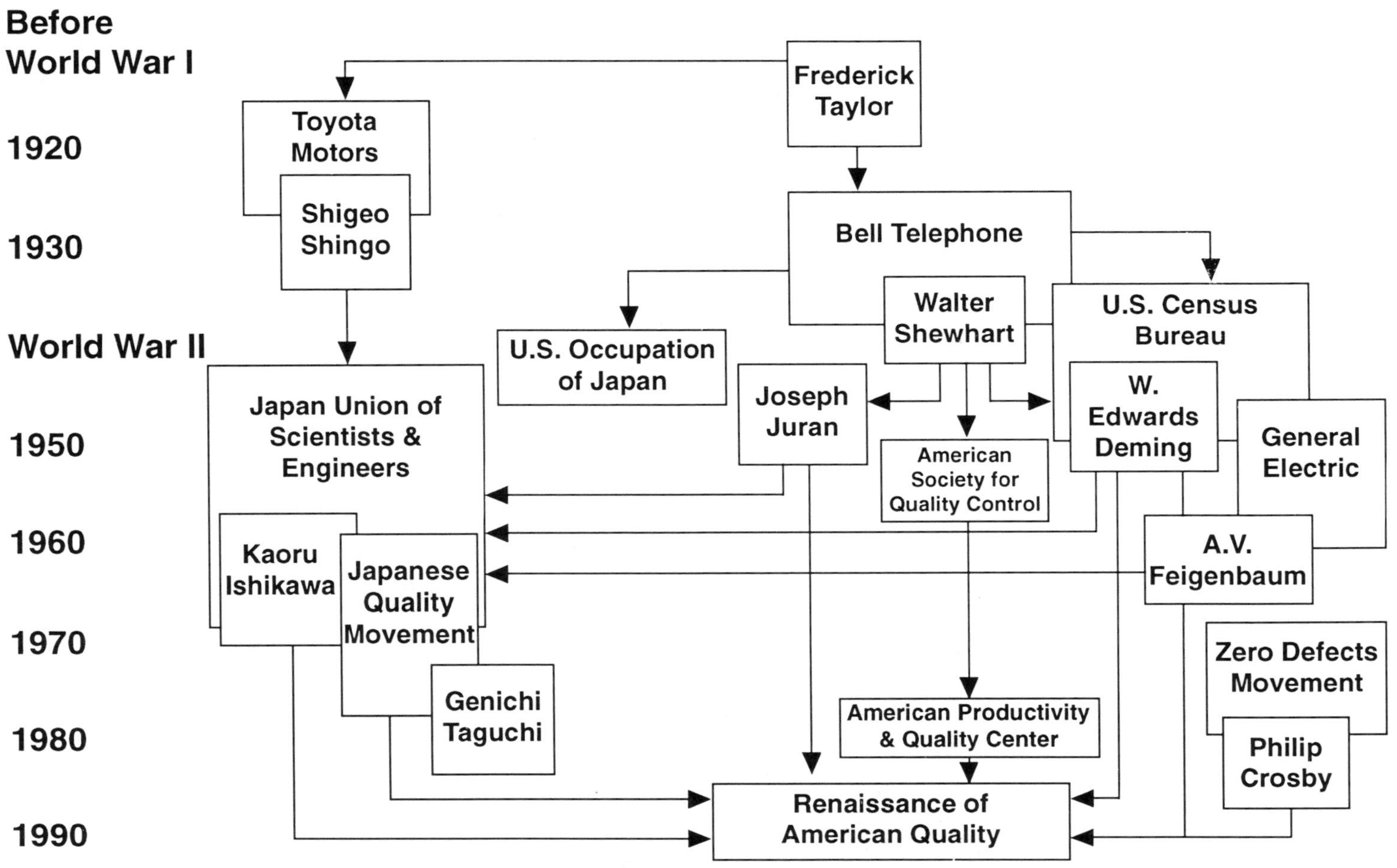

to planning and information resources. Naturally, it also embodies quality assurance, customer satisfaction, and the overall results achieved. Both cultural and process/outcome improvements are significantly affected by the factors included in this definition.

Many factors are responsible for a company's results, and the standards it sets are critical to its success. Total Quality defined broadly is an excellent standard because it goes beyond management practices to the heart and soul of the organization. TQM efforts instill new values such as teamwork and collaboration, develop new and fuller partnerships with both internal and external customers and suppliers, and make continuous improvement a way of life as people understand that customer expectations are a target that is constantly moving upward.

These new organizational principles support the need for lifelong learning, improved listening and foresight, and dedication to breakthrough thinking and innovation. Increased involvement of company employees leads to increased motivation. As stakeholders in their business, whatever the business is, employees find their creativity tapped. Rewards change to meet the new challenges work teams are facing. An understanding of the long-term goals of the business is realized, and performance shifts to include that vision. Bottom line, a transformation in a company's driving forces and the way it does business takes place.

TQM in Action

Everyone connected with the organization is responsible for TQM. Executives are expected to be involved both internally and externally with customers, suppliers, and key stakeholders. Many employees are given increased accountability for knowing what the customer wants and how best to deliver it. Teams of employees work on quality-related issues using any and all business information that is available. Those performing supervisory roles act as boundary spanners and resource garnerers for their employees. Coaching, not controlling, is the managerial way of life.

In a top TQM company, the traditional pyramid organization structure has been inverted. The needs voiced by the customer, and then naturally by the customer contact employee, are heeded as never before. Training is funded in knowledge and skills necessary to do the best job one can to satisfy the customer. Work is redesigned and organizational structures changed to meet marketplace demands. Power is shared and doors of communication opened so that all employees can respond quickly and effectively. All this is quite different from a traditional organization where layers of approval are needed.

While there has been some "TQM bashing" in the press, corporations that have properly implemented the effort as a management system ardently stand by it. Even in the largest organizations where TQM and its participative management component have had years to take hold, there are still pockets where managers act as heroes on whose shoulders all decisions must lie. But TQM companies are fast-tracking those who are building empowered work teams. And rewards beyond promotion have changed substantially.

TQM also supports the concept of employees improving and measuring their own work processes. Concern for such factors as quality, cost, timeliness, and schedules are reflected in the values of the people and the way they perform. These employees have been given the tools to develop their own measures of quality and even to conduct their own customer surveys or complaint analyses.

The use of information has changed in these organizations as well. All levels of employees in a TQM organization have more usable and available data upon which to make sound decisions. As a result, there is more employee input to both operational and strategic planning, and there is a greater understanding of short- and long-term goals and objectives. Increasingly, interactive communication is a natural outcome of such a management system.

It is crucial to understand that TQM is not a short-term proposition. In the United States particularly, many find it hard to accept that it can take three, five, or even ten years to truly change an organization. Quality professionals are sensitive to this, and most TQM efforts take dual tracks—one that brings continuous improvements and even breakthroughs within the first year and another that focuses the strategic quality plan on several years of initiatives, including cultural shifts.

One of the most valid questions about TQM is, "How do I know, or how does my organization know, that TQM is worth it?" Real statistics make a sound case for implementing TQM. In 1991 a long-awaited study came out of the U.S. General Accounting Office showing that twenty-two Malcolm Baldrige National Quality Award finalists had displayed significant improvements in four major areas:

1. Market share and profitability
2. Customer satisfaction
3. Quality and cost
4. Employee relations

The average market share of the finalists increased by 13.7 percent. Average annual customer satisfaction ratings increased by 2.5 percent, and quality and cost indicators showed exceptional gains. For example, reliability increased 11.3 percent, order processing time decreased 12 percent, and errors were reduced by 10.3 percent. (These statistics reflect annual averages.) One of the key indicators of employee relations was the number of employee suggestions submitted. An increased annual average of 16.6 percent was realized by the twenty-two companies.[3]

These impressive results speak for themselves and support the need for all organizations to consider TQM seriously. Hopefully, they also spark a realization in human resources professionals that taking up the gauntlet and encouraging immediate and strategic action toward effective TQM planning and implementation is a worthwhile human as well as business endeavor.

The History of HR as a Champion for Employee Involvement

As the United States entered the 1970s, headlines were asking "Is the Work Ethic Dead?" and "Has the 'ME' Generation Given Up?" Labor productivity was viewed as a problem. It was then that the United States began to look to Japan for creative management practices that could enliven the workplace.

Participative management began to take hold in a good number of organizations, and the results of employee involvement efforts began to show bottom-line improvements. The quality circle movement, which led to employee problem-solving teams, was advanced. These strategies may have been seen as driven by the chief executive officer, but studies show that staff departments such as HR championed these efforts in more than 50 percent of the cases.[4]

In the early to mid-1970s, forward-thinking HR professionals also began to understand and act on the need to become more integrally involved with strategic planning. Increased emphasis began to be given to human resources planning. Looking to the future even included sophisticated computer models developed to simulate an organization's demographics as far ahead as ten years. Succession planning was implemented broadly. Career development took its rightful place as a component of the annual performance appraisal system.

These efforts act as evidence of the importance of the HR function to a "well-oiled machine." Yet in regard to Total Quality Management initiatives, it *has* been the CEO who is the driving force. Corporate leaders have been on the cutting edge of TQM as a weapon in the race against global competition. Where and how often has the HR executive been the turnkey? In talking with colleagues around the country, and even some around the world, I found HR to have been the catalyst no more than a quarter of the time.

The HR Function as a TQM Champion

It is in many ways hard to understand what stopped many U.S. HR leaders from influencing their institutions to implement Total Quality. Perhaps the technical aspect of quality improvement is the barrier. If so, HR professionals will be relieved to know that the basic statistical tools of TQM require only elementary math skills and are easily taught to and learned by all levels of workers. (Chapter 5 on training and development shows clear examples of this.) But TQM goes beyond technical factors; it also involves cultural change, and it is here that a TQM effort needs the experience of HR. For example, the HR function has led many such efforts in the past. The HR function has consistently used survey feedback techniques to monitor overall measures such as organizational climate and employee attitude. The HR function also led the march toward participative management. It only makes sense that the HR function play an integral role in TQM efforts.

Perhaps it is the lack of familiarity with TQM that keeps so many HR leaders from championing its start-up in their companies. Perhaps it is the "wait and see" attitude that many people have about new efforts. If it is necessary to become familiar with TQM, that has become easy. Granted, some of the early texts on Total Quality look forbidding, but now there are many articles and books that provide simple roadmaps. And the TQM consulting field has mushroomed into a multimillion dollar industry, so there is plenty of help. If a cautious attitude is the reason for HR professionals' reluctance to champion Total Quality, then it is time for HR to step up to the table, given the excellent results provided by organizations that truly embraced TQM and implemented it well.

But the reason does not matter. If you are reading this book, you are already aware of the critical contribution TQM can make to your organization. Perhaps you are even one of its champions. If your organization has initiated a TQM effort, research shows that you will be involved in several key aspects of it, whether you want to or not.

This book is meant for any and all of you. Chapters 2, 3, 4, 5, and 6 highlight where the special expertise of HR professionals will be a necessity for successful TQM implementations. Chapters 7, 8, 9, 10, 11, and 12 highlight where your expertise will be a boon to the effort, and Chapters 13 and 14 show you what you can do in your own function to lead the way in your organization. My hope in writing this book is that you will not only consider championing this effort in your organization but, as you journey through it, you will look forward to developing the skills and knowledge that ready you to respond.

Chapter 2

Human Resources and Total Quality Efforts

The human resources function has been supporting Total Quality efforts in one way or another since their inception. In reviewing more than 100 case studies about productivity and quality written since the late 1980s, before Total Quality became well-known, different companies were experimenting with different approaches that affected the way people worked, the way they were paid, the way they were recognized, etc. The HR staff was often asked to assist in one or another aspect of the change. Even if an outside consultant was brought in—say, to create a gain-sharing program—an HR representative most likely sat on the team to help. This chapter gives an overview of the major areas of HR involvement in Total Quality and briefly discusses other areas of the HR function that are being affected in today's Total Quality movement.

Primary Areas of Involvement

Four areas in the typical charter of human resources are clearly primary areas of involvement in quality efforts. These four areas are:

1. Employee involvement
2. Employee recognition
3. Training and development
4. Compensation

Let's look at each of these from a macro perspective.

Employee Involvement

The employee involvement (EI) movement of the 1970s was instigated as often by staff groups supporting participative management techniques as it was by the executive management team. This shows that the human resources function was carrying the banner for increased productivity and a better labor-management climate well before the introduction of TQM. Why? Perhaps it was because HR is the function that is closest to one of management's key customers—its employees. Perhaps it was because HR's training divisions are generally partly responsible for management development, and the results of early research supported participative techniques—so naturally, training professionals did too. Perhaps productivity decreases had become so rampant and inflation such an obstacle to employee satisfaction with pay that the HR function had to bring creative solutions to the table. These early efforts helped organizations to develop some skills and gain some experience that will help them to make the changes inherent in a Total Quality culture.

There are many ways that human resources professionals have been supporting EI efforts. The four most common are (1) idea generation programs, (2) employee surveys, (3) teaming efforts, and (4) other participation opportunities. Let's cover each one separately.

Idea Generation

Idea generation is most closely linked with suggestion programs, which have long been a common way of soliciting employees' ideas. However, suggestion programs have not always been totally successful. Employees complain about how long it takes to see if their suggestions are adopted. Supervisors sometimes feel the programs are just a way to get them to implement something they have already heard about and turned down. Higher-level management believes in the principle behind suggestion programs but sometimes questions if they are worth the money.

The recent evidence supporting suggestion programs comes from Japan. Once again, the effectiveness of similar programs in that country teaches America a lesson. Not only are significantly more suggestions per employee submitted in Japan, significantly more are adopted.

In the United States, suggestion systems have not been given the top-management support or recognition they deserve. Enhancing them now is important because of the need to harness the creativity of the work force. In addition, suggestion program processes and results are receiving more attention since becoming one of the measures of human resources effectiveness for the Malcolm Baldrige National Quality Award.

Maybe the motivation is not as important as the outcome. The General Accounting Office study cited in Chapter 1 showed an average increase of 16.6 percent annually in the number of suggestions submitted in the responding companies.

Other methods of ferreting out employee suggestions have been attempted. Special promotions asking employees for their ideas about a specific issue are somewhat common. Usually there are prizes for the best idea; sometimes everyone submitting an idea gets a prize. Or instead of a prize, the best idea giver might get a letter of commendation in his/her personnel file.

You can probably think of other types of idea-generation initiatives you have been involved with. You can probably also remember just being asked for your ideas, or just asking others. It is surprising that this simple concept has not always been a common method. Some examples of exceptional idea-generation efforts are outlined in Chapter 3. For now, suffice it to say that the time has finally arrived for excellence in these efforts.

Employee Surveys

The employee opinion survey is another technique that has been around for many years, but again, its use has not necessarily been optimized. General morale and job satisfaction questions have been the focus of most climate surveys, with questions on management effectiveness, communications, wages and benefits, etc. Only recently have organizations begun to look at employees as internal customers and asked their opinion about quality or other actual business issues.

Another data-gathering technique gaining momentum is the focus group. Initially a market research technique with consumers, this way of soliciting feedback is perhaps less scientific than a solid random sample of employee surveys, but it does bring rich information to management relatively quickly about a whole host of issues. Even more powerful is combining the above two techniques by distributing a reliable sample of surveys and following that up with employee focus groups that can elaborate on the written results.

One of the most creative outcomes of survey results I've seen was the 1991 creation of action teams throughout a major decentralized food supplier. The company had kicked off its Total Quality effort with management and supervisory training to prepare them for new expectations regarding their future roles. During this time, a large sample of employees across the country were surveyed—not with a typical climate survey, but with a survey whose questions mirrored the content of the Malcolm Baldrige National Quality Award criteria. The analysis of results naturally highlighted many strengths and areas for opportunity for the company. Top management then made the survey data the basis for initial quality improvement projects systemwide, asked managers and supervisors to coach the improvement effort, and used the survey results as the initial baseline against which to measure progress over time.

However a company decides to collect employee feedback, its *use* is the critical component of effectiveness. No manner of communicating the results will have any meaning over time if employees don't see and experience any change from their input. There are thousands of cynical people in organizations not only because they are poorly motivated, are managed inappropriately, or work in ill-designed jobs or work structures. They are also cynical because they have given their input and been ignored.

This is not always the case, and I am not indicting all of American industry for asking for and then ignoring employee feedback. I am merely saying that it happens much more often than it should, and that when it does, it adds more fuel to the fire that Americans just don't care. However, there is evidence in organizations implementing Total Quality that employee surveys are excellent indicators of satisfaction and, just as important, solid baselines for measuring both management and system improvement.

Teaming Efforts

On the surface, one would think that the United States would have a very simple time instilling organizations with teamwork principles and structures. Look at the nation's love of sports. Sure, individual sports are admired, such as golf, tennis, and swimming. But team sports—football, basketball, and baseball—are an American tradition. Team language is common in plants and officer: who is quarterbacking this effort, who will catch the ball if someone needs help, etc. Yet the typical organization is run more like a military operation than a football team. There is a general, a chain of command, a hierarchy of authority, and so on.

There seems to be a paradox here. The military is needed in times of crisis. A regimen is crucial when in danger. The purpose of the military is to protect in times of need, and so it must operate a tight system. But do corporations need this type of operation on a daily basis when working routinely, when responding to customers quickly, and when solving problems either creatively or systematically?

In the 1970s, several forward-thinking companies began to experiment with team structures. This early form of teams included the already mentioned quality circles, which were formed from members of a work unit who met on a regular basis to solve problems. These teams were often led by the supervisor, who facilitated the weekly or biweekly meet-ings. As often, actual facilitators were trained to manage the process.

Quality circles were borrowed from the then touted Japanese man-agement techniques. But as indicated earlier, many of these efforts did not work well, and quality circles fell out of favor in the 1980s. Taking a moment to look at why they often failed and what was learned from them can help with successfully implementing Total Quality. It may also help us to avoid seeing quality teams and self-directed work teams as fads that will pass with time.

Most often the circle groups dealt with quality-of-work-life issues such as smoking in the workplace. Too seldom did the teams look at work processes and recommend improvements. Too few bottom-line results, like cost savings or customer service improvements, were reported. Those companies that really armed their workers with problem-solving skills and techniques fared better. In these companies, circle groups still exist and have management support.

The United States didn't understand that once these employee groups managed to have success with smaller projects that improved the quality of work life, they could evolve to improving work processes. Also, many circle groups were trained by in-house trainers who could teach facilitation skills, effective problem solving, and even cost-benefit analy-sis, but had little exposure to either industrial or quality engineering tools and techniques that would help the staff to bring home improvements more prone to receive management attention.

The other obstacle to effective implementation of quality circles was the lack of a managed shift in the culture of many organizations to sup-port this involvement initiative. Too often the participative techniques learned in regard to quality circles were not transferred back to the work-place, where it was business as usual. And even in some departments that truly attempted to imbue their culture with a new way of looking at and treating the work force, department heads spearheading the effort received mixed reactions from their own peers and superiors. They weren't following the unwritten rules of behavior; they weren't sticking to the long-held beliefs and norms of traditional management.

If the entire organization was not involved in the shift to a more participative culture, quality circles were viewed as just another program, and the rewards were seldom in place to support the effort over time. Management found that it had to stand up for working differently and sometimes even buffer its teams from someone higher up in the organi-zation who felt uncomfortable with or even threatened by such change.

There are other dimensions of quality circles that could be discussed here, but enough of the variables have been covered to draw a clear pic-ture of some of the problems that led to the demise of this movement.

The important difference between quality teams and the circle groups that needs reiteration is that the quality teams that are put in place in a Total Quality effort are sponsored by top management and meant to initiate a shift in the culture that makes continuous improvement a part of team members' daily lives; the use of the tools and techniques becomes a standard part of the way they work. Those that are temporary in nature—e.g., cross-functional teams—are also expected to transfer knowledge and skills back to the natural work units.

More complicated than quality circles is the movement to self-directed work teams, since this structure not only takes a shift in the culture but also threatens the actual jobs of managers or supervisors. I contend that as teams become empowered in Total Quality efforts, organizations will naturally flatten, and fewer layers of management will result. Not many people really say that out loud yet. But as self-directed work teams evolve, that reality will have to be faced. This may well be the primary obstacle to broad implementation of self-directed teams in the United States. But if our senior managers are as brave as they are smart, they will begin moving their organizations in this direction and rewarding those management teams that move toward more responsive structures and fuller empowerment of employees.

I have worked with enlightened work groups of managers who actually planned the flattening of their organizations. They believed it was better to act proactively as architects of the future than to continue in the current mode of reacting to competitive pressures or fighting fires. A more detailed discussion of self-managing teams appears in Chapter 3. I believe they are part of the wave of the future and deserve more than a cursory introduction in this book.

Other Participation Opportunities

Other important participation efforts have surfaced over the last decade in unionized settings. There are many reasons for the loss of influence of unions in the United States. Yet, if unions embrace the need to empower employees and take a leadership role in championing Total Quality efforts, their influence can again grow. When unions partner with management to improve the company, its competitive position is strengthened. TQM offers this opportunity.

I've stopped being surprised when I work with union stewards to gain their support at the beginning of a Total Quality implementation and find that they are excited and supportive. Many say that Total Quality embodies the very principles and practices that they have been seeking all along. So important are these players to the game that an entire chapter (Chapter 11) is dedicated to labor-management partnerships. For now, suffice it to say that if you are a human resources professional in a union company, don't withhold your interest or your organization's interest in Total Quality from your union. Educating union officials as you become more knowledgeable yourself may well be a step in the direction of building one of your strongest alliances. And large-scale change efforts have a greater chance of success if all key stakeholders are involved in the earliest stages and work toward the future together.

Other efforts have arisen that offer participation opportunities as well. One of the key components of Total Quality that has been in the forefront, even if a company is not yet ready to institutionalize a total effort, is customer satisfaction. Many companies have begun customer service–oriented efforts that use customer action teams (known as CAT teams) to look for ways and/or methods to improve satisfaction or better fill consumer needs. Perhaps some sincere thanks are in order to today's renowned experts such as Tom Peters or Karl Albrecht for familiarizing us with these concepts. Wherever the credit goes, CAT teams have been a positive movement in the right direction.

There are many other examples of participation activity, from placing an employee on a company's board of directors, to bringing employees more fully into the decision-making process, to establishing cross-functional task forces that address business issues. Regardless of the activity, employees are beginning to be viewed as key stakeholders in U.S. organizations who have the right and responsibility to be involved in improving both how the customer is satisfied and how the work is performed.

Employee Recognition

Some observers question the viability of recognition programs as true motivators. Perhaps this is because, generally, only a small percentage of employees are singled out for recognition. Perhaps this is because the criteria for selection are often viewed (rightly or wrongly) as too subjective. Perhaps the value of the recognition award is too insignificant. Whatever the reasons, there is mounting evidence that recognition programs do work if they are well designed and managed. For those who believe that pay is the only reward of value to today's work force, successful and motivating recognition programs will be discussed that serve a valuable purpose for both organizations and their people.

Let's try to put recognition programs in their proper place. In the world of motivational theory, recognition for a job well done still holds its ground as an important intrinsic satisfier. Yet employees I talk with in doing my initial assessment prior to a TQM implementation say all too often that they do not receive adequate recognition for the part they play in their organization's success. Even increased involvement in making the operation run more smoothly is a form of recognition of their worth, let alone formal or informal programs.

To further support the need for effective recognition programs, I want to cite responses to a July 1988 poll of 383 members of the American Productivity & Quality Center (APQC) on job-related motivational factors. Fifteen common factors were ranked. Recognition for a job well done landed in third place, with 90.9 percent giving this factor a four or five ranking on the importance scale. (Five equalled "very important.") Yet when asked about the extent of that factor's availability in the workplace, respondents said recognition for a job well done existed in only 54.5 percent of their companies.[1]

If you take into account that companies that are members of the APQC may, in fact, be more aware than the average of motivators that increase people's productivity and quality, that 54.5 percent may be uncharacteristically high. Another factor that could be making a significant impact on the obvious lack of successful recognition efforts is uninformed management. Edwards Deming says 85 percent of all our organizations' problems are related to management, so perhaps questioning management's commitment or even understanding of the importance of recognition to the human spirit is not as out of line as it may initially appear. Certainly, all human resources professionals understand the impact of this need in people and the inherent value that would be gained by both the organization and its people if recognition were freely given when deserved.

Flexibility can be built into a formal recognition program. This can be seen in the monthly performance award banquet held in the Service Product Group of the First National Bank of Chicago. At this impressive evening, the bank not only recognizes the most superior performance, but also the most improved, the most effective in a changing environment, etc. The teams recognized vary in structure from natural work groups to cross-functional issue teams to individuals on a team.[2] Several formal recognition programs will be cited in more detail in Chapter 4, which is dedicated to this subject. Right now, the focus needs to remain on the importance of recognition as a factor in an organization's success.

In fact, just for a moment, take recognition down to its simplest component—that of verbally expressing appreciation for a job well done. Human resources professionals sit in chairs of influence with managers, and yet, when holding heart-to-heart discussions with them, how often do the HR professionals recommend giving plain, old thank-yous? This is done at McDonald's, where both formal and informal recognition appear to be part of the culture. McDonald's management is trained to follow the company's 20/20/20 rule. When a manager arrives at a store, he/she takes twenty seconds to chat with every crew member. Then, during the shift, the manager takes another twenty seconds to observe every employee. Finally, at the end of the shift, another twenty seconds is taken to thank every employee for a job well done. Not too complicated, but certainly this behavior sends a "you are important and noticed" message to everyone.

Another incentive program at McDonald's encourages minors on the payroll to stay with their job. Unlike typical incentive programs, this one awards points just for every hour the employee works. The points earned can be exchanged for cash, merchandise, or even a college scholarship. And the program appears to reduce turnover early on in the employee's tenure, so there is organizational benefit, too.[3]

Recognition is important. Whether it is in the form of a cash reward, a letter of commendation in an employee's file, a special formal occasion, a plaque, or an informal handshake and "thank you," it appears that this is an opportunity area in the United States. And it is an area that most certainly can be considered part of the human resources function's charter.

Training and Development

To make this segment a quick and easy overview of the importance of training and development in a Total Quality effort, it seems wise to break training down into some of its critical components and show where it supports the change to Total Quality. There are three phases in a full shift to Total Quality. First, there is an initial planning and assessment phase. Second, there is an implementation phase, where teams start up; they evolve and grow as the organization seeks not only to learn, but also to reap returns. Finally, there is a renewal or transition phase, where an assessment of successes and opportunities to that point are blended with future planning.

The Planning and Assessment Phase

Assessment can take many shapes in a Total Quality effort. It may come in the form of a cost of quality assessment or an internal/external customer assessment. Another common form of assessment is to complete an internal audit against the Malcolm Baldrige National Quality Award criteria. Whatever form the assessment takes, internal teams of employees are often chosen to learn the methodology used so that the organization can become self-sufficient in repeating the assessment in the future. As teams analyze the data collected during this phase, they uncover areas for improvement. Assessment tools, such as interviewing and data collection techniques and skills are among the items that require training during this phase.

The results of the initial assessment lead directly into strategic quality planning, for which no special training is needed. (Facilitation of the planning session is, however, vital.)

Awareness training often begins during the planning and assessment phase. This training can include basic quality theory, an overview of the approach the company has chosen to take, statistical quality tools, and the manager's changing role. While application is not the goal, understanding and buy-in usually are. All management, along with any specific segment of the company that will be involved in the initial pilot effort, attends this training. Some companies provide awareness for all employees at this time.

The Implementation Phase

Most TQM efforts begin to be implemented in targeted segments or with selected projects. Those employees who are part of the pilot teams need more in-depth training and ongoing coaching in order to optimize the return on their investment of time and energy. Effective team and meeting skills along with quality tools training are generally part of a core curriculum. The ongoing coaching that is generally made available as part of the process serves both a development and a role model function. Depending on the topics of the pilot projects, specific training and development might be required to optimize the probability of successful outcomes.

Cultural change is an important part of the implementation. These changes only begin in the first year of a TQM effort: Generally, long-term cultural change takes three to five years to be fully institutionalized. Initial shifts start to appear in just twelve to eighteen months, but total systemwide change takes longer. During this first eighteen months, many different training and development efforts might ensue. For example, a leadership development program may be started to help managers learn new skills in participation and motivation. There may be training in variable pay systems, such as gain sharing or a pay-for-knowledge system. Coaching of top management teams may be needed to help the executive group change its own behavior. This group, along with selected organizational segments, might need increased understanding of supplier partnerships, benchmarking techniques, or a myriad of other quality-related topics.

Sometimes, having an outside coach is the only way that managers can experiment with new behaviors and have someone to talk with candidly during the transition. One of the important principles to keep in mind regarding the training and development support needed is that while there are some core topics and skills that must be understood and applied, each organization has its own special needs, and some customization will certainly be in order.

The Renewal or Transition Phase

If the principle of continuous improvement has truly been taught, then conceptually, Total Quality Management is a circular rather than a linear effort. Continual renewal and reinforcement are part of the process. As management, along with the company's employees, steps back to take a look at its own progress, it may see that for the organization and its people to continue to grow, there may be more advanced development needs and not just the recycling of initial topics or tools.

During the initial quality thrust, several other types of on-the-job or technical training needs may have been uncovered, such as literacy or computer training. It is also common to have discovered that a formal cross-training plan would have immense benefit. Finally, there may be internal consulting skills or other needs that have surfaced for the line managers or other internal quality staff. Actions toward accomplishing these objectives could well begin at this stage of the effort.

The training and development needs of an organization as it begins to implement a Total Quality Management process are significant. Chapter 5 is devoted to this topic and includes recommended curricula along with examples of some of the tools and techniques that HR professionals will be expected to know.

Compensation

The final major area of involvement for the HR profession has to do with the broad-spread change in pay systems. Variable pay systems abound today and challenge HR professionals continually to improve their skills. Not only have group incentives found their way into the workplace, but there is also a large array of gain-sharing programs. Gain sharing is not the same as traditional profit-sharing programs. Rather, it is a type of compensation program where on a monthly or quarterly basis, a formula that includes the outcomes of real-time performance results in a bonus (generally to all employees) reflecting the period's experience.

Another exciting pay system gaining acceptance is called pay-for-knowledge. This technique is related to the rise in multiskilling in the workplace. As employees learn more and more work unit tasks and can handle an increasing number of jobs within the work group, their pay rises to reflect their increased value. Both gain sharing and pay-for-knowledge are being instituted at an increasing rate. There are other innovations in the compensation arena beyond those discussed here; they are covered in Chapter 6.

One compensation success story involves a plant in Texas that discovered from its employee opinion survey that workers at all levels were dissatisfied with their compensation. Management knew that it could not afford an across-the-board pay increase. In a sincere effort to solve the problem, management embarked on an effort to install a gain sharing plan. A task force formed to look over the possible measurements determined that overall plant measures would be used so that all employees would feel that their work played a part in the outcome.

At the time of this writing, the plant is twelve months into the effort. Thus far, it has paid a bonus three out of four quarters, and the business environment looks favorable. Some initial confusion has been cleared up, communications have improved, and everyone knows what they are working toward. The measures appear to be sound, and the employees support the plan. The plant manager is encouraged by the progress that has been made and plans to ask operations to take a hard look at how they are organized and structured—a move he thinks will meet with a more positive response since improvements may pay off in higher bonuses for everyone. By the way, there are no longer any special management incentives in this plant. The gain sharing plan replaced all bonuses for any employees who had them, and so far, no one is complaining. This gain sharing plan succeeded because of the considerable planning, time, education, and care taken with the program's development.

Another success story involves a pay-for-knowledge system. In this plant, there was a large minority population who wanted career development but were thwarted because of literacy problems. The compensation manager decided to tackle both problems with one strategy. He determined that a cross-training program could be developed that included basic reading and math skills along with the technical tasks that needed to be learned by a certain group of work teams.

He was open and honest with the minority employees about the fact that because of the added curriculum, it would take them longer than some of their counterparts to move into the multiskilled area of the factory. But he was able to gain their trust, and as the first couple of employees were able to move into the higher paying multiskilled jobs, more of the minority population began to seek the opportunity. Over the three years that I watched his progress, the turnover of my colleague's minority work force decreased, the output of the work area moved from good to excellent, and recruiters had to spend less time in outreach activities to attract minority workers.

Secondary Areas of Involvement

There are several areas where the HR profession's expertise will come into play beyond the four primary areas discussed above. The consultation and facilitation skills of organizational development (OD) professionals are needed in holding top management planning sessions and meetings. OD experts are needed in enabling teams to develop fully and assume responsibility for their work processes. They could well be called upon to assist in organizational redesign efforts. OD professionals' knowledge of system change is invaluable in the cultural shifts that will be occurring in the total organization and in its various work units.

As a company evolves toward its TQM goals, the HR professionals who have expertise in succession planning and personnel planning will be called upon to identify the types of workers that will be needed at all levels. They may also be asked to simulate the organization charts of the future. They will help to develop transition plans or programs for workers who may be displaced. Or their creativity may truly be tapped as they are asked to develop a personal plan that finds a value-added place for all current staff in a flattened organization of the future.

Many HR professionals have expertise in performance management. Don't be surprised if performance appraisal systems go through a total revamping in the 1990s as a result of TQM. New research shows that multi-rater reviews are more accurate than traditional appraisal practice; with the downward cascading of supervisory responsibilities to teams, a shift to peer involvement in performance appraisal is already occurring. I cover this in Chapter 8. Another major impact of TQM on managing performance is the improvement of both standards and measurements. As work processes are aligned with customer requirements, outputs of the process will necessitate changing current expectations and, therefore, measurements.

Even very traditional HR functions such as selection and job evaluation will be affected by TQM. Work teams will be intimately involved with hiring and even disciplining and firing team members. Different skills will be needed in the workplace as cross-training efforts increase. Multiskilled workers will become the norm, and competencies of applicants will need to be assessed as never before in order to ensure that new hires have the capability to learn the varied tasks that will be required. Job evaluations will become more complex but may well lessen in number as this multiskilling effect takes hold. Whether the number of jobs to be evaluated lessens or not, those performing the evaluations will be dealing with more varied tasks within the job and tiers of levels of a job as a person comes on board and is progressively trained to perform all tasks of the work group. These issues are covered in Chapter 9.

A key to success in any Total Quality effort is a well-planned internal communications strategy. Some companies will house this responsibility in the public relations or corporate communications function, but even so, HR will be involved. A benchmark communications plan is outlined in Chapter 10.

Conclusion

A great and exciting challenge faces not only the organization embarking on the Total Quality journey, but also the human resources professional lucky enough to have a seat on the train. This book is meant to help you make the journey easier as well as more pleasant. When the way a person has worked for a long time begins to change, resistance or at least frustration is natural. TQM will mean changing the way the HR professional works. But inherent in that change is the possibility that the vision of a better tomorrow for the people of the organization—so long an important principle of the human resources profession—can actually become a reality.

Chapter 3

Employee Involvement: Moving Toward Self-Managed Teams

Employee involvement efforts in the United States are still relatively new. While we ushered in participative management because of our preoccupation with Japanese management in the 1970s and early 1980s, the majority of U.S. companies did not begin to change their cultures until the mid-1980s. Prior to that time, we tended to use survey feedback techniques to elicit employee opinions and suggestion systems to solicit their ideas. The advent of TQM, however, accepts full employee involvement (EI) as a cornerstone.

This chapter offers a basic model of employee involvement efforts, gives evidence of their results, and cites specific program initiatives. Finally, a roadmap is given for moving organizations along a continuum toward self-management. This chapter concentrates on the organizations and techniques paving the way toward greater empowerment of the work force because many companies are implementing involvement efforts as a feasible strategy for maintaining competitive advantage.

According to *Employee Involvement in America*, a major study completed by the Center for Effective Organizations at the University of Southern California, the revolution in employee involvement began with participation groups such as quality circles and has more recently progressed to even more dramatic work design and structure changes such as self-managing teams.[1]

A total of 476 *Fortune* 1000 companies responded to the USC survey, equally split between the manufacturing and service sectors. The four primary reasons cited for implementing employee involvement strategies were:

1. To improve quality
2. To improve productivity
3. To improve employee motivation
4. To improve employee morale

Interestingly, corporate staff groups led the way in being cited as the original stimulus for EI. Fifty-eight percent of companies said it was a staff group (e.g., human resources) that initiated the effort, followed by a corporate executive, VP level (47 percent). The chair or CEO was cited by 41 percent of the companies as the catalyst. Obviously, multiple responses were allowed, which indicated that executives and staff groups collaborated to bring about these changes. But this does not diminish the critical role played by staff groups in this revolution. Finally, the USC study demonstrated the positive impact of EI on organizational performance indicators, as shown in Figure 3-1.

Moving Toward Employee Involvement

Worker satisfaction and organizational effectiveness are key responsibilities for the human resources function, so fostering movements in your company toward EI and peak performance should be expected of HR professionals. However, many organizations' cultures act as barriers at this time. The cultural shift needed to make TQM a way of life is somewhat frightening, yet it must occur. Once again, HR professionals have the opportunity to act as the catalyst for the changes that must be made. Educating oneself about TQM, planning the strategy, getting the chief executive to commit to it, and beginning the implementation is called for now.

The following model offers a roadmap along with further evidence of the outcomes of moving across the "EI continuum." Figure 3-2 shows how companies progress from programmatic techniques to parallel structures to processes that are integrated into organizations. Thus, since survey feedback and suggestion systems are programmatic techniques, they fall to the left of the continuum. And since self-managing teams are a way an organization performs its work, they fall to the right of the continuum.

The Skills Needed

Varying knowledge and skills are required to move your organization across the EI continuum; they will be discussed more fully in Chapter 5.

(Text continues on page 28)

Figure 3-1. Impact of employee involvement on performance indicators.

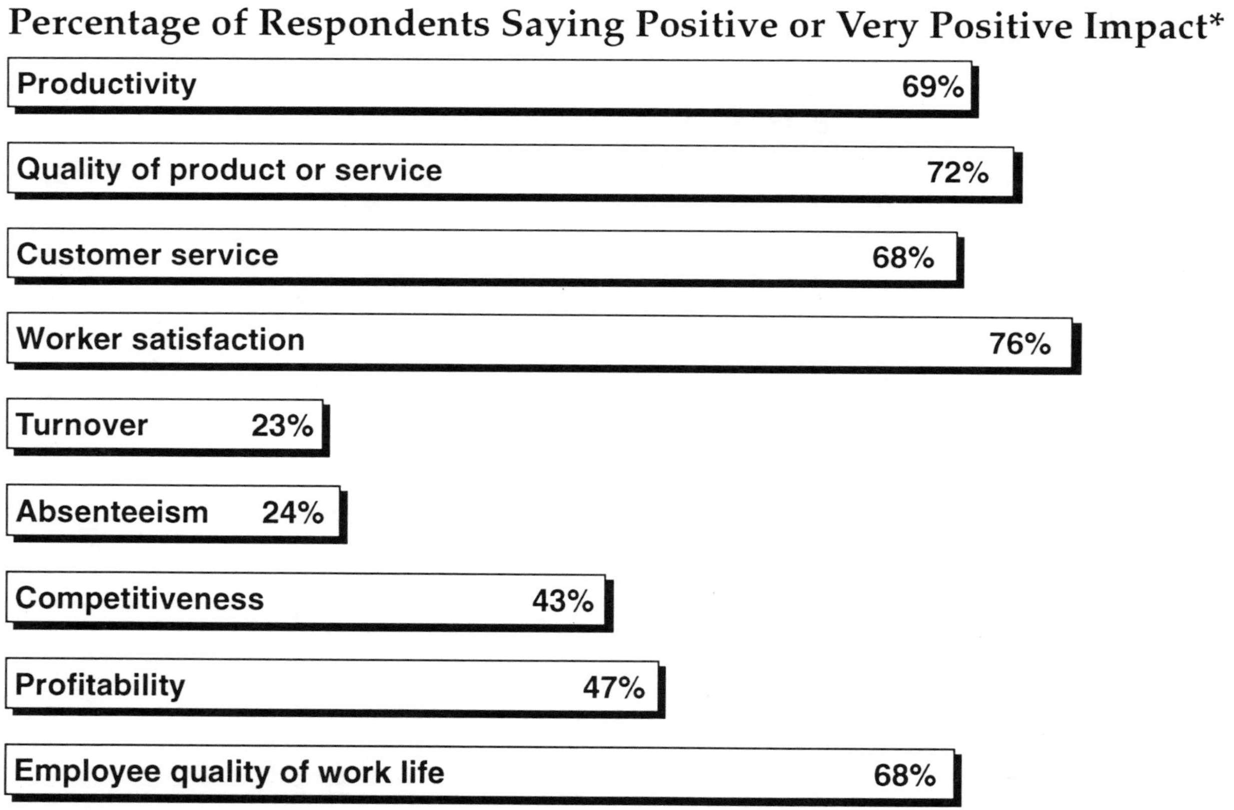

Percentage of Respondents Saying Positive or Very Positive Impact*

Indicator	Percentage
Productivity	69%
Quality of product or service	72%
Customer service	68%
Worker satisfaction	76%
Turnover	23%
Absenteeism	24%
Competitiveness	43%
Profitability	47%
Employee quality of work life	68%

* 4 or 5 on 5-point scale: 1=very negative,   5=very positive   Does not sum to 100 because multiple responses allowed

Source: Edward E. Lawler III, Gerald E. Ledford, Jr., and Susan Albers Mohrman, *Employee Involvement in America: A Study of Contemporary Practice* (Houston: American Productivity & Quality Center, 1989).

Figure 3-2. The employee involvement continuum.

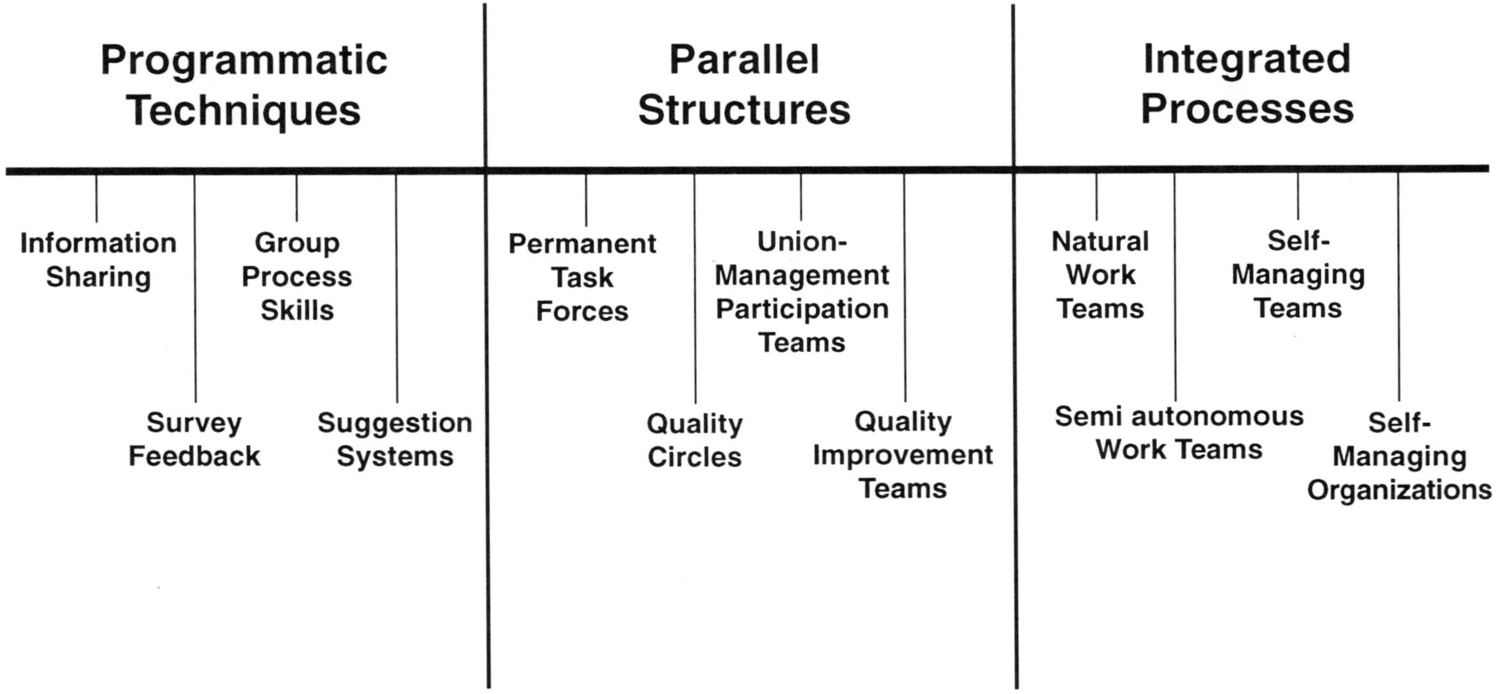

Programmatic Techniques	Parallel Structures	Integrated Processes
Information Sharing	Permanent Task Forces	Natural Work Teams
Group Process Skills	Quality Circles	Self-Managing Teams
Survey Feedback	Union-Management Participation Teams	Semi autonomous Work Teams
Suggestion Systems	Quality Improvement Teams	Self-Managing Organizations

However, the basic needs are mentioned now, as you and your organization will want to consider the current sophistication and involvement level of your work force as you begin to envision a new work organization. For example, most companies do not have inside experts to conduct surveys, so they hire outside consultants to design them or buy prepackaged surveys. Employees need basic skills such as communications and language proficiency in order to complete the surveys. With suggestion systems, employees need analytical and critical thinking skills. (In some suggestion programs, workers are also asked to do cost-benefit analysis, but many programs leave that task to the supervisor or approval committee.) Supervisors are also usually responsible for mastering group process facilitation techniques; workers do not usually need them until you are ready to move across the continuum toward team structures.

As you move toward self-directed teams, many other skills and an opening of the organization's "information doors" are needed. If you assign an organization goal to a task force or problem-solving team or ask a team of employees to improve their work processes, employees need skills in interpersonal relations, assessment techniques, group problem-solving tools, quality tools, team dynamics, and cost-benefit analysis. They also need access to customer requirements, supplier requirements, and short- and long-term corporate strategies. You can see that parallel structures (like permanent task forces or quality improvement teams) help employees become partners in the business of the organization.

The Structure Needed

Parallel structures refer to the new organizational structure that is instituted while the old one remains in place for the time being. The specific structures tend to mirror the current hierarchy in that senior management is involved, but they differ in that often other levels in the organization are represented. Once management establishes parallel structures, it finds itself being asked if its vision is eventually to integrate those structures more fully into the organizational process. The answer is generally *yes*, but on an evolutionary timeline.

These new processes and shifts in the culture often take three to five years to become instilled. (And in government, five to ten years is common.) In the meantime, parallel structures are devised to give focus and attention to efforts like TQM. Most people in organizations are busy, and with the short-term orientation of U.S. companies, these new efforts must be in the spotlight and seen as a priority. Creating a parallel structure, such as a quality council that has quality teams reporting to it, can help an effort succeed by keeping it near or at the top of every involved party's agenda. Otherwise, the effort could be short-lived and become "just another program." If designed and managed well, however, parallel structures prove effective and can progress to full institutionalization.

As you move to the right of the continuum in Figure 3-2, you can see that employees need knowledge of organization structure, work redesign, business systems, and personnel practices. In self-managing work teams, for example, employees are responsible not only for scheduling work, but also for hiring, discipline, performance management, and even budgeting. Therefore, skills that we used to assume were "managerial" are now needed by all players on the team. Leadership skills are expected now at all levels of the organization as the supervisor's role changes to one of a coach and boundary spanner. Employees take on more traditional supervisory duties themselves. This means fuller ability to apply conflict resolution and negotiations skills as well.

The HR function's strategic plan ought to include training all levels of employees so they can reach the place on the EI continuum that matches the organization's long-term goal. But before we head all the way across the continuum to self-management, let's go back to the beginning and cite some of the continuous improvements and changes that are implemented along the way.

Suggestion Systems

Suggestion systems—shown to the left of the continuum in Figure 3-2— are a traditional method undergoing change because of TQM. Winners of the Malcolm Baldrige National Quality Award have made current statistics of suggestion program effectiveness common knowledge. In December 1990, it was reported that the average number of suggestions per employee in the United States was .14 per year. In Japan, the average was more than twenty, with leading companies' averaging nearly fifty suggestions per employee each year.[2] There are reasons for the difference. One of the biggest complaints about U.S. suggestion systems is the long lag time between an idea offered and a response received. If management really wants employee ideas, it has to let employees know by how responsive the system is. Also, poor implementation percentages in the United States have an impact on the number of employees submitting suggestions.

One U.S. benchmark company is Milliken & Company, a Malcolm Baldrige National Quality Award winner. Milliken has what it calls the 24/72 rule. An employee's idea must be responded to within twenty-four hours and an action plan for implementation explained within seventy-two hours. This rule was adopted to show management's commitment to the suggestion system. Milliken recently averaged nineteen suggestions per employee, with an 88 percent implementation rate. The company began with a baseline average of .5 suggestions per employee per year, only slightly higher than the national average. This is a living, dynamic suggestion system with few peers in the country.[3]

In an innovative approach to suggestion systems, the Carl T. Hayden Veteran's Hospital in Phoenix added a unique process to its standard suggestion system. Once implemented, suggestions affecting a work group or department that fall within the purview of that work unit can be submitted to the QUEST Program, which awards $10 to both the employee making the suggestion and the supervisor approving implementation. All implemented suggestions submitted in the month then compete for a $50 award for the employee and supervisor. Finally, a QUEST Suggestion of the Year award of $250 is given to the winning employee and supervisor. Another year-end award of $5,000 is given to the department having the highest number of suggestions implemented.

This program is unusual for several reasons:

- It does not judge the worth of the suggestion. The suggestion has already been approved and implemented.
- A financial incentive is given to all suggesters *and* the approving supervisors.
- Dollars are returned to the department having the largest number of substantive suggestions, encouraging further creativity and improvement.

Teaming

Let's move on to more focused team activities, shown in the center of Figure 3-2. The First National Bank of Chicago provides an interesting example. Employee involvement is a vital element of the bank's quality process, and in the early 1990s, there were thirty active quality improvement teams in place. An example of how First National uses teams is shown in its response to external forces. In 1990, Illinois Bell announced a new area code for the suburbs surrounding Chicago, and an improvement team was created at First National to guarantee a smooth transition. Customers experienced no delays due to the diligence of this team.[4]

The Wallace Company of Houston, Texas, also uses employee teams for focused purposes. Its on-the-job training teams analyze steps of the work process—for example, the sales order process. Eventually, this type of team creates the ideal process flow, determines how best to measure the process, writes procedures, and trains all sites on the new process. Wallace also uses what it calls Point Teams to take on projects and address focused issues. For example, Point Teams were established in 1991 to handle the issues raised at a retreat on human resources. Teams looked at performance evaluation, employee assistance programs, career development, new employee orientation, and other HR issues.[5]

On a larger scale, Corning is committed to teams. Some are ongoing teams; others are brought together to solve particular problems. The organization's goal is eventually to have 100 percent of its employees involved in teams. In 1990, 40 percent of employees—10,000 people—were on 2,200 teams. Some are on quality improvement teams, some on quality circles, and some on corrective action teams. All are an ongoing part of Corning's culture and a way that the organization performs work.

In a report to the Conference Board, James R. Houghton, Corning chairman, said, "The secret is to simply encourage participation. With such a high percentage of employees participating, peer pressure takes over and others, not wanting to be left out, join in." Interestingly enough, Corning is also having better participation in its suggestion system. In a recent year, 8,000 of 16,000 suggestions were implemented.[6]

Teams also occur in unionized settings. Vickers AMD (Aerospace-Marine-Defense), in Jackson, Mississippi, is represented by the International Union of Electrical Workers Local 792. Unlike some unionized companies, Vickers was not in trouble before moving to labor-management participation teams; it just wanted to be more competitive. Its improvement effort includes a steering team made up of seven white collar workers and seven union members. Ron Modreski, former director of quality and now a general manager, says, "I always realized that teams were powerful, but I did not realize the absolute power of teams that are properly trained, that clearly understand the direction and are given accountability to make things happen—what they are capable of achieving." An example of this company's success with teams was an increase of first-time-through product of 15 percent, from 70 percent to 85 percent.[7]

Wheeling Pittsburgh Steel turned to teams because of crisis, including bankruptcy. Labor and management joined forces in a team effort that has turned the manufacturer around. After years of struggle, the company now sits in the number-two position in world market share in its product line and is regaining financial strength. I spoke with several members of the labor-management team, and they believe they would not have made the turnaround without the partnership. However, they admitted that they might not have taken such bold steps had they not been in such dire straits.

Analog Devices in Massachusetts proudly displayed the results of its efforts at a 1991 Super Teams Conference sponsored by the Manufacturing Institute, a division of the Institute for International Research. Analog says it keeps on track by linking team goals to end-customer needs, gives teams the methods and incentives needed to create impressive improvements, and has a system in place that provides performance measurement, feedback, and corrective action. Many of those initiatives certainly are linked to the types of tasks HR professionals want to be involved with. Let's look at the results.

Analog Devices looked at external measures such as defect levels, on-time delivery, and lead time in addition to price and responsiveness. Then it took a measurement of manufacturing cycle time and yield. For each measure, a steering team was formed with a number of cross-functional improvement teams under each. With results such as on-time delivery increasing from 80 to 97 percent and overdue orders decreasing from 1,300 to 100, the results speak for themselves.[8] Teams work! And, as a key principle of TQM, employee involvement is definitely a winning strategy.

Self-Managing Work Teams

Perhaps the most challenging of all EI initiatives is the movement to self-managing work teams, shown to the right of the continuum in Figure 3-2. With the barrage of downsizing in the 1980s, middle managers are naturally concerned with their own job security. The loss of power and status, generally hard earned, also doesn't bode well with traditional managers as they first consider the prospect of self-managing teams. So why have as many as 600 U.S. companies already made the shift to self-managing teams?

Cost savings is not the only reason. Improving productivity and quality, meeting new levels of customer satisfaction, and improving the quality of work life for employees are also reasons for the move. TQM will also accelerate the move to self-direction. And results from such efforts clearly show the benefits. Moving organizational structures toward self-management includes all employees; the efforts are no longer found primarily on the factory floor, as they were in most early implementations, but in all sizes and types of industries. And HR professionals will be looked to as key players in the game of implementing self-management.

As an HR professional, you will be involved in the transition in many ways. You will be called upon to transfer people from one role to another. You will be expected to know the implications of multiskilling the team members. You will be expected to recommend and make changes in your company's reward system. You will be involved in reorganizations that affect facilities design, job classifications, and displaced workers at all levels. All this means that HR professionals must develop new conceptual understanding and skills.

The insurance industry is one of the leaders in the move to self-managing work teams. One of the most interesting tales comes from the Aid Association for Lutherans (AAL), one of the healthiest insurance companies in the United States. During AAL's first year of transformation, business volume processed rose 10 percent, while a work-force reduction of 12 percent took effect. That same year, AAL inaugurated a new health care line of business that necessitated significantly different underwriting skills as well.

AAL completed its transformation in approximately three years, faster than most total systems change efforts of this magnitude. Today its work is performed by approximately seventeen self-managed teams of twenty to thirty employees each. The organization structure is aligned toward four regional areas. Teams are expected to complete all tasks from issuing new policies to processing claims.[9]

The role of the HR professional is needed during such a transformation. Besides your normal role regarding transfers, outplacement, or training, you might be called on to be part of an assessment or design team that diagnoses the current organization and builds a vision of the future. In a company moving toward increased employee involvement, many people could be asked to participate in developing the overall measures/indicators of effectiveness, establishing the baseline at the beginning of the effort, creating the vision, and implementing the changes. Top management often looks to the human resources function for help in such efforts.

In another insurance industry example, quality circles began at Shenandoah Life in 1981. Two years later, the company decided to pilot its first self-managed work team. After experiencing success, key players (including an HR staff member) held brainstorming sessions to develop the overall needs of the organization as it moved to total implementation of the functions involved in the pilot. In three years, Shenandoah's further deployment of self-managed teams resulted in a 53 percent increase in the average skill level of employees, a 33 percent increase in total work volume with a 10 percent decrease in the number of employees, a 37 percent decrease in processing time for all transactions, and a 48 percent increase in average number of service requests processed per employee. Employees at Shenandoah are proud of the gains made, and the company has received national attention for its achievements.[10]

Self-managed work teams are effective in other industries as well. Amoco Corporation is creating self-directed work teams in various segments of its operations. For example, at the Amoco Customer Service Center in West Des Moines, Iowa, a design team was created to analyze customer requirements, the organizational system, and the social environment. The team is employee-driven and makes recommendations to both optimize and control system variances. But beyond the quality-related activities, the team has taken on the responsibilities of shared management. Team members organize, plan, manage behaviors, and recognize performance. Their responsibilities also have grown to the point where they allocate resources, including the physical layout of the work area.

Figure 3-3 shows a blueprint of the work area before the layout was changed. Figure 3-4 shows the redesigned layout. As you can see, there is an increased customer focus with all functions moved together and teams created for quick response and total care of the customer. Both dollar savings and improved service have been the result.

Employee decisions related to their work have also changed at Amoco. Prior to being redesigned into teams, employees had only three basic decisions to make: what to send or say to the customer, how much work to do daily, and when to report work-related problems to the supervisor. Today, the following decisions are made by employees:

- Who does which work tasks
- When the team meets
- When and how to give feedback
- Scheduling work, lunch, and breaks
- Scheduling vacation
- When and how to conduct cross-training
- How to take a customer's request to completion
- How to monitor daily productivity
- How to solve work-related problems without supervisory involvement
- How to make and implement improvement recommendations

The manager of the customer service and collections area eliminated that position and has moved on to other responsibilities at the center. The majority of the design team goals were met and this new process has allowed for continued improvement. Success in the above area has led to further use of the process and establishment of more teams at the center. Other Amoco facilities follow in their Iowa sister's footsteps. For example, in a petrochemical facility in Texas, both the laboratory functions and the engineering functions have recently moved to team structures.

Thus far, I've provided examples that involved changing existing organizations. It seems fitting to share one now about a start-up organization—a Minnesota paper mill called Lake Superior Paper Industries (LSPI). Lake Superior began operating in the late 1980s and amassed impressive statistics from the start. Rather than operate with an expected multimillion dollar loss in the first year, the mill made a $3 million profit.

Figure 3-3.   Original layout before it was changed by the team.

Physical Layout for Credit Area

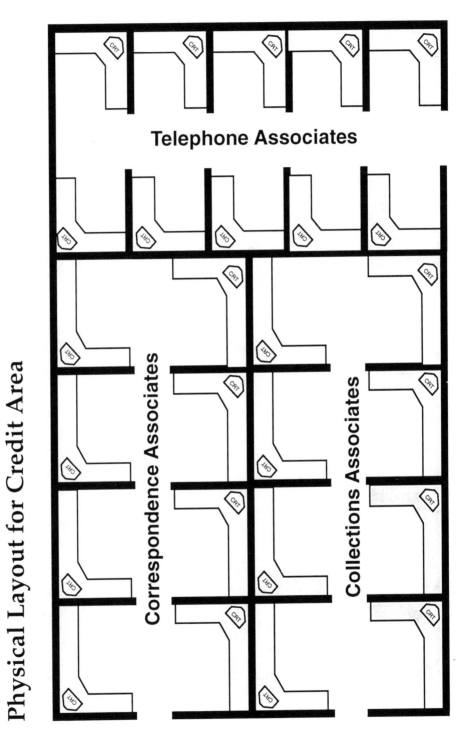

Figure 3-4. Redesigned layout.

Physical Layout for Customer Business Unit

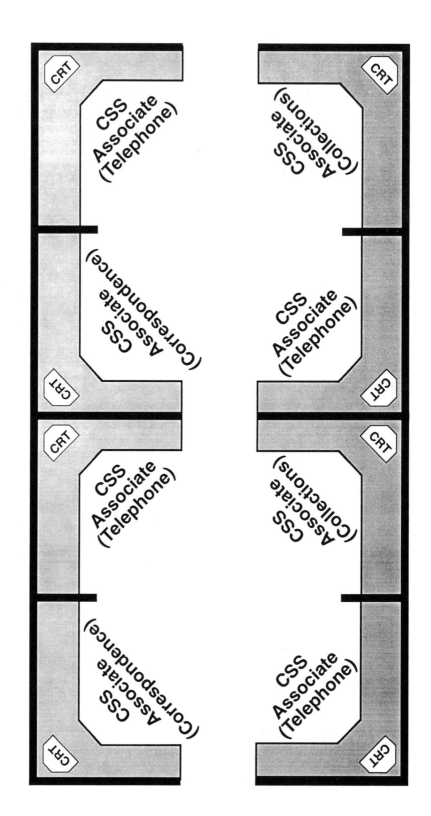

Shipments of 400 tons of paper per day were projected; over 500 tons was averaged. The mill is in the top 25 percent of paper mills in safety. As for absenteeism, the industry average is 3 percent; Lake Superior's is 0.6 percent.[11] Teaming is not the only factor in the mill's success, but it is certainly an important one.

LSPI's advantage of being a start-up operation and beginning with a clean slate cannot be underestimated. Managers for the different areas of the plant were hired first, and then the work force was brought on board. Management was educated in many of the concepts and skills we have already discussed, but it was also given an in-depth orientation to sociotechnical systems design. The sociotechnical system at LSPI was created by a design team that included the VP of human resources. The design team at Lake Superior is a permanent task force. Even once teaming is brought to an organization, effective design needs to be viewed as evolutionary—hence, the permanent nature of the design team.

Today, the manager's role at LSPI is one of an information provider, resource, and buffer. Employees make decisions on work schedules and assignments, performance feedback, team goals, and overtime. In addition, some of the more mature teams make hiring, terminating, training, and even budgeting decisions.[12] This is an especially good organization to look to for understanding how teams progress at different rates and how the team manager role shifts throughout the maturation process, since all teams were formed at start-up but are now in different stages along the continuum.

Words of Caution

Before providing you with a roadmap and checklist of critical tasks that need to be accomplished when making the transition to any kind of empowered teams, let me include a few words of caution. If management support for the change is lacking when a company is looking at the feasibility of moving to teams, then stop to build management understanding and support of pilot teams where there is a champion. Team structures do work. The evidence has already been provided, and everyone at all levels finds increased satisfaction with their new working environment. But as in all large systems change efforts, the effort is doomed without a sponsor or champion who will support the shift. And since teams have significant impacts on culture, a committed sponsor is a necessity to make it through the transformation. Especially in the case where a pilot is meant to provide on-site evidence to the rest of the organization, ensuring the highest probability of success is the wisest road to take.

Making the transition to teams takes time. Give yourself a minimum of eighteen months to begin to see some permanent culture shifts. (It is wise to build in shorter-term project results and celebration opportunities.) Culture change is not a three-to-six-month proposition. Don't begin with unrealistic expectations, and don't give them to anyone else either! A year and a half is like a millisecond in the life cycle of an organization, and the changes are worth a short wait.

The Change Process

According to the American Productivity and Quality Center, there are two phases in the process of moving organizations toward self-direction. In this adaptation, the first phase is targeted at management; the second is targeted at the work site itself.

Phase One

Step 1: *Educate senior management.* As with all major change efforts, initial education and determining the purpose of the change are critical for both direction setting and commitment. Management must see how the change integrates with current and future goals or it will not effectively perform its role as sponsor of the effort.

The role of senior management is time-consuming, especially during the earlier phases of the change. Not only do senior managers need to learn about teaming, they must determine the fit with the strategic vision. Once a "go" decision is made, resources must be sanctioned, target units selected, and an organizational structure established. Finally, in order to serve as effective advocates, top management must model team principles and visibly support the effort in word and deed.

Step 2: *Assess readiness.* A clear understanding of the current state will aid change agents and senior management in the timing and nature of the effort. Obstacles and barriers to self-direction need to be identified.

Certain key issues must be assessed, including management commitment levels, productivity/quality improvement history, resource requirements, organization climate, and critical success factors. A structured interview guide should be customized for use by an assessment team, which will conduct interviews and analyze and report the findings. This effort is worth the time because it will allow for development of an improved change management strategy.

Step 3: *Establish the needed structure.* A steering arm is generally needed to give focus and attention to the effort. This team, generally made up of senior management, often creates a vision of the future and determines the values underpinning the effort. The steering arm will guide and educate a design team or teams that will build and help manage the implementation plan. The steering team ensures the fit between the redesign proposal and the business needs. This body also governs resources as necessary and looks at the overall reward system or other corporate systems to ensure that they support the effort. The steering team can also be involved in benchmarking successes in other organizations.

The design team is made up of some senior managers and a diagonal slice of the organization's key players at all levels. The design team needs to get close to the customer and outline a recommended organization that will effectively and efficiently meet the customer's needs. The steering team also may be involved in talking with the customer regarding their future needs and visions. You can see that these two teams work very closely together. Their interdependency and constant communication is critical to the effort's success.

Step 4: *Select target units/review design options.* The steering team, in response to the design team's recommendations, makes the final decision on selecting target areas and on which design or designs for teaming to pilot. A communications strategy also needs to be developed at this time in order to position the effort well and keep employees informed throughout the change.

Once the organization determines whether it will move through the EI continuum to natural, semiautonomous, or self-directed work teams, the implementation is begun. It is generally feasible to implement change through the current organizational structure in order to enlist the support of middle management and frontline supervision. Training and educating these two groups is just as critical as training and educating the target area employees. Middle management and frontline supervisors must support cross-training of the work group, of course, but they must also support change in the organizational structure and in their own roles.

Step 5: *Educate work unit management.* Since I've already discussed the targets of training and education efforts, let me reinforce the need to increase team dynamics skills and knowledge of sociotechnical design, as well as to encourage awareness and skill building toward leading and coaching for management. In addition, the move to the concept of inclusion needs addressing. Middle management and supervisors of the target area need to be involved in planning the scope of the effort and implementation steps for their work units. Employee representatives should also be included early on. If your company is unionized, union representatives ought to be involved now as well.

Phase Two

Step 1: *Involve supervisors/work teams.* General mapping of current and ideal work processes is a good starting point once initial training efforts are completed. Customer feedback also needs to be communicated. General information sharing about the business issues and challenges also helps employees to support the change. Clarification of roles and responsibilities is essential at this time. The creation of action planning teams can now follow logically as initial efforts are kicked off.

Step 2: *Assess work team needs.* As employees get close to finalizing what the current work process is, it is helpful if they are involved with supervisors in gathering information from all stakeholders. This will allow inclusion of the important considerations in the creation of the ideal process and team design.

Skill building is critical, so conducting a needs assessment is a logical step. Rather than only formal training, I recommend that informal coaching by the supervisor in critical skills be developed in the work unit as needed throughout the effort. I call this just-in-time training, and its beauty lies in the instant application of skills needed to the work at hand. It will be discussed in more detail in Chapter 5.

Step 3: *Set direction.* Initial action planning teams focused on a key work process. Now, more teams can be created to fulfill many improvement objectives. These may include quick fix opportunities that were uncovered in the assessment. They also include teams whose objectives are to create the overall mission and vision of the new work unit based on information gathered in earlier steps. Finally, additional teams will be formed to look at the work unit's other work processes.

Step 4: *Develop measures.* Now that many teams are operating, training in measurement is necessary. It is critical to measure current and improved processes to determine whether and how well the change effort is succeeding. It is not uncommon for teams to discover that unessential work is being performed. Teams also often find a reduction in cycle time and a significant increase in customer satisfaction. If the efforts are not measured, their value may be difficult to determine, and the changes may not stick.

Measurement has other purposes besides building evidence for the new status quo. Measures help to set continual goals for increased performance and, therefore, for continuous improvement. They also are very important to the recognition and reward systems that need to be established. Finally, improvement measures can help to identify other problems that need to be addressed.

Step 5: *Finalize work process improvements.* Any work that needs to be completed in analyzing the key work processes must take place now.

Recommendations for changes should be prepared to present to management. Depending on the roles and scope of authority established, these recommendations may not need to be given to senior management, but rather to the highest levels of management affected by the recommended changes. However, the steering team needs to be informed early on about the overall content of the recommendations and to whom the presentation will be made. (Don't be surprised when at least some senior managers want to be present to hear the recommendations.)

Step 6: *Develop work redesign plan.* The final implementation plan should be detailed and should include consideration of everything that affects both the processes to be changed and the organizational structure needed to best facilitate the new order of things. This implementation plan should be supported by senior management so it can continue to gather resources, support the shift, and deal with any further obstacles.

A complete plan will also include the levels of decision authority that are being delegated downward. This includes decisions on topics like work scheduling, work methods, work hours, team membership, discipline, performance feedback, and information flow between teams. Any changes in reward systems should be implemented at this time as well.

Step 7: *Evaluate the results.* The final step occurs after implementation, and it measures the success of the effort against the baseline. This evaluation acts as a refueling for the organization to address the needs that are raised at this time in order to ensure ongoing progress.

Conclusion

As you can see, moving your organization toward employee involvement and self-direction is not a simple process, and the abilities of human resources practitioners can greatly aid the effort. Supporting the steering, design, and work unit teams is critical since the human factors are as or more important than the technical factors in achieving the visions set forth by the teams.

The following checklist is a brief summary of events and is included as a tool for ensuring the success of the effort. It can also be an effective communications tool for all organization members involved in the change effort.

Checklist for Transformation to an Employee Involvement/Team Culture

☐ Create a change management structure (e.g., advisory/steering council, design teams).

☐ Hire an expert if there is not one on staff to help guide the process.

☐ Determine membership and roles of change management teams (include all stakeholders).

☐ Educate members of the above teams.

☐ Involve key others in early discussions (including union officials if they are not on the advisory/steering council).

☐ Build a shared, tangible vision of the future.

☐ Develop an assessment strategy focusing on customers, employees, and suppliers.

☐ Create overall measures of effectiveness.

☐ Baseline the current situation to determine results of the effort.

☐ Complete the assessment.

☐ Create an implementation plan, and assign accountabilities.

☐ Allocate resources as required.

☐ Unblock obstacles to success.

☐ Provide necessary training.

☐ Develop and implement a communications strategy.

☐ Revise reward and recognition systems as needed.

☐ Clarify performance expectations as needed.

☐ Monitor and revise the plan as needed.

☐ Celebrate milestones along the way.

☐ Continually reinforce the effort.

Chapter 4
Employee Recognition

Clearly, rewards and recognition go hand in hand and play a great part in successful TQM implementation. This chapter focuses on recognition programs that are not part of the company's formal compensation program. It is assumed that the formal compensation program takes care of the individual's basic financial needs and that other forms of recognition are necessary to a comprehensive strategy that seeks to motivate people to high levels of performance. The more we learn about people, the clearer the relationship we draw between their performance and the systems that reinforce and recognize behavior. Therefore, mastering the ability to develop effective recognition systems that support quality improvement is critical to the human resources professional championing TQM.

Recognition is broadly defined in this chapter to mean any display that acknowledges, approves of, or shows appreciation for a person's or a team's actions. This definition allows exploration of everything from small, simple recognition efforts to elaborate, formal programs.

Recognition as a Motivator

There appears to be a dearth of books on the subject of recognition programs. Books on motivation, on the other hand, abound. As a result, making the link between an employee's need to be recognized and what are considered primary motivators seems a pertinent entry to the subject of this chapter.

All HR professionals have seen small, thoughtful acts such as conscious "pats on the back" motivate and inspire people to the same degree that formal events do. In fact, there are employees who are motivated merely by the realization that their superior entrusts them with responsible tasks and then leaves them alone, counting on them to perform. Since it is easy to draw the relationship between such forms of support and employee performance, one would expect there to be a plethora of such behavior in the workplace. Yet these types of actions, let alone formal or informal programs, are not as pervasive or effective as they could be.

TQM efforts are often a good place to experiment with recognition strategies that can later be deployed beyond achievement of quality improvements. But in order to build a firm case for increasing employee recognition actions to a strategic level, let's first look at the results of various employee attitude surveys as they relate to key motivators. Of course, money is usually in the top five answers on such surveys, but surprisingly, it is seldom first. Other motivators that vie for the top spot are being included in decision making that affects work or the workplace, sharing business information, growth and learning opportunities, approval/acceptance by others, and interesting/challenging work. This supports the thesis that job satisfaction indicators compete well with money as a motivator. (There *are* employee surveys that show pay as the most important motivator. Yet right behind it are feeling "in" on things and doing interesting work.)

The American Productivity & Quality Center completed a member survey on the subject in 1988 which mirrors many others. Most APQC members are well educated and gainfully employed; therefore, one might expect a different mix of findings. Instead, the Center found that its members mirrored the general responses shown elsewhere. Challenging work ranked first, and recognition for a job well done was third. Pay-related factors ranked fourth and eighth out of fifteen.

The interesting finding from this survey was not the ranking of motivators, but rather the responses about U.S. organizations' effectiveness in building these motivators into their operations. While 97 percent of the respondents ranked challenging work as important, 88 percent felt that it existed in their workplace. Not a wide gap here, but one showed up on another factor: 91 percent ranked recognition as important, but only 55 percent said it existed in their workplace. Another significant difference was identified when 96 percent of respondents said it is motivating to know their opinion matters when decisions are made, but a disappointing 68.5 percent said that this motivator exists in their workplace.[1] Results such as these show that American organizations have a long way to go in optimizing all that is known about unleashing people's potential. TQM offers a powerful opportunity to do it right—to build recognition programs and processes that have true meaning. Let's review some simple efforts first.

Informal Recognition Programs

If people's needs are taken into account when developing recognition programs, one can begin to see why and how the old cliché "small things mean a lot" remains true today. Pats on the back, while slang for praise, also represent an informal recognition program—one that met with considerable success among government employees in a major city that was beginning a culture change effort to become more customer focused in the late 1980s.

In a division of several hundred people, one manager seemed to understand the value of small, significant acts. She began a ceremony in the monthly staff meeting that publicly praised employees for exceptional service to each other as internal customers or to the public as external customers. Employees received a paper hand that represented the "pat on the back." The employees' pictures were taken with the manager for the bulletin board and department newsletter. This simple but powerful miniprogram did as much to reinforce high levels of customer service performance as did a more elaborate implementation of better electronic communications linkages between headquarters customer service and field representatives.

Another example of a small, informal program that supported idea generation comes from my days as the productivity manager for Arizona's Bank of America. The impact of this one program did more to convince me of the importance of recognition as a motivator than anything else in my career to date. The internal consulting team I was part of was responsible for establishing a productivity and quality effort. We felt that some form of ongoing recognition would help the effort to succeed. Our simple idea was readily accepted by both our customers and our boss.

Small blue satin ribbons, printed with "I Had a BRIGHT Idea," were presented to employees by high-level managers in informal ceremonies in the workplace. All good ideas, whether implemented or not, were recognized. Employees displayed their blue ribbons proudly at their workstations, and the little ceremony was looked forward to and discussed widely by everyone in the work unit. I realized how important this recognition was when I finally earned my own blue ribbon. I still have it.

A wonderful adaptation that combined pats on the back with blue ribbons was put into place at Katy Medical Center, a unit of EPIC Healthcare Group, located in Texas. After adopting the strategy to make "service at the bedside" its competitive advantage, Katy started many initiatives. One of them, the Blue Ribbon Service award, asks for nominations from patients, visitors, employees, and the medical staff. Employees who are selected receive blue ribbons. Those who are selected more than once receive a gold star for each subsequent award. Again, these employees proudly wear their ribbons or pin them up at their workstations.[2]

TQM has led to similar programs in all types of businesses from department stores to blood suppliers. Everyone I talk with says they work. These easy-to-implement recognition programs belie the need to develop expensive, formal programs. Yet many companies have them, and they too have value. Let's move on to a few good examples of these more elaborate programs.

Formal Recognition Programs

Formal recognition programs fall somewhere between innovative financial reward systems and the informal programs described above. They are generally organizationwide and run by a steering committee or staff function. Such programs usually begin with a big bang. There may be an elaborate kick-off meeting, write-ups in the company newsletter, and even awareness training. But this initial visibility can quickly wear thin if management doesn't actively support and encourage employees to meet the criteria established for receiving the recognition award. And as soon as employees (and even managers) see compromise in selecting the winners because of politics or other nonmeritorious reasons, recognition programs lose meaning.

This has happened with many Employee of the Month programs, where the selection committee acts upon a belief that equal distribution among departments is as important a criterion as performance. This dilutes the effectiveness of the award by choosing lesser performing employees just because "it's time someone from department X wins." Nothing will kill enthusiasm or credibility faster than recognizing people who don't deserve it.

Formal recognition programs' criteria demand careful attention from the start. Since many employees seek opportunities for recognition, management must carefully consider what performance or results it wants to reward, because a well-designed motivational program *will* influence behavior. Whether teamwork, ideas, or improvements are the goal, the program must be guided by clearly communicated and easily measured standards. Formal programs usually have clear winners. Not everyone submitting an idea, providing exceptional service, etc., is chosen for recognition. Many employees put in earnest efforts and are disappointed when they are not selected. This emphasizes the very real need to take special care with such programs, since the winner/loser aspect can be counterproductive.

The many components of such a program must be developed well. For example, even the people selected to act on the panel that chooses the winners are important: It is wise to appoint a cross-section of the organization so that all types of functions and employees are represented. (Of course, formal recognition programs within functions can be decided by the personnel of that function.) The diagonal slice of the organization can symbolize to employees that this program is not another "same old thing" that recognizes the "same old people."

A communications strategy should be part of implementing TQM, and a portion of it should focus on the tactics used to foster new reward and recognition programs. The goal of the communications effort should be to bring the right message to the right people at the right time. Promotional campaigns to encourage nominations and publicize winners need to be the cornerstones for continuing momentum, along with consistently sustained emphasis by top management as to the worth of the recognition. In fact, receiving such an award would be an excellent point for review at performance appraisal time.

Selection of the award itself is also key. A trip to Sea World in San Diego will excite employees of an operation in Lincoln, Nebraska, but it may well be unsatisfactory for employees based in Los Angeles. Whatever the award, it must have value to the recipient.

Planning the recognition event is another important consideration. Depending on the organization's culture, the event can be held in as simple a place as the company auditorium or as fancy a place as an expensive restaurant. No matter what the location or how elaborate the event, it must be well orchestrated and played out.

Here is a summary of the key components of a successful formal recognition program. The necessary steps are:

Step 1:   Develop the purpose of the program.
Step 2:   Create criteria for selecting winners that reflect program goals.
Step 3:   Develop the process for program administration and determining award winners.
Step 4:   Communicate the program goals and standards of measurement.
Step 5:   Select a panel of judges.
Step 6:   Offer appropriate training, if necessary.
Step 7:   Select the awards.
Step 8:   Plan the recognition event, if applicable.
Step 9:   Select the winners.
Step 10:   Celebrate!

Model Programs

There are many examples of excellent formal recognition programs. Citing only a few is a challenge. Let's start in the banking industry with a program called Legend in the Making. Baybanks, a New England holding company, decided in the late 1980s that a qualitative, subjective program would motivate frontline employees to deliver exceptional service. A traditional kickoff was held, followed by training for the branch managers, who would in turn communicate the details of the program to their employees. "Superior service" was left loosely defined and could be reported by a peer, a manager, or a customer. Both a form and a phone line were established for making nominations.

Several levels of prizes were created, for which employees received credits toward progressively nicer rewards. The first level of reward was a tote bag; the second was a Baybanks watch. Many employees earned these.

Two further levels of recognition were established. Every month, a small number of Legend Makers were named, and they dined with senior management and earned special plaques. Every fourth month, five top performers were selected to be Baybank Emissaries. They visited companies noted for exceptional service, such as Federal Express and McDonald's. The trip wasn't for pure fun; the emissaries wrote formal reports to top management about what they learned. This gave the employees a sense of mission as well as a reward; it also gave top management excellent benchmarking information on exceptional service.[3]

The only unfortunate aspect of this program, in my opinion, was that it was developed for a predetermined time only. Its purpose—to reinforce superior service by bank employees—was fulfilled, and the kind of behavior elicited by Legend in the Making has now become the norm in the Baybanks culture. Nonetheless, I was so impressed by this program that I hate to think it was not continued.

Another effective formal program is from the public sector. The City of Phoenix Excellence Awards, given annually, are a sought-after honor. Both individuals and teams can be nominated by management or employees for recognition for a job that far exceeds expectations. A special breakfast, attended by many city officials, is held to celebrate the success of the award recipients. Professionally done photographs are displayed in the main administration building, and stories appear in the employee newsletter.

Great care is taken to see that all winners are deserving. Criteria are tough. Often, department managers have to wrestle with many deserving employees or work groups before choosing which to nominate. The criteria that follow are a good example from which to springboard, but it is important to remember to customize your criteria to fit your organization's culture. The recipients of the City of Phoenix Excellence Awards are chosen on the basis that employees or employee groups are eligible after meeting one or more of the following:

1. Continued and repeated excellence in overall job performance
2. Solving an extraordinary problem, achieving or exceeding a significantly difficult goal
3. Successful implementation of an innovative idea where the result was identifiable
4. An outstanding act that brings the city recognition from the public

Moving into the manufacturing industry, we return to Vickers AMD in Jackson, Mississippi, which has special recognition programs for perfect attendance and team progress. The results of the perfect attendance program provide evidence that focusing attention on desired behavior does reinforce and increase it. In the first year of the program, three employees earned the award. In the next year, twenty-eight employees were recognized! The award—a special jacket—was not overly expensive but returned a great deal on the organization's investment.[4]

Team progress is recognized in many ways, with tangible awards ranging from trips to jewelry. But Vickers also chose to use various communications tactics to recognize employees. Bulletin boards display results, a special newsletter spreads the word about quality achievements, and every employee belongs to a Success Sharing team that meets monthly to hear news from the team leaders.

In addition, top management sponsorship of the teams is visible in a special annual newsletter where it shares its goals and accomplishments. The newsletter discusses team progress, of course, but more interestingly, it also recounts team frustrations. This keeps the report realistic as the employees who read it certainly know that teams do not always reach their goals without some uphill climbs.[5]

In general, formal programs can take the form of monthly, quarterly, or annual events. Not all awards go to "the best." Often, award programs also recognize such positive accomplishments as "most improved," "best sustained superior performance," and other characteristics deemed important.

Awards vary, too. Examples given in this chapter show the diversity, but there are many more to choose from. Other types of awards include letters to the manager, sabbaticals, prime parking spots, earned time off, movie tickets, best-selling books, training seminars, shares of stock, tickets to sporting events, or upscale calculators. These awards can also be used for informal recognition. Just let imagination and creativity be your guide.

On-the-Job Recognition

The concept of recognizing people on the job makes us think of praise from our bosses, merit salary increases, and promotions. There are many more recognition opportunities available than those three, and many of them have been around for quite some time.

The word *participation* means many things to many people. I would like to give you, again, a broad definition that fits the context of this chapter. Anything that results in increasing the level of mental, physical, and emotional involvement of people falls under this book's definition of participation. This includes such managerial behaviors as communicating more than just what people have to know to do their jobs to soliciting employee input and involvement. And, of course, it extends to giving away a choice assignment with lots of visibility and sharing or delegating decision-making power with or to individuals.

Broadening the scope of an employee's or a team's job also shows confidence, builds esteem, and motivates people. The cross-fertilization of ideas and skills can revitalize workers. Also, allowing employees to start new projects or ventures or to innovate and experiment can be wonderful rewards.

In many companies, being assigned to special task forces that address unique organizational problems or initiatives often offers special recognition opportunities to employees. Sharing such assignments goes a long way toward reinforcing the efforts of superior employees. These opportunities are also a way for managers to say "thank you" for a job well done.

The newer concept of creating a dual career ladder is a way to recognize and reward employees with special technical expertise. Giving people a career path to a job—management—that is only a mismatch for them is not showing them that we value what they love and what is important to the survival of the enterprise. For years, scientists, engineers, pension specialists, lawyers, and yes, even HR professionals, have been given only one path. Now they can stay within their technical or professional areas and still benefit from increased recognition, status, and compensation.

Representing the organization at conferences allied to various professions or writing for their professional journals also motivates, but many organizations don't support these types of activities. Yet they can enrich people's jobs and lead to higher levels of performance by keeping them from stagnating and/or reinforcing their value as professionals. In the age of flatter organizations, such techniques will likely become common practice.

Another good example of recognition is the delegation of an important presentation to one or more members of a team. Does it always have to be the highest manager of the work unit who gets to speak? What's in it for team members who get to attend such sessions? The answers are obvious.

A participative management environment provides another important on-the-job application. In crisis, turnaround, or other such times, a more traditional approach may be warranted, as the company may well need a "captain at the helm of the ship." But in normal times, American managers who refuse to involve employees more completely in the day-to-day and even long-term visionary work of the operation miss a great chance to build commitment and motivate people. Remember, almost all the studies cited early in this chapter show that feeling "in" or "a part of" decisions is important to today's work force.

There are many other opportunities that you as an HR professional can influence. By risking these types of changes in your own organization, you can lead by example as well. Then, when you encourage the promotion or recognition of individuals who are adapting to the changing needs of today's work force, you can add your own insights or point to your own operation as evidence of the levels of performance that participatory opportunities bring to the organization. A word of caution, though. If visibility or sharing responsibility is viewed negatively by top managers as taking the spotlight from them, you will need to do some work to change that view.

Conclusion

In today's and tomorrow's environment of global competition, uncommitted and uninformed employees neither care nor understand the challenges facing their organizations. By creating an environment that maximizes the important contributions of people, the HR professional can improve the organization's ability to meet world-class standards and competitive challenges. Focusing on recognition is one of the important pathways. Recognizing people builds a sense of pride and increases the probability of higher quality, increased productivity, and concern for the customer.

If your organization has recognition programs in place, it would be wise to review the type and nature of these programs in light of the need to support quality and customer satisfaction–oriented performance expectations. There likely is a great deal of improvement that can be made. The HR professional has the influence necessary to move recognition initiatives to a more effective, even strategic level.

Since motivating and rewarding today's work force is a human resources responsibility, top management will likely listen to an assessment of the company's needs in this important area. Looking for opportunities to visibly say "thanks for a job well done" will reap great benefits for your company and its people.

Chapter 5
Training and Development

Perhaps it is in the arena of training and development, more than any other, that human resources professionals can make an easy transition to the role of Total Quality champion. Since the mid 1980s, an entire curriculum has been created to support Total Quality efforts. From teaching quality awareness to "the seven basic quality tools" to team leader/facilitator roles to customer contact to the manager's changing role, training programs have been an integral requirement in developing a Total Quality capability and culture. As quality efforts become more mature in some leading organizations, these companies have begun to offer sophisticated programs in order to advance more fully their people's skills and abilities as they forge new ground. Some of these skills include quality function deployment, benchmarking, design of experiments, and designing self-managing work teams.

This chapter focuses on the basic course curriculum needed to institute a Total Quality effort. It outlines the content needed to work with the senior-level quality leadership team, assessment teams, and the pilot quality improvement teams. The roles and responsibilities of these teams are also clarified. Finally, the chapter closes with an in-depth discussion of the seven basic statistical tools used by quality improvement teams.

Senior Quality Leadership Team Training

The senior quality leadership team (QLT) is a high-level, policy-making body that is also often called the quality council or executive steering committee. It reflects the natural organization and generally includes the company's top management—those at the first and second levels of the organization. If the top HR professional does not report directly to the top of the organization, it is advisable that this individual sit on the quality leadership team. If the company is unionized, the union president should be a member. It is wise to keep the membership to a number that can effectively participate in group discussions. As such, eight is optimum; twelve is maximum. Thus, if the second level of the organization has more than twelve members, representatives of the key segments should be selected for the QLT.

The role and responsibilities of the QLT vary, but a general list contains these steps:

1. Develop or refine the mission, vision, and values of the organization
2. Conduct an organizationwide quality assessment
3. Develop the organization's strategic quality plan
4. Charter and monitor quality improvement teams
5. Develop a communications strategy to support the effort
6. Coordinate and provide resources for quality improvement efforts
7. Create an initial training plan
8. Develop an overall measurement plan for the Total Quality effort or even all critical process and outcome measures
9. Develop a reward and recognition system that reinforces teamwork
10. Establish and monitor quality policy
11. Continually update and renew the Total Quality effort

The quality leadership team is typically not enamored with the idea of classroom training. Members have attended numerous classes and seminars over the years. As a result, the training offered to these organizational VIPs must be interesting, experiential, and entertaining. Yet it is critical that a baseline of quality knowledge and skills be imparted to each QLT member. Readings, discussion, seminars, networking, survey feedback, and experimentation with behavior change on the job are six common ways that top managers learn about quality.

Another consideration in working with executives is the need for an outside expert to lead their workshops. Like other programs brought in for this level, Total Quality training and planning often needs the experience and perspective brought by a professional outside consultant.

The curriculum for executives includes awareness training in Total Quality Management, a working session to prepare for the kick-off activities, and a strategic quality planning session. Any other training can occur just-in-time, meaning that the leadership team members learn about concepts and/or skills needed as they continue their management of the Total Quality process. Such training might include further practice in the basic quality tools, sessions on benchmarking, and models of measurement.

Executive Awareness Training

The purpose of executive awareness training is to orient the senior managers to the principles of TQM and to clarify the comprehensiveness of the effort. Other objectives often include influencing increased support for the effort and clarifying the need for a change in the leadership role. A typical agenda for an initial awareness training session would be:

1. An overview of the principles and beliefs of at least the three quality "gurus," W. Edwards Deming, Joseph Juran, and Philip Crosby
2. A perspective on the payback for TQM efforts, preferably based on real experiences of other companies
3. An overview of what a typical TQM implementation includes
4. A brief refresher on large-scale systems change
5. A briefing (preferably including some action planning) on the leader's role in TQM

This session could last for a half day to two full days. If a full day is doable, it would be helpful to add a more complete discussion of the quality improvement teams' systematic problem-solving process and a brief introduction to the basic statistical quality tools. If two days can be found, enhancing the understanding of the gurus and actual practice of the basic statistical tools would be advised. The more days that can be committed to learning about TQM, the better. Content that is not included in this early session would most likely have to be covered at some later date.

Quality Leadership Team Workshop

The purpose of the leadership team kick-off workshop is to complete a strategic mission and vision statement that will guide the organization, to finalize the structure that will support the effort, and to complete initial planning for the first phase of the TQM effort—assessment. A typical agenda for this work session for executives might be:

1. Developing or refining the organization's mission/vision statements
2. Creating the overall structure for the effort

3. Discussing the need for a values statement from the senior management team, and if needed, developing it
4. Explaining the need for comprehensive assessment as a basis for strategic quality planning
5. Refresher training in the definition of *process* as it relates to work performed in the company
6. Identifying and prioritizing the major processes that support the company's vision
7. Identifying the above processes' major customers and suppliers
8. Determining and prioritizing all external customer segments
9. Discussing methods to assess employee perspectives of quality and overall morale, and if needed, planning it
10. Developing the timeline for assessment
11. Determining sponsorship/support for the assessment team
12. Identifying assessment team members

Strategic Quality Planning Workshop

One of the common mistakes an organization makes is to create improvement teams without a strategy in mind. Joseph Juran says that implementing quality project by project, team by team, is the best way to build a critical mass of support while returning success to the company for beginning the effort. Yet there is a greater payoff and stronger commitment if the effort is focused on improvement opportunities that have been uncovered as a result of objective assessment rather than people's opinion. The strategic quality planning workshop is the result of such an effort. An aggressive agenda for a two-day strategic quality planning workshop would be:

1. Overview of the roadmap for planning a TQM effort
2. Review of strengths and areas for opportunity found in the quality assessment
3. Generation of the organization's critical success factors
4. Development of a matrix rating major process opportunities against the critical success factors
5. Review of the above results against customer feedback, which adds a validity check
6. Review of the results from number 4 against employee feedback, which adds another measure of accuracy
7. Final prioritization of quality improvements needing initial attention by the company
8. Development of improvement team charters
9. Identification of potential improvement team leaders

10. Establishment of timeline to confirm leaders, solicit team members, and communicate direction to the company

This is usually an intense two days, and often teams need to move numbers 8, 9, and 10 to subsequent QLT agendas depending upon the extensiveness of the information covered.

Beyond these formal workshops, coaching and facilitating the leadership team throughout the implementation process is advisable. Chapter 7 on organization development shows what this entails and how it is played out.

Management Training

The organization is made up of other layers of management that need to be brought on board for the Total Quality effort to succeed. Even though the executive leadership team focuses implementation efforts in just a few major areas, the nature of the pilot projects is usually cross-functional. As a result, most management staff will be involved in supporting the pilot teams' activities in some way or another. For example, team members may need access to information that is normally held at higher levels in the company. Another example might be that one or two team members come from within a manager's department, and the people who are filling in for them will want to know what is going on and must see the managers' support of the effort as a top priority.

As a result, the commitment of managers at all levels is necessary and their understanding and buy-in crucial for the effort to succeed. Managers should receive the same awareness training as the executives, but in addition, the priorities that were established during the strategic quality planning workshop should be detailed for their understanding. They also need to comprehend what will be expected of them. For instance, an inherent precept of Total Quality is the movement to participative management, with involvement of employees as stakeholders of their work processes. If the organization has not moved in that direction already, it needs to offer both conceptual and experiential training for managers. (Of course, it would be wise to conduct a similar training session for the executive team since its members will be leading the way.)

The Manager's Changing Role

The curriculum for this course must be built on what has gone before. There are many excellent management and supervisory development courses that have been offered to employees at this level. A review of common themes from past courses should be conducted so that this training program integrates well with past efforts.

Here is some of the essential content that needs to be covered:

1. A "big picture" overview of the payoffs of employee involvement, using actual case studies and bottom-line impact on results
2. An outline of the evolutionary movement of manager as conductor/director to developer/coach/boundary spanner
3. Review of the process of developing individuals as it relates to developing teams
4. Review of the stages of team development and skills to grow teams to maturity
5. A segment on building visions for the future, with actual steps that a manager leads the team through in building that vision
6. An introduction to the characteristics of leadership, preferably including a survey feedback instrument that can act as an initial baseline for each participant
7. An action planning model for management that outlines a development strategy for each participant that can be reinforced back on the job with his/her supervisor

Team Training for Managers

If only a brief overview of Total Quality was offered as awareness training, managers now need to have a fuller understanding of the team problem-solving process and the seven basic quality tools that will be used by the teams. I will discuss that in the section on training needs for teams, as the content does not differ. Managers should attend the complete team leader/facilitator course outlined in the following section if at all possible. If they can, they would not only understand the basic quality tools, they would also get a closer look at the teams' group process.

Team Training

One of the differences between quality improvement teams and typical committees and task forces is that on quality teams, employees from all levels are generally members. That means that different mixes of people and different levels of status are brought together to assess or improve the organization's work. This necessitates training in team dynamics and skills along with training in the statistical tools used in the quality improvement process. It is common to have classes in conducting an assessment and in team leader or facilitator skills. A shorter version of the team leader/facilitator class is generally offered for team members. Let's look at the content of some of these classes now.

Assessment Team Training

The purpose of conducting an organizationwide assessment is to identify the areas of strength and opportunity that will become the focus of the quality effort. It is from this assessment that initial improvement teams will be chartered. The first question an organization must ask is what assessment method the team will use. Many internal assessments are being conducted against private industry's Malcolm Baldrige National Quality Award criteria. In government, the criteria of both the Prototype and President's Award are often used. (These award criteria are similar to the private industry Baldrige criteria.)

There are some other methods that deserve mention. For example, Philip Crosby's financially based cost of quality method is sometimes used. (This method looks at rejects, inspection costs, and prevention costs.) There are some models that just identify the most important major processes and assess them in conjunction with garnering customer feedback. There are methods that use an internal employee survey or an external customer survey to identify organizational improvement priorities.

It is evident that the strategic underpinning for a TQM effort can take many forms. Whatever the approach, the assessment team members need a preparatory workshop in order to accomplish their objectives successfully. The use of the Baldrige criteria is very common, and because of its comprehensiveness, this outline for training will assume its use. A typical curriculum for such a course is:

1. An introduction to assessment as an approach to identifying strengths and opportunities
2. An introduction to the Malcolm Baldrige National Quality Award criteria
3. A case study of assessment using the above criteria
4. An introduction to the company's highest priorities for assessment
5. Clarification of subteam membership (where actual people are assigned aspects of the assessment)
6. An overview of questioning techniques
7. Development of questions to be used in the assessment
8. An overview of interviewing techniques
9. Practice in interviewing
10. Data/report identification (for current information on topics that are being assessed)

11. Subteam action planning
12. Total assessment team action planning

An outside expert is often brought in to conduct this workshop and coach and support the team during this phase. However, more and more classes are being given on how to conduct an internal assessment so that companies do not have to rely on outsiders to help them through this process. Organizations such as American Society for Quality Control, the Association for Quality and Participation, and the American Productivity & Quality Center are good places to start looking for help.

Team Leader/Facilitator Training

Quality improvement teams differ from traditional committees and task forces in other ways as well. The quality team has a leader, but that leader does not act as a facilitator of team meetings. Thus, the leader, while setting the agenda and running the meeting, can be a contributor and not have to focus on the group's team dynamics. The facilitator is a separate person who does not have a stake in the outcome of the work improvement, but rather in the team's group process and the members' abilities to solve a problem well. This duo is in partnership, moving the team forward and helping it to grow and mature while addressing an organizational need.

Since there is such a close partnership, training for team leaders and facilitators is often offered as one class, although there may be classes just for facilitators. My personal preference, to train these partners together, is based on experience with more than 100 teams. The following curriculum will fill the needs of both:

1. A brief overview of the quality effort and how improvement teams fit into the overall structure
2. Steps in launching teams such as creating the team mission, meeting ground rules, and setting action plans
3. A definition of the concept of work process with actual organization examples
4. An introduction of a systematic problem-solving model, preferably showing where the seven basic quality tools are used
5. Quality tool number 1: Process flowcharts
6. Quality tool number 2: Cause-and-effect diagrams
7. Quality tool number 3: Pareto diagrams
8. Quality tool number 4: Scatter diagrams
9. Quality tool number 5: Histograms
10. Quality tool number 6: Run charts

11. Quality tool number 7: Control charts
12. Brainstorming/problem-solving tools and techniques, e.g., nominal group technique, affinity diagramming, criteria matrix, multi-voting, and force field analysis
13. Communications exercises in consensus, win-win negotiation, listening, feedback, and interpersonal styles
14. The role of the team leader, facilitator, member, and scribe
15. The stages of team development

It is very important that team leaders and facilitators receive experiential training, and the more practice, the better. If customized case studies can be developed that fit the company, it can really pull the content into place for participants. Such courses can last four or even five days. Three days is a minimum one should expect in actual class time without the special case study.

Team Member Training

Team members are generally trained in one of two ways. The first way is traditional: Team members are brought into the classroom to learn tools and techniques together. The other is just-in-time training, where members are given an overview of their charter, training is offered as part of the regular meeting format, and learning/practice is completed using the team's actual content/data. The benefit of the latter method is that teams are learning as they progress through the problem-solving model. The weakness in this approach is that knowledge transfer may be spotty depending on the team leader's or facilitator's skills or his/her perception of the team's need to learn all of the course content.

The curriculum is virtually the same as that for the team leaders and facilitators, although not as in-depth. Two to three days is typical.

Just-in-Time Training

The terminology *just-in-time (JIT) training* is becoming popular in TQM circles. Since this method of training is most used with team member training, it makes sense to address it here before moving into specific curricular content. The JIT approach to training is most like technical on-the-job training. It assumes that adults learn the most in a real-time setting, where they can immediately apply the skills learned in the actual setting where they will be used. This holds true for JIT training for the seven basic quality tools and even for team interaction skills.

Quality teams often have to manage progress while carrying a full-time workload. In initial stages of the Total Quality effort, being assigned to a quality team may be exciting and worth doing, but it is still often viewed as additional work. This is because the culture and, therefore, the workplace has not yet viewed time for continuous improvement as part of everyone's job. The result of this reality is that getting two entire days off (the minimum needed) for team member training is often viewed as impossible. Besides the typical training alternatives, such as two one-day sessions or four half-day sessions, the JIT training concept seemed a natural for quality teams.

Here is a scenario of how JIT training could occur. A team meets every other week for two hours. As part of their agenda, the members go beyond information sharing and do actual wok in their meeting sessions. Let's say that the agenda coming up includes establishing the team's ground rules. The facilitator is the support of the team leader and the technical expert. As such, in the meeting he or she would likely be the one to describe what team ground rules are, check for understanding, and move the team through actually creating them.

In a future meeting when the team has advanced to using the basic quality tools, data can be gathered by team members between meetings. The agenda for the next meeting can include an item like "Turning data into a histogram." The meeting would begin with training in histograms, followed by the creation of the actual histogram that the team needs to complete some stage of analysis.

Just-in-time training is simple and can be used effectively. The major caution is that training can get lost, be skipped, or have a low priority unless the JIT process is clearly laid out and both team leaders and facilitators are held accountable for the training of teams, with actual completion dates or sign-offs as part of the process.

The Seven Basic Quality Tools

The seven basic statistical tools used by quality improvement teams are:

1. Process flowcharts
2. Cause-and-effect diagrams
3. Pareto diagrams
4. Scatter diagrams
5. Histograms
6. Run charts
7. Control charts

These tools take only basic mathematics ability. Except for control charts, there is nothing more complicated than simple adding, subtracting, multiplying, and dividing. Team members help each other in developing the charts and graphs so there is seldom a need for literacy classes in an organization undertaking a Total Quality effort. (However, the team environment can act as an observation method of needs assessment if a particular company does have literacy needs.)

The following discussion of the basic tools includes the steps needed to complete each chart or graph. In addition, completed pictorial representations of each tool, taken from courses I have taught for the American Productivity & Quality Center, are provided. (The tools appear again in Chapter 13, where they are shown in specific HR applications.) Many of the examples in this chapter come from various industries in order to reinforce that the tools can be transferred from one industry to another.

Process Flowcharts

The process flowchart comes out of industrial engineering and has been in use for many years. It is a symbolic representation of the steps that must be taken to result in a work process output. The most common symbols are a rectangle or square for an action step, a diamond for a decision step, and an arrow to show the flow from one process to another. There can be a slight variation in the symbols used from one text to another or from one software program to another, but these symbols are pretty standard. The simplest flowchart symbols are shown in Figure 5-1.

The benefits of flowcharts go beyond merely understanding the steps in a work process. The flowchart helps people see the interdependencies in the process, highlights redundant steps, identifies delays in the process, and points to causes of variation. It can also identify areas of potential automation, but one of the key principles of flowchart experts is to simplify and improve the process first before automating a deficient process.

There is one final thing that needs to be understood about flowcharting. A flowchart can be created for differing levels of detail. A simple macro flowchart would describe large segments of activities, such as research, design, test, redesign, and standardize. Many actions can take place underneath those five breakdowns. The next flowchart can be more detailed and go to the activity level, where all the activities under research would be charted, then all the activities that complete the design segment of the process, then the test segment, etc. This second level of flowcharting is generally a must in order to make real improvements. It is also possible to go to a third level of detail, the task level. A team would go to the task level of detail if that was needed to make improvements,

Figure 5-1. Flowchart symbols.

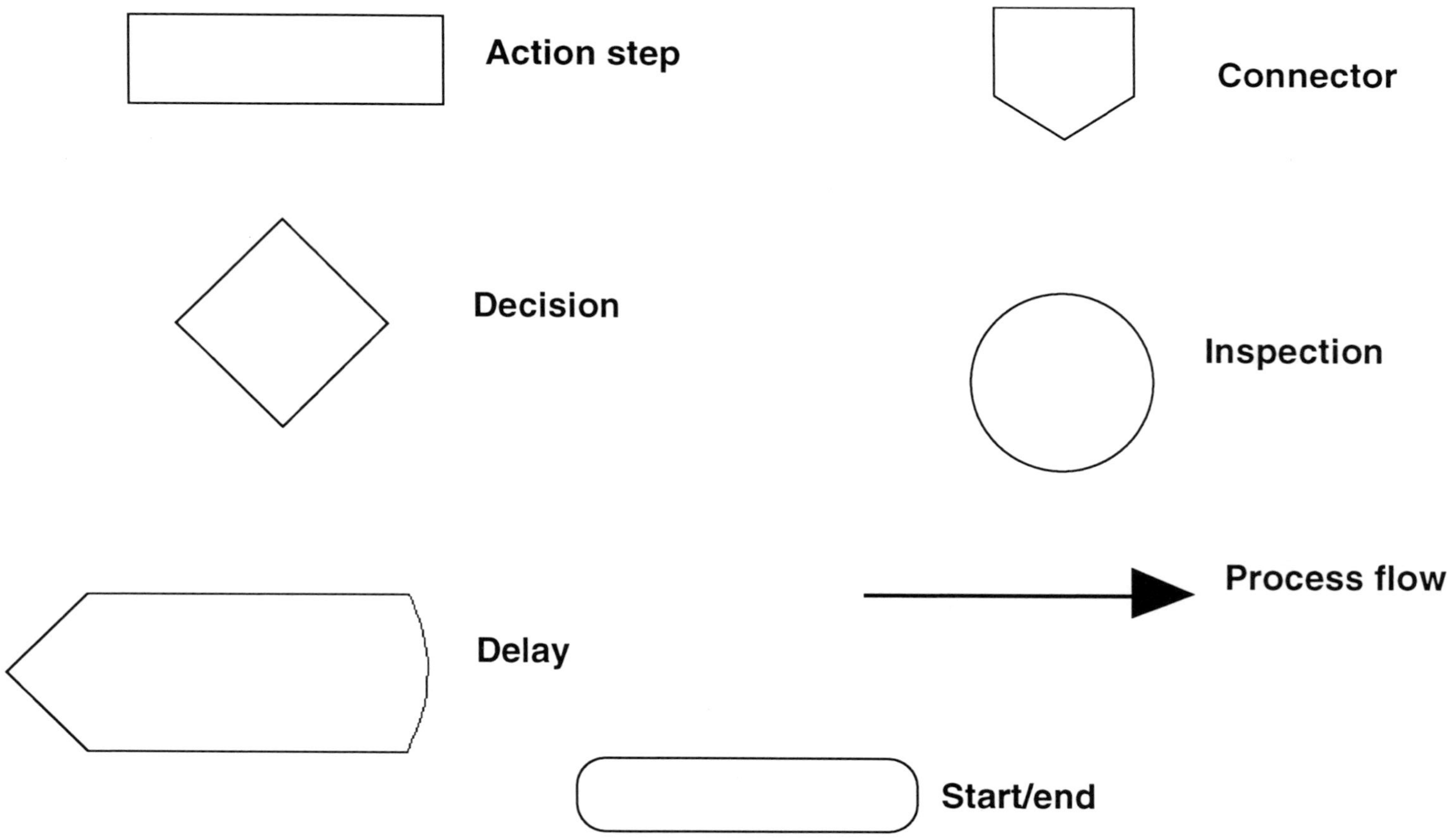

Action step

Connector

Decision

Inspection

Delay

Process flow

Start/end

and many do. A typical second-level flowchart depicting a production process is shown in Figure 5-2.

The steps in the flowcharting process are:

Step 1: Identify the beginning (the very first step) in the process.

Step 2: Break down the process to the activity level and determine the second action.

Step 3: Continue completing the steps in the process until the output (whether a product or service) is delivered.

Step 4: Review the finished chart and gain consensus that it is accurate.

Some hints for coaching teams through this process include:

- Be careful where the process begins. Identifying the input that kicks off the first step in the process is important and can help to establish the proper boundary.
- The process owner (the person who has the authority to change the process) should be a team member or be in close communication with the team leader in order to be involved with the findings of the team. Often, the process owner does not know in detail what is going on inside the process.

Cause-and-Effect Diagrams

Cause-and-effect diagrams come from Japan. They are sometimes called Ishikawa diagrams after their developer or fishbone diagrams because of their shape. Cause-and-effect diagrams are a useful tool for identifying the root causes of a quality effect. For example, if the effect being studied is late lab work, brainstorming all the potential causes would result in a very long list that may be difficult to make sense of. But a cause-and-effect diagram would point out potential causes, help a team to categorize related causes, and help to display the causes in such a way that a plan of action could be created to determine which causes truly are root causes. Another way to look at this is to understand that the goal of the quality improvement team is to treat causes and not symptoms, so that the changes made will be long-lasting and not just a Band-Aid. A cause-and-effect diagram showing the potential causes of late lab work is shown in Figure 5-3.

The steps in completing a cause-and-effect diagram are:

Step 1: Determine the quality effect/characteristic the team wishes to improve, e.g., late lab work.

(Text continues on page 68)

Figure 5-2. Second-level flowchart depicting a production process.

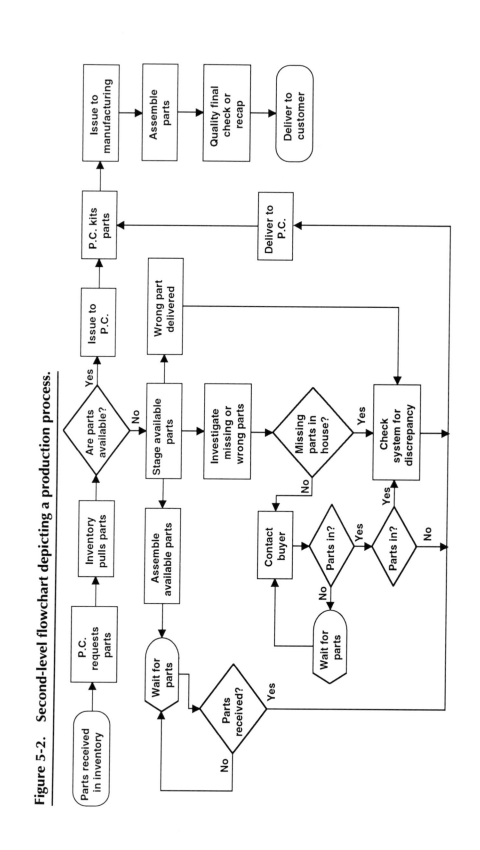

Figure 5-3. Cause-and-effect diagram of late lab work.

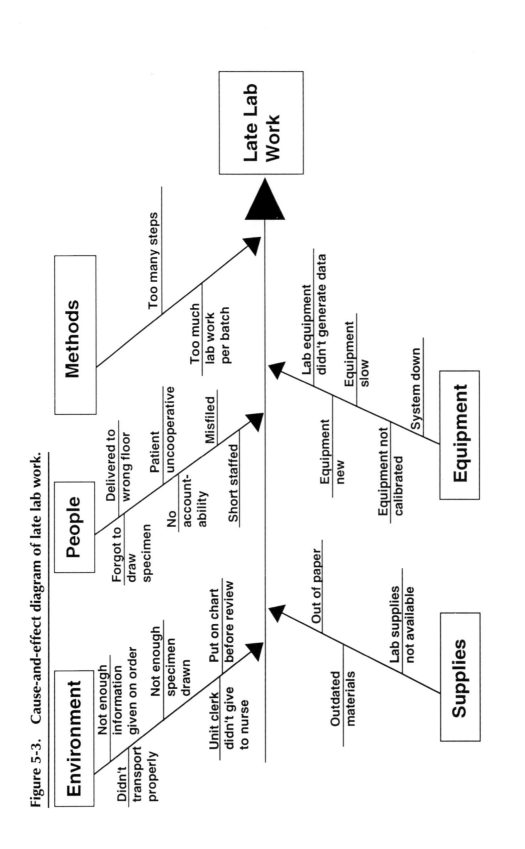

Step 2:   Write the characteristic in a box on the right side in the middle of the chart.

Step 3:   Draw an arrow pointing to the characteristic from the left side of the chart.

Step 4:   Brainstorm all potential causes of the effect.

Step 5:   Cluster all the causes that appear to be related into categories. (The most common categories are people, methods, supplies, equipment, and environment, although the team members drawing up the list should determine the right categories for each diagram.)

Step 6:   Write the names of the categories in boxes above and below the arrow, leaving room to depict the specific causes.

Step 7:   Draw arrows from each category to the main central arrow.

Step 8:   Write the specific causes relating to each category, and draw a line to the appropriate branch.

The team should continue placing causes on the diagram until all the potential causes are displayed. Once the diagram is complete, the team members need to evaluate the potential causes so that they can reach a decision about which causes they want to take action against, those they believe are the root causes.

Pareto Diagrams

A Pareto diagram—named for its developer—is a way of showing which problems occur with the most frequency. It supports the well-known 80/20 rule, that 20 percent of all problems take 80 percent of the fix-it time in any work process. Pareto diagrams are useful for prioritizing, choosing starting points, and measuring as well as displaying relative importance. They show how to display a series of problems in descending order, so the resulting bar graph has the tallest bar on the left and the shortest bar on the right. This is always how a Pareto chart (just a specialized bar graph) looks. A typical Pareto chart depicting customer complaints looks like Figure 5-4, but it can be taken a step further. For now, let's look at the first series of steps.

The steps in constructing a Pareto diagram are:

Step 1:   Select the problems to be measured.

Step 2:   Determine what standards to use to compare data, e.g., frequency of occurrence, cost per unit.

Step 3:   Determine during what time period the data to be displayed will be collected.

Figure 5-4. Partially complete Pareto diagram depicting customer complaints.

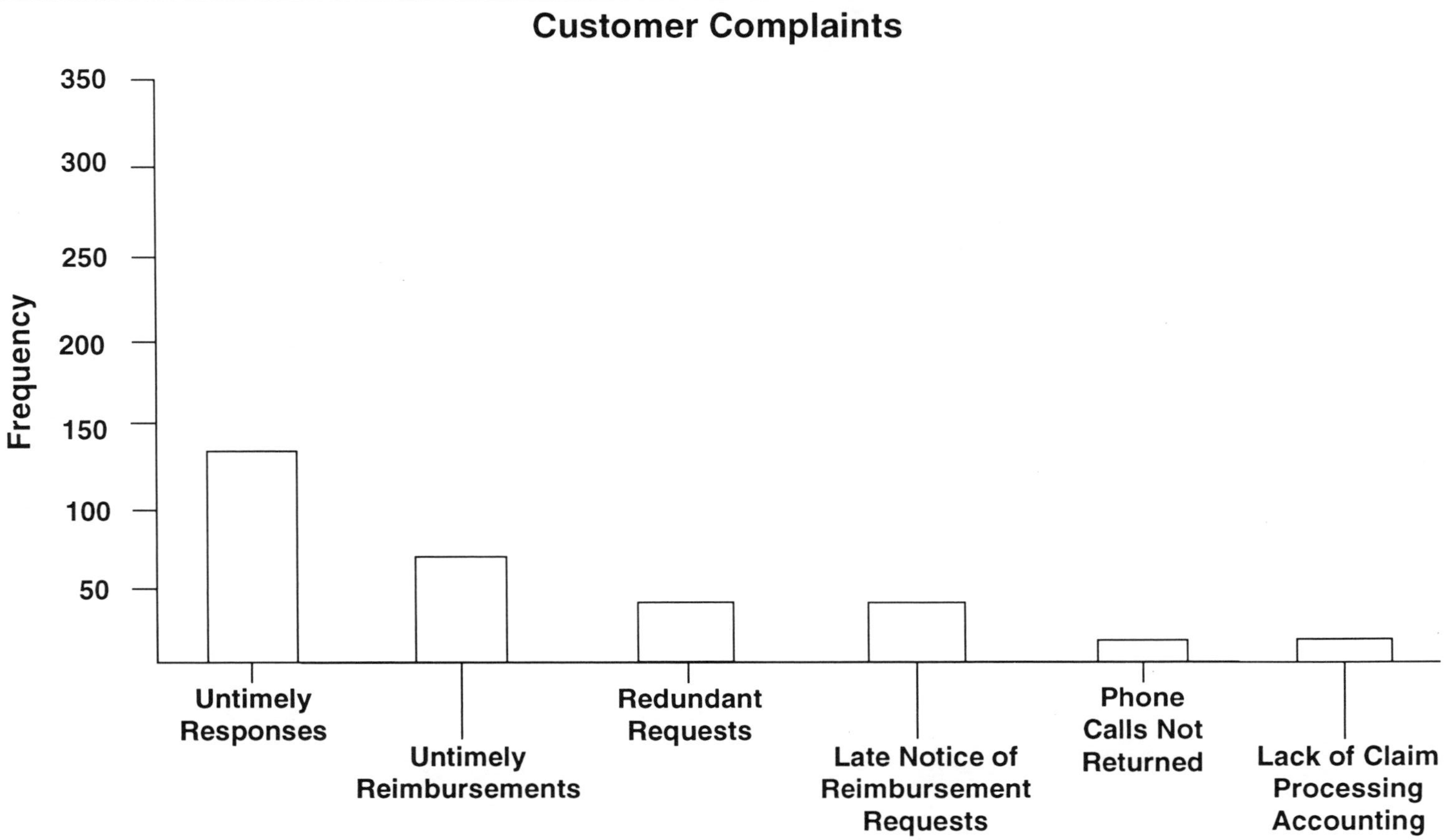

Step 4:   Collect data.

Step 5:   Calculate the total frequency, cost, etc., for each category of data.

Step 6:   Organize the categories in descending order.

Step 7:   Draw and label a horizontal and vertical axis.

Step 8:   Label the vertical axis with the measured standard selected in Step 2, e.g., frequency.

Step 9:   Separate the horizontal axis into equal intervals representing each problem category and label them from left to right, with the category of greatest frequency to the left.

Step 10:   Complete construction of the bar graph.

There is a further step in the construction of a Pareto diagram that results in identification of cumulative values leading to 100 percent of the problems reflected. This is done by calculating the number of each category's problems against the total number of problems captured during the time period. This additional step aids in displaying which 20 percent of the problems occur most often. This completed Pareto diagram would look like Figure 5-5.

Often, a category that has been selected can be further broken down into specifics. For example, if a category of customer complaints is "order late," there can be various reasons for late orders. These can be checked and frequencies graphed and displayed as well. As in all quantitative methods, it is wise sometimes to step back from the data and use some common sense. If a problem does not occur with much frequency but has dire consequences, you may want to focus initial action there rather than on the problem cited in the tallest bar. The Pareto diagram is a tool in decision making; it does not make the final decision for you.

Scatter Diagrams

Scatter diagrams determine the possible correlation between two variables. With data for two variables plotted on an X and Y axis, the graph shows whether a relationship exists and what that relationship is. Scatter diagrams are not held to prove or disprove a relationship, but rather to indicate relationships between variables. Usually, at least fifty data points are plotted to find a pattern that tells if there is a relationship between the two variables. A common relationship used in teaching this tool is that between height and shoe size.

One of the teams I worked with in a business setting used a scatter diagram to determine if there was a relationship between the volume of work and the number of errors. A scatter diagram of the two variables—

Figure 5-5. Complete Pareto diagram depicting customer complaints.

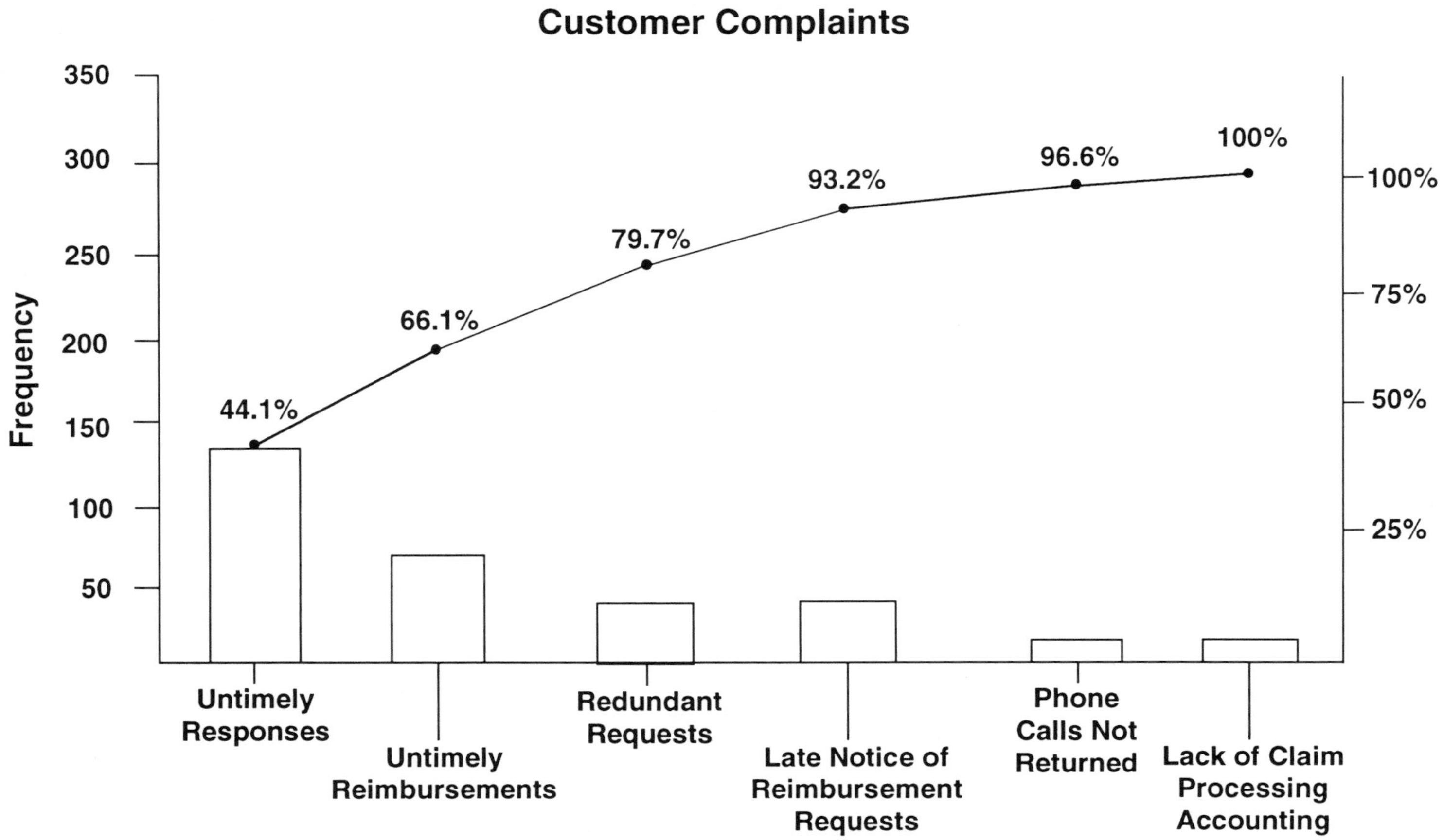

Customer Complaints

Figure 5-6. Scatter diagram depicting relationship between number of orders and average time to process orders.

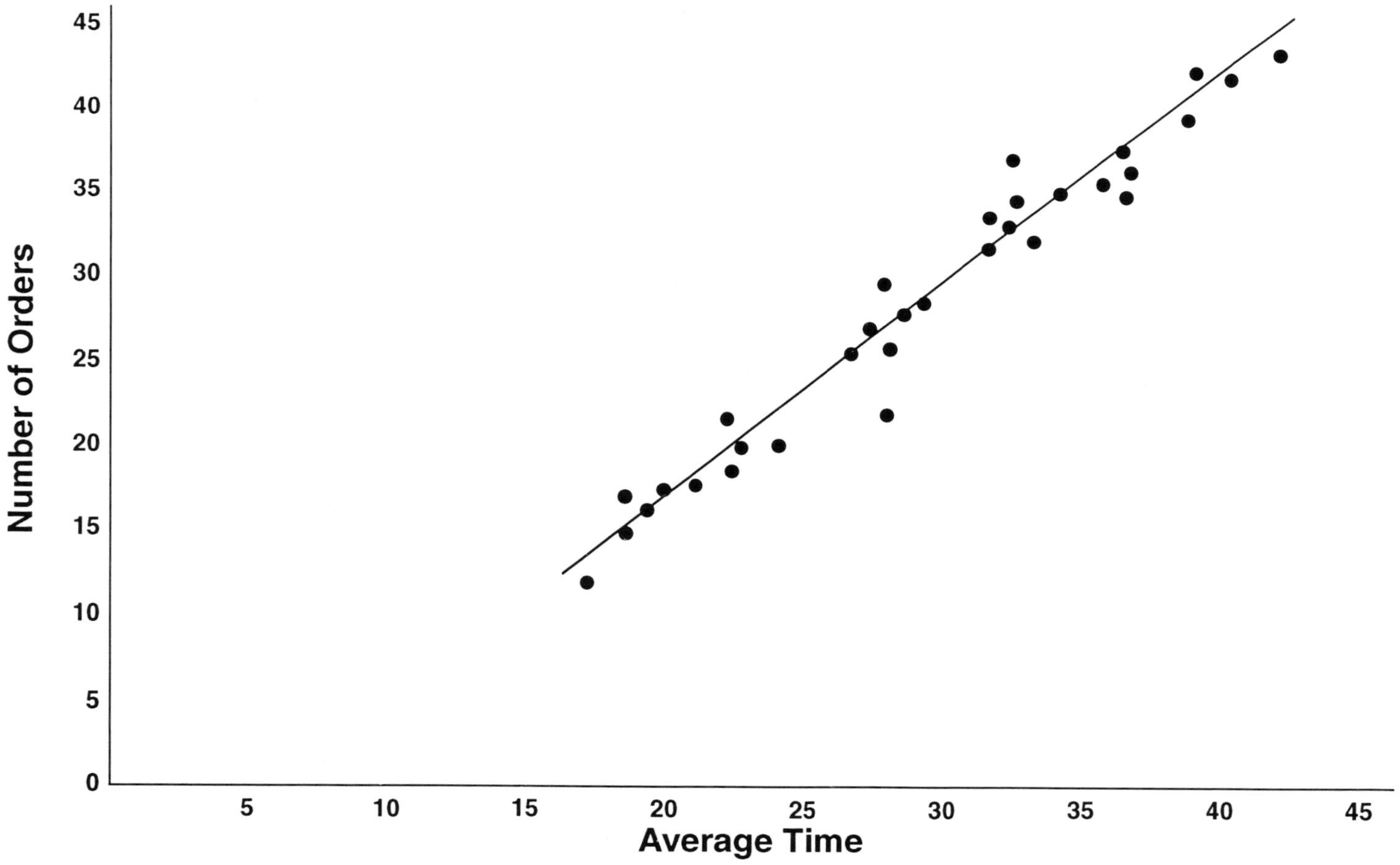

number of orders and average time to process orders—shows a positive relationship in Figure 5-6.

The steps in constructing a scatter diagram are:

Step 1:   Determine the two variables to be compared.
Step 2:   Construct a data sheet for each variable.
Step 3:   Gather fifty to one hundred data points for the two variables.
Step 4:   Draw a graph with a horizontal and vertical axis.
Step 5:   Label each axis.
Step 6:   Plot the data points.

Once the data points have been plotted, the shape or pattern of the dots will describe the relationship, as shown in Figure 5-7. The relationship may be positive or negative, or no relationship may exist.

Histograms

Histograms represent the distribution of data and can show variation. Each bar of the graph indicates the number of data points falling at a particular level. In human resources, a good example is the use of a bell curve (a histogram shape) in the merit rating procedure generally tied to performance appraisal. The profession has traditionally taught that there should be a normal distribution among performance levels of employees, with 66 percent falling in the midrange, and lesser percentages outside the middle. A histogram in the shape of a bell curve that reflects normal distribution looks like Figure 5-8.

The histogram is not an exact, scientific tool. There are several formulas used for its construction. One that is particularly easy takes the following steps:

Step 1:   Count the number of data points.
Step 2:   Determine the range for the data set.
Step 3:   Determine the class width for each category.
Step 4:   Determine the class boundaries.
Step 5:   Make a frequency table.
Step 6:   Construct the graph.

Steps 2 and 3 need elaboration in order to be completed. To determine the range (Step 2), the smallest value must be subtracted from the largest

(Text continues on page 76)

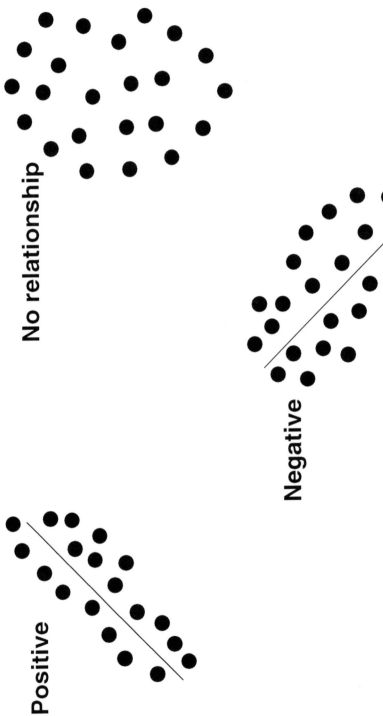

Figure 5-7. Relationships depicted in a scatter diagram.

Figure 5-8. Histogram in the shape of a bell curve.

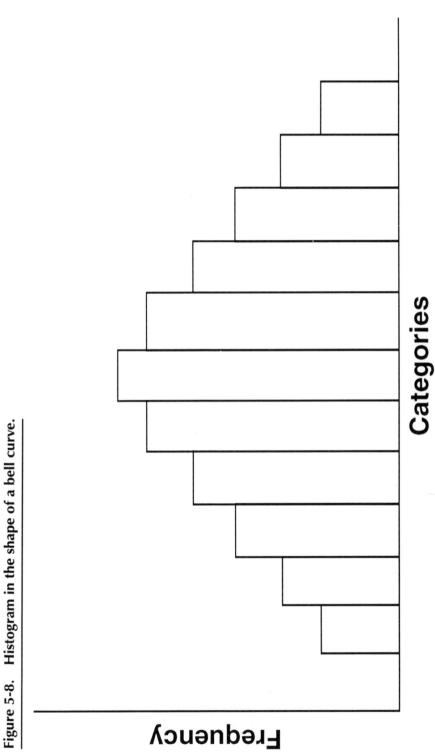

Categories

Frequency

value. Then the range must be divided into a designated number of classes using the following table:

Number of Data Points	Number of Classes (K)
Under 50	5–7
50–100	6–10
100–250	7–12
Over 250	10–20

Step 3, the class width (W), can now be determined by dividing the number of classes (K) into the range (R) as follows:

$$W = R \text{ divided by } K$$

A tip is to round numbers up to the nearest whole decimal.

Step 4 is to determine the class boundaries. In order to do this, the smallest number of the data set begins the first class. For example, if the smallest number is 10, and the class width is 7, the class boundary is 10 + the next 6 numbers, which makes 7 numbers (the class width). This makes the class 10–16, with the next class starting at 17. That next class would be 17 + the next 6 numbers, or 17–23, with the next class width starting at 24, and so on. Add any leftover numbers to the last class. (Remember that histograms do not have to be exact to get the shape of the curve and that the shape holds the information.)

The next step, Step 5, is to make a frequency table. This is simple. Each class is listed with the number of measures that fall into it located across from the class as follows:

Class	Frequency
1	3
2	10
3	13
4	11
5	6

Constructing the graph, Step 6, takes drawing an X and Y axis with frequency on the vertical axis and the other measure on the horizontal axis. The bars are then filled in, and their shape gives the information. Figure 5-9 shows the normal distribution (bell curve) and a bimodal distribution. The bimodal shape indicates that two processes are being performed, that two shifts are operating with different results, that two people are operating the equipment, and so on.

Figure 5-9. Histograms showing normal distribution and bimodal distribution.

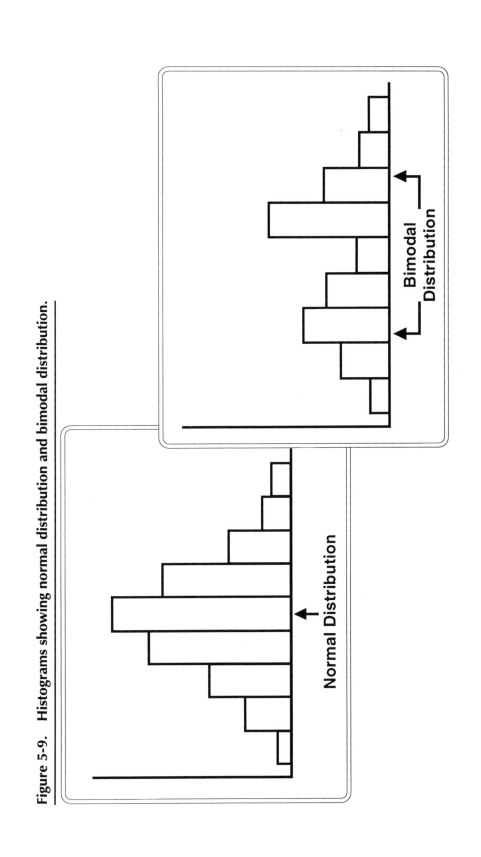

Figure 5-10 shows shapes that are called skewed. These shapes indicate that something is happening with greater frequency on one or the other side of the average. Usually this is an indicator for concern, since there is more than the normal variation. Once in a while, though, we would be glad to have this type of variation from the mean. For example, who would complain if his or her company had all high performers and, therefore, a negatively skewed histogram showing most ratings at the high end, as at the right of Figure 5-10? Well, it would probably throw the merit compensation plan out of whack, but this is the kind of "problem" most chief executives would like to address.

There are other shapes that might be found. Flatter shapes that are not skewed would show a large range of variation in the process, and tighter shapes that reflect clustering around the mean show a small range of variation. Wide ranges generally imply that there is too much variation in the process, which offers an opportunity for improvement.

Run Charts

Run charts are just trend lines over time. They are commonly used and do not take much explanation. A graph is developed that plots time on the horizontal axis and the other measure on the vertical axis. This shows the variation over the time period. Run charts are not that helpful when it comes to assessing the variation in the process because it is not clear whether the innate variation is within or outside the control limits. (Control limits identify deviations from the mean or average.) As seen in Figure 5-11, there appear to be many peaks and valleys in the time it takes to complete authorizations. Yet without the control limits, we cannot be sure if action needs to be taken.

Control Charts

Control charts draw a more complete picture in that they illustrate the stability of the process and show if a special cause is occurring that is pulling the process out of control. *Out of control* means that special causes are responsible for inconsistency (lack of stability) in the process. Those beginning to use control charts need to understand a few basic precepts about work processes. For example:

- All processes fluctuate with time.
- These individual fluctuations are not predictable.
- As long as points fall within predictable boundaries, the process is performing stably.
- When points fall outside the predictable boundaries, action can be taken to correct the special cause of variation.

Figure 5-10. Skewed distributions.

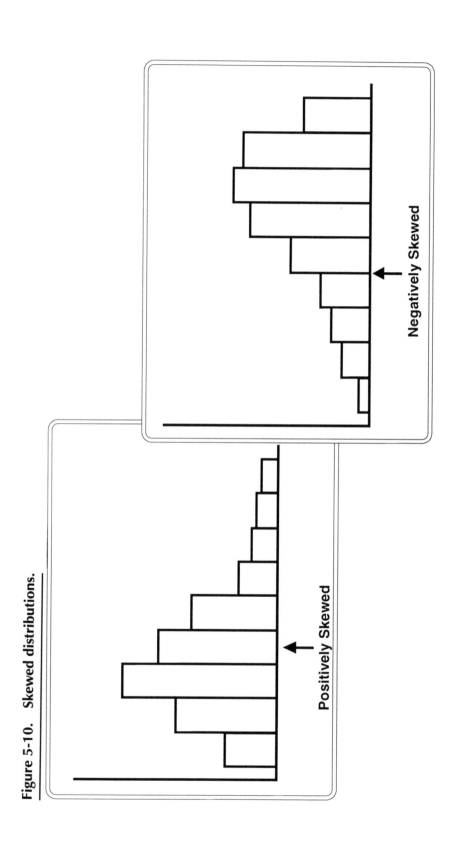

Positively Skewed

Negatively Skewed

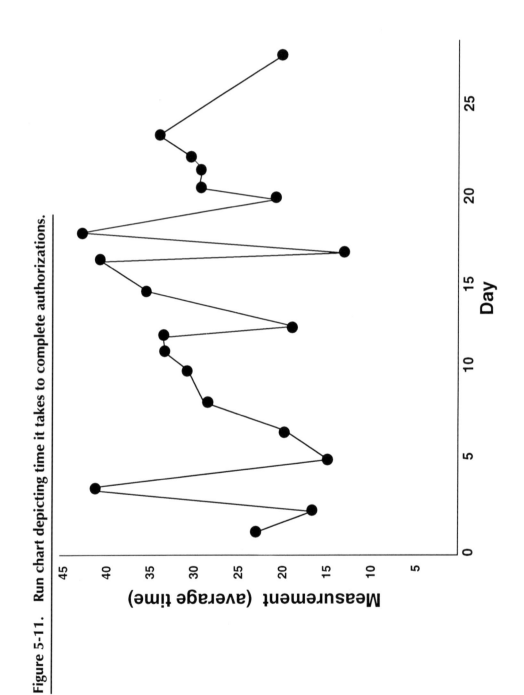

Figure 5-11. Run chart depicting time it takes to complete authorizations.

The control chart depicted in Figure 5-12 was created from the run chart shown in Figure 5-11. It shows that no points are out of control and that the process is stable over the time period measured.

Steps in creating a control chart are simple. Points on the chart represent data, and they are spaced at equal horizontal intervals, each interval usually representing a time period. That time period can be hourly, monthly, or any other logical measure that makes sense for the process being studied. When drawing the vertical axis, the values plotted should be greater than the largest and smallest values to be placed on the graph.

The centerline of the control chart is the average of the plotted values, and the upper and lower control limits are created based upon standard formulas. Most control charts show that two-thirds of the plotted points fall within the center third of the chart since most distributions are normal. The remaining points fall outside of this center. (You can visualize this by imagining a bell curve on its side.)

In Figure 5-12, there were no points out of control, or outside of the upper or lower limit. There is no need for action unless the work team and its leader want to reduce variation further. However, there are guidelines to help people know when to pay close attention to the process. For example, when seven points fall above or below the centerline or eight points are steadily increasing or decreasing, the process may be headed out of control.

The various formulas for control charts can be found in many quality texts. There are formulas for averages, ranges, proportion defective, number defective, and number of nonconformities in constant or varying sample sizes. Manufacturing companies particularly are concerned that averages and ranges are in control. The following steps will assist in developing this type of control chart, called an $\overline{X}$ and R chart:

Step 1:   Collect data.

Step 2:   Calculate $\overline{x}$ for each subgroup.

$$\overline{X} = \frac{\Sigma X}{n} \qquad n = \text{\# of samples}$$

Step 3:   Calculate R (Range) for each subgroup, from highest to lowest.

Step 4:   Plot the range for each subgroup of the R chart.

Step 5:   Calculate centerline for the R portion of the chart.

$$\overline{R} = \frac{\Sigma R}{k} \qquad k = \text{\# of subgroups}$$

Figure 5-12. Control chart depicting time it takes to complete authorizations.

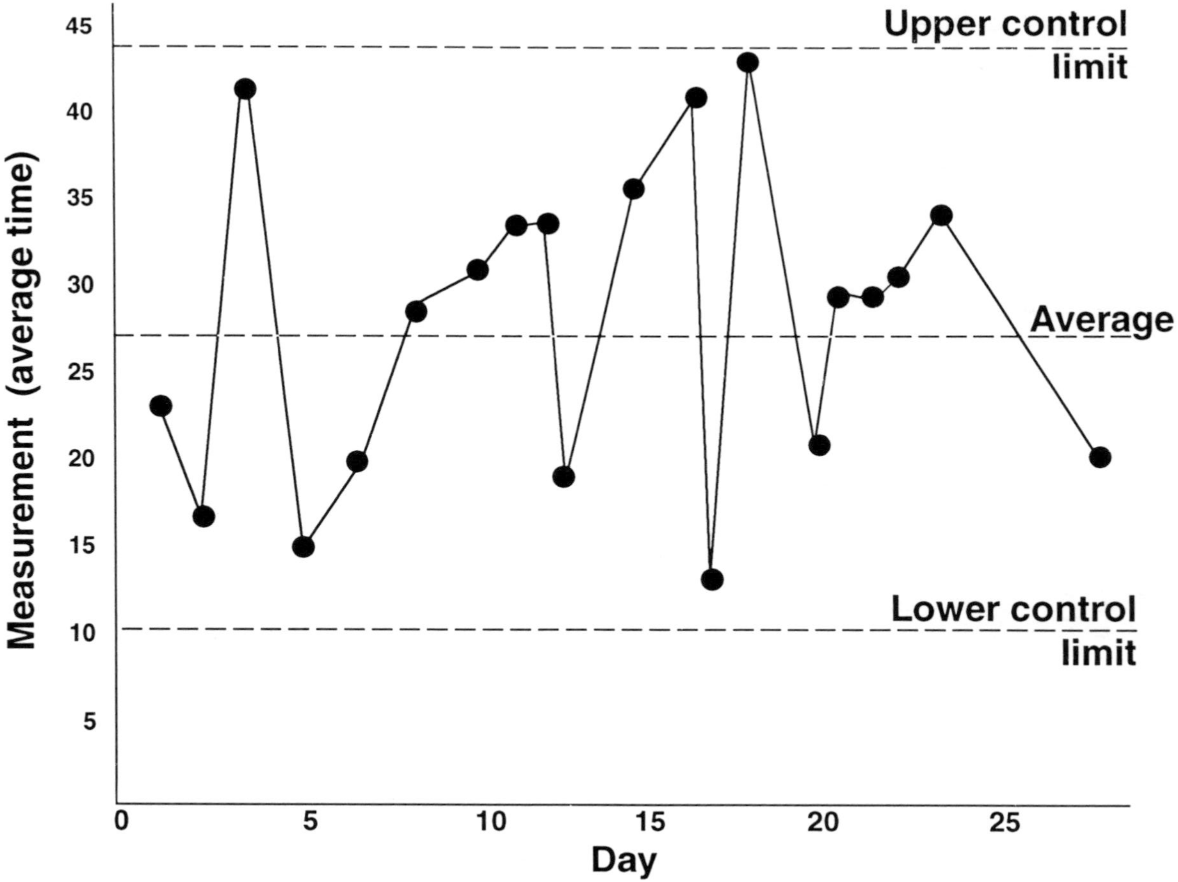

Step 6: Insert the centerline for the R portion of the chart.

Step 7: Calculate upper and lower control limits for the R portion of the chart.

$$UCL_R = D_4\bar{R} \quad LCL_R = D_3\bar{R}$$

Step 8: Insert the control limits for the R portion of the chart.

Step 9: Plot the average for each subgroup of the $\bar{x}$ chart.

Step 10: Calculate centerline for the $\bar{x}$ portion of the chart.

$$\bar{\bar{X}} = \frac{\sum \bar{X}}{k}$$

Step 11: Insert the centerline for the $\bar{x}$ portion for the chart.

Step 12: Calculate upper and lower control limits for the $\bar{x}$ portion of the chart.

$$UCL_{\bar{x}} = \bar{\bar{X}} + A_2\bar{R} \qquad LCL_{\bar{x}} = \bar{\bar{X}} - A_2\bar{R}$$

Step 13: Insert the control limits for the $\bar{x}$ portion of the chart.

The formula is self-explanatory except for the symbols D_4, D_3, and A_2. These are givens, and often control chart samples are taken in fives ($N = 5$). When $N = 5$, $D_4 = 2.114$ and $A_2 = .577$. $D_3 = 0$ up to a sample size of seven.

The formula for a type of control chart used more frequently in administrative operations shows the number of errors (defects) in subgroups versus the number inspected in the subgroups. It is known as a p chart for proportion defective, and the formula is as follows:

$$p = \text{proportion defective}$$

$$p = \frac{\text{number of rejects in subgroups}}{\text{number inspected in subgroups}}$$

$$\bar{p} = \frac{\text{total number of rejects}}{\text{total number inspected}}$$

$$UCL_p = \bar{p} + \frac{3\sqrt{\bar{p}(1-\bar{p})}}{\sqrt{n}}$$

$$LCL_p = \bar{p} - \frac{3\sqrt{\bar{p}(1-\bar{p})}}{\sqrt{n}}$$

Here are some final tips on control charts:

- Generally, twenty to twenty-five groups of samples need to be collected before calculating the control limits.
- Upper and lower control limits *must* be statistically calculated.
- Variation of the process can be reduced between the control limits, but common causes of this variation necessitate management involvement because something standard inside the process will need changing.
- Being in control does not always mean that the process is performing the way it is needed, e.g., if it consistently makes parts outside of specifications.

Other Training

The above courses and instructions on the quality tools should provide a headstart for any HR champion. Yet all needs may not be covered in this chapter. For example, basic meeting management skills were not suggested since most companies have such a course in place, and the meeting ground rules set with a facilitator support productive meetings. Likewise, pure communications courses were not suggested because communications classes already held often determine how much of this topic is included in a customized team leader/facilitator course. More advanced tools such as quality function deployment or benchmarking are not included in most basic classes.

Here is some key content that the HR professional will want to ensure is covered if the organization lacks these skills:

- Win-win negotiation
- Conflict resolution
- Building consensus
- Group problem-solving tools
  - Affinity diagramming
  - Nominal group technique
  - Force field analysis
  - Criteria screening
  - Multi-voting techniques
- Active listening
- Effective questioning techniques
- Giving and receiving feedback

Exercises or readings in creativity and innovation can also be helpful.

Conclusion

Training is not all that is needed for a successful TQM implementation, although some espouse it as *the* major tactic. On-site coaching and consultation is the key; studies show that only 50 percent of skills trained in the classroom are applied, and a company cannot expect successful implementation with its people only 50 percent enabled. Nonetheless, training is critical on the road to Total Quality.

Human resources executives can and do often use training as a means to raise awareness of the need for action and to begin the employees' education with that purpose in mind. That would be an excellent starting point for the HR professional to use, whether in management training, supervisory training, or executive retreats. The forces of change that move organizations forward come from many arenas, and training is an established forum for new ideas.

However, if the purpose of training is to take the organization to the level of on-the-job application, classes offering lots of practice, followed by on-site coaching, are critical for success. A comprehensive training strategy should be developed that addresses, at a minimum, the needs of the organization over the TQM implementation timeline.

Chapter 6
Compensation

Compensation professionals have long been involved in developing pay systems that motivate workers to produce goods or deliver services. However, too often, these systems have relied on traditional philosophies such as merit pay, which do not effectively link pay to performance over time and do not satisfactorily motivate workers. So why do U.S. organizations continue to manage employee rewards and motivation with such traditional methods? And since the pressure of global competition continues to squeeze profits and thus makes cost containment and increasing productivity and quality top priorities, how do HR professionals deliver compensation systems that provide the balance necessary between a company's financial success and a stimulated, productive work force?

These difficult and challenging questions form the basis for this chapter, which looks at the revolution occurring in employee reward systems across the United States. Concise explanations of the types of variable pay systems most commonly used, along with basic formulas for developing and implementing them, are also offered. Reward systems are related to a company's management philosophy, which is also discussed. Finally, examples of successful implementations are given in order to provide a network of resources for HR professionals to tap.

Evolution or Revolution in Reward Systems?

The 1980s was a watershed decade for American business in that executives finally recognized intense competition as the most pressing issue of the time. Even successful businesses had to face an uncertain future and begin to look for new ways of operating that maximized productivity and, therefore, profit. It was during this decade that significant experimentation with new reward systems began. (*New* is not necessarily an accurate description. Many of the variable pay systems discussed in this chapter were developed much earlier in the century but had not met with broad acceptance.)

If you accept that business needs a motivated, informed, and involved work force to face future challenges, and that reward systems play a substantial role in sustaining such a work force, then the basis for experimentation in reward systems is quite logical and expected. Yet despite the many national surveys that show employee dissatisfaction with current reward systems, a revolution is obviously not in progress. Here is where progressive HR professionals can champion efforts that will add momentum to the changes that need to happen quickly if America is to retain its world economic leadership role. TQM can act as a positive catalyst for these changes.

According to numerous surveys, employees do not find their reward systems "rewarding." Most see little relationship between pay and performance. Also, employees generally do not see that they will benefit financially from quality and productivity improvements in the workplace. But with the rash of mergers, downsizings, and the like that began in the 1980s and continued into the 1990s, employees began to see the link between their organization's financial success and their own job security.

Let's focus on the challenges and responses that developed during the 1980s. Perhaps the greatest challenge facing companies was the need to tie pay more clearly to performance, with such programs as gain sharing. Business looked to the sales function as the model for individual incentives, and industries as unlikely as banking began to motivate tellers to sell customers new products. Plus, completely new territory was forged with the establishment of pay-for-knowledge systems.

Another major challenge facing U.S. industry had to do with reducing compensation costs. Both compensation and benefits managers were looked to for solutions. In the compensation arena, professionals introduced the lump-sum bonus. And U.S. companies followed the lead of the Japanese, who had for decades institutionalized two-tier pay plans. Other innovations were attempted, such as all salaried plans, and by the time the 1990s began, various variable pay systems had something akin to a track record.

So where do U.S. compensation plans stand today? I like to rely on one highly authoritative source when looking for statistics on the newer reward systems: *People, Performance, and Pay,* based on a 1987 national survey distributed by the American Productivity & Quality Center and the American Compensation Association. Its major findings show that the 1980s did result in striking growth in a number of companies adopting nontraditional reward systems and that the more competition an organization reports, the more likely it is to use a nontraditional approach.

Figure 6-1 shows the number and percentage of companies using nontraditional rewards. The study also indicates that all companies reported a positive impact on performance linked to the new reward system. Last, the findings show that some organizations have eliminated or reduced more traditional approaches such as COLA, merit pay, pattern bargaining, and even executive perquisites.[1]

Other significant findings from the survey include the types of reward systems being used with various employee categories. Gain sharing and profit sharing appear as the leading types of variable pay systems used for all employees, with more than 50 percent of responding organizations offering both options to all classifications of employees. Pay-for-knowledge programs are focused on production workers more than on other classes of employees, and the all salaried work force has grown beyond the managerial and professional ranks to include over 80 percent of responding companies' administrative and clerical staff and over 40 percent of production workers.

Individual and small group incentives are most applied to managerial, professional, and production workers. Like pay-for-knowledge, the two-tier system is focused on the production worker and not that commonly applied across employee classifications. Finally, lump-sum bonuses appear to be used with managerial, professional, and technical employees more than with administrative, clerical, production, or service workers.[2]

One note of caution about the statistics from this study. The sample population includes members of the American Productivity & Quality Center and the American Compensation Association, which may mean that they are primarily larger organizations with possibly a more sophisticated approach to compensation issues than smaller companies. (This is not just a gut reaction. As recently as 1991, I listened to presentations of survey results by compensation consultants that included a larger percentage of respondents in the small to medium-size category. Generally, these results point more to the use of bonuses and lump-sum payments than to two-tier or knowledge-based pay systems.)

With regard to pay-for-knowledge programs particularly, I don't believe these statistics portend the future. The success stories that follow will explain why I believe pay-for-knowledge programs will become popular. In addition, in national surveys that ask companies if they plan to use these types of nontraditional reward systems, the answers by a majority of respondents are consistently affirmative.

Another excellent source of data on variable pay is a 1990 study by the Conference Board, where 435 companies supported the findings of the 1987 study described above. Individual incentives and lump-sum merit bonuses topped the list of variable pay options in use. In fact, the

Figure 6-1. The use of nontraditional reward systems.

Number and Percentage of Companies*

Nontraditional Rewards	Total (N=1,598) #	%	Goods (N=741) #	%	Services (N=741) #	%
Profit Sharing	507	32	274	37	208	28
Lump Sum Bonus	484	30	229	31	216	29
Individual Incentives	440	28	199	27	211	29
Gain Sharing	211	13	151	20	60	8
Small Group Incentives	223	14	111	15	112	15
All Salaried **	174	11	94	13	58	8
Two Tier	171	11	112	15	50	7
Pay for Knowledge	85	5	59	8	18	2
Earned Time Off	101	6	34	5	53	7
Total Number Using at Least One Nontraditional Reward	1,190	75%				

* Columns sum to more than N and 100% because of multiple responses.

** Only includes companies using system with production and/or service workers.

Source: Carla O'Dell, *People, Performance, and Pay* (Houston: American Productivity & Quality Center and American Compensation Association, 1987).

data support the trend that a "pushing down" of executive incentives is in the making for all managerial levels in the United States and that gain sharing is the system most under consideration by these respondent organizations.[3] For now, suffice it to say that experimentation with these variable systems is on the rise and will continue to be, for just as competition is not likely to cool down, neither will the sophistication of the human resources profession as it ties itself more and more to the strategic business objectives of the organization.

And finally, as recently as 1992, the American Compensation Association's research report, "Capitalizing on Human Assets," supported the evidence that variable pay systems were becoming a major business strategy with the objectives of developing the human asset of the company and shifting the corporate culture.

This report looked at 2,200 plans that focused on nonmanagement employees and were designed with a clear link between organizational performance and rewards. The report reinforces that regular communications of company performance to employees, employee feedback processes, and employee involvement efforts are factors that support the pay plans' success.

While traditional methods of pay adjustment, such as negotiated increases or merit pay, continue alongside these plans, the report shows that variable pay systems provide satisfaction for such business objectives as:

- Improving business performance
- Fostering teamwork
- Improving performance-reward linkage
- Improving morale
- Improving communications
- Creating an empowered environment[4]

With such major studies supporting variable pay systems, the challenge for the HR professional is to become adept at and to champion these pay plans. TQM fosters employee involvement and teamwork in the quest for increased productivity, quality, and profits. It just follows that TQM offers you a perfect scenario to accept the above challenge.

Let's look in more detail at some of the more common variable pay systems meeting widespread acceptance.

Individual Incentive Compensation

Incentive compensation is defined as a portion of an employee's pay that is directly linked to performance, usually to output. Individual incentive compensation has a long track record, especially if one looks at the concept of sales commissions, which have been used effectively for decades. This history is likely one of the reasons why individual incentives are expanding well beyond either sales or executive compensation programs. In many of today's organizations, the traditional individual piecework arrangements for production workers are still in place. But beyond that, incentives for administrative employees and incentives for managers (based on individual contribution to profitability, achievement of objectives, and the like) continue to grow.

Incentives for nonexempt employees became common in the 1980s, such as the aforementioned incentives for tellers in bank branches across the country. But that's not all. In addition nonexempt workers in banks who are engaged in processing items are also often given incentives. Unlike the tellers, who receive credit for the number of new sales or number of referrals of existing customers for new products, the incentives for these workers are generally based on individual standards such as items processed accurately per hour, day, or week. These incentives for nonexempt and even professional employees are found in all industries. Other measures of performance against which incentives are credited might include collections for accounts receivable, customer satisfaction ratings, meeting timetables, and implementing scientific discoveries.

Later, this chapter addresses the measurement challenges facing professionals who are being asked to assist with developing such programs. For now, the point is that incentives for individuals at all levels of the organization are becoming more and more commonplace.

Incentive plans may make the compensation professional's job more challenging, but the related increases in productivity, quality, service levels, and employee satisfaction—all cited by the companies responding to various national surveys—prove their worthiness. Creative professionals can achieve many objectives with either individual or group incentive programs.

Obstacles to Incentive Programs

For those who are beginning such programs, consider a few important obstacles. One is the traditional hierarchy of the organization and its inherent dependencies. These types of structures generally maintain a certain level of authority and, therefore, a certain level of inequality. Social psychologists have shown that if the distance between boss and subordinate declines, whether it be social or economic distance, then automatic deference and respect also decline. This equalization of power and authority, along with a smaller gap between salaries, erodes the very basis of the hierarchy.

This is not to say that some erosion might not be helpful in achieving higher or even peak performance levels. Nonetheless, the rationale for resistance becomes more understandable. The bright side to this is that now the resistance can be better managed. Cultural change and managerial style are not simple challenges, but superior service, superior products, and superior results overall are goals worthy of facing the challenges resistance brings.

Another obstacle to implementing incentives is the increase in administrative paperwork necessary to track performance measures. I have personally implemented individual and group incentive programs in operations that I managed. It did take a little extra effort, but focusing employees toward the critical aspects of their performance definitely improved their results, both individually and as a group.

A third obstacle to providing incentives for a broad spectrum of the work force has to do with the values the program will espouse, whether stated or not. When the banking industry began to incite tellers for sales or referrals, most banks found that the service values that had been instilled in their work force were in contradiction to the new message—sell! This was distasteful to many, and the values of the people had to be shifted to see sales as a service.

A fourth obstacle has to do with the traditional manner in which we evaluate performance. In traditional approaches to performance appraisal, evaluation can be quite subjective. In moving toward identifying critical performance parameters, the outcome of incentive programs often results in more quantitative measures. Long-held attributes such as tenure (loyalty), cooperation, and belonging cannot be integrated easily into the equation. Also, it becomes more difficult for management to explain unsubstantiated differences in rewards between employees when the measures of performance are based more on quantifiable results. It also becomes more difficult for managers who choose to treat almost everyone the same to continue not making distinctions between individuals' results.

My personal bias regarding new pay systems is to integrate the best of both worlds and create incentives that reward both individuals *and* groups. This is not that common, but it takes into account the best of the American culture that rewards individual achievement while supporting the need to instill teamwork and collaboration. In any walk of life, achieving that delicate balance is not easy, but it certainly can be accomplished. This approach necessitates a managerial focus on both group and individual development and recognition as part of the job in today's world.

Small Group Incentives

Let's veer from individual incentivs and look at the growth and effectiveness of small group incentives. These endeavors, while growing in number, are less common than their individual counterparts. Yet as Total Quality and other involvement efforts continue to gain momentum, the number of small group incentives will grow dramatically. This belief is supported by many of the national surveys that have been conducted since the late 1980s. Small group incentives generally cover groups of seven to twenty employees. The reason the number of employees is small is because of group cohesion and synergy. Often, natural work teams are the logical choice. Groups can sometimes be larger if a cross-functional effort is being incited or, as is sometimes the case in service and manufacturing organizations, the entire department (e.g., customer service) is.

Usually incentive awards are based on financial performance or production criteria. National studies do show that as the incentive moves into the nonexempt/hourly ranks, production and not financial performance frequently becomes the basis for the reward. There are many logical reasons that organizations are moving in the direction of small group incentives. One of the most common is the organization's need to promote teamwork. Another is to increase the productivity and quality of the work group's output. Linking pay more closely to performance and achieving company goals are other common reasons. When the group incentive is tied to the continuous improvement effort, the reasons may be to increase cost savings or improve service levels. And sometimes, small group incentives are put in place to support a shift in the corporate culture.

Let's look at a fictitious case study that incorporates both individual and small group incentives.

Case Study

The target population of this incentive program is the nonexempt work force in a division of a banking operation that has two functions. One function closes loans, and the other puts the approved loans on the books. The criterion for the incentive is a production-based outcome that includes a quality checklist, which is completed by the worker. A random sample of checklists is reviewed by supervisory staff to ensure that both quantity and quality are acceptable prior to payout. The premise of this program is to promote not only productivity, quality, and customer service, but also divisional pride and teamwork. The following standards were set:

Job	Production Standard	Quality Standard
Closer	60 loans per month	100% accuracy
Booker	400 loans per month	100% accuracy

Standards were established based on the time it took to process various types of loans, including complexity and current quality levels. Both closers and bookers were involved in setting the standards and in designing the incentive plan. All employees were asked for input and concurrence with the plan before it was put into place.

The plan provided the following incentives:

Job	Monthly Standard (per person)	Incentive
Closer	Production over 60/month	$15.00@
Booker	Production over 400/month	$ 5.00@

One-third of the dollars are paid based on productivity, one-third of the dollars are paid based on quality, and one-third reflect the group outcomes. The quality portion of the incentive is to be paid in arrears due to the need to review a 10 percent random sample per employee.

Once an employee reaches standard in any given month, the incentive program activates. Incentives are paid separately for productivity, quality, and group outcomes. For example, the closer's $15.00 would come from $5.00 for productivity, $5.00 for quality, and $5.00 for overall group performance.

Sample Payout

1. Closer exceeds quota by 15 loans with no quality errors:

    15 loans × $5.00 = $75.00   Production incentive
    15 loans × $5.00 = $75.00   Quality incentive
    Total $150.00   Individual incentive

2. Booker exceeds quota by 50 loans with no quality errors:

    50 loans × $1.66 = $83.00   Production incentive
    50 loans × $1.66 = $83.00   Quality incentive
    Total $166.00   Individual incentive

3. Group exceeds quota by 100 loans in closing and by 200 loans in booking:

    100 loans × $5.00 = $500.00   Closer portion
    200 loans × $1.68 = $336.00   Booker portion
    Total $836.00   Group incentive

    Group formula: $836.00 ÷ 24 employees = $34.83@

4. Closer monthly incentive   Booker monthly incentive

        $150.00 $166.00
          34.83   34.83
        ―――――――   ―――――――
        $184.83 $200.83

I have not provided the checklists used for each position. A simple listing of pertinent information needed will suffice. When a staff member is trying to close a loan in order to send it to be approved, all numerical figures must be accurate, the spelling of the buyer's name must be accurate, the street address of the property must be accurate, the fees must be paid, the loan application must be filled out completely, etc.

In the case of the staff member putting on the loan on the books (or into the main database), the account number must be correct, the first payment due date must be accurate, the term and interest rate of the loan must be correct, the principal balance must be verified, and the payments must be accurate and complete. These are the types of items found on the quality checklist that each employee and the supervisors use as a personal and internal audit. Any errors found by the supervisor would eliminate the quality portion of the incentive from being paid since the team decided that the quality standard was to be 100 percent.

The Question of Overtime

What about overtime considerations when it comes to creating incentives for nonexempt personnel? William E. Buhl, the compensation manager for HEB Corporation in Texas, addressed this issue in an article written for the American Productivity & Quality Center's *Manager's Notebook Series*. He states that the Fair Labor Standards Act requires that regularly paid bonuses be included when calculating nonexempt or hourly employees' regular pay rates in order to determine overtime pay rates. This might obviously drive up the costs of overtime pay and increase the administrative burden of calculating such pay. Buhl's recommendation is to design incentives as percentage-of-wage bonuses that will protect against liability for any additional overtime pay under the Act. He cites examples for individual incentives and group incentives.[5]

This first example is of an individual incentive using the percentage-of-wage formula, here set at 4 percent:

Employee	Monthly Wages		Percentage of Wages		Individual Incentive
Sue	$890.46				
	70.10 (OT)				
	$960.56 total	×	4.0%	=	$38.42

This second example is of a group incentive using the percentage-of-wage formula:

Employee	Group Incentive Over a Quarter	Three-Month Wage	Percentage of Wages
Joe		$3,400.00	
		510.00 (OT)	
	$450.00	$3,910.00 total	11.5%

Gain Sharing Plans

Gain sharing programs are another type of variable pay system that is gathering momentum. Simply put, gain sharing is an incentive plan that rewards participants for increased productivity on the basis of a predetermined formula. While it appears that gain sharing blossomed in the factories starting with employee involvement efforts throughout the 1980s, the model company was then little-known Lincoln Electric of Ohio. As early as 1982, magazines such as *Forbes* were talking about the Cleveland manufacturer. And in February 1983, the company held a press conference to call attention to its success and to concentrate attention on the plight of America's heartland. While Lincoln Electric was prospering, its management was watching its neighboring industries suffer. Lincoln's managers wanted other organizations to consider the Lincoln incentive system as a catalyst to redesigning their own reward systems.

Perhaps you have heard this story of Lincoln Electric. Perhaps you know that since 1934, Lincoln employees have been earning bonuses that averaged 97.6 percent of regular earnings! The bonus system was begun at the request of the workers, who were denied a pay raise in 1933 because of the Depression. The employees themselves suggested the alternative—that the company share any profitability increases with them.[6] Even in the early 1980s, Lincoln workers outpaced the average annual earnings of workers at like manufacturers by more than three to one and continued to outpace them (but not by so much) even during recessionary times.

As long ago as the Depression era, two of the historical bases for modern-day gain sharing, Rucker and Scanlon plans, were developed. The only other model gain sharing program, Improshare, was developed in the 1970s. At the beginning of the 1980s, these three types of plans dominated the systems in place. But by the end of the decade, customized plans were more commonplace, and few "cookie cutter" programs existed.

Here are the key distinctions among the three historical models mentioned above:

1. *Rucker plan.* This plan uses a calculation based on an historical relationship between labor and value added, with a bonus generated in any month where actual labor costs are less than a standard percentage of production value.
2. *Scanlon plan.* This plan establishes a base ratio related to the experience of the past several years. Then it measures the labor costs of the unit against sales and applies the base ratio to determine the bonus payable.
3. *Improshare.* This plan establishes a measure of work hours saved for units produced in comparison with the work hours required to produce an equal number of units during a base period.[7]

I will downplay the role of the above models as current surveys show that most gain sharing plans today are customized to fit a company's specific needs. However, many plans still involve certain productivity improvements over a base period. Other factors that can be considered include financial achievement, cost control, improved service levels, and even safety records.

While payments can be made monthly, quarterly, biannually, or even annually, it appears that most plans pay out quarterly. Some plans hold a portion of the payout in reserve in case of unpredicted declines in the factors used as measures; these reserve dollars are usually paid out at the end of the plan year. There is mixed information about the amount of actual dollars actually paid out, but the 1990 Conference Board study on variable pay (mentioned earlier), cities a range from 2 to 8 percent of annual wages and salaries, with the median payment at 3 percent.[8] This is substantially less than the average 5 percent merit increase of the last few years and explains why most companies using gain sharing still set base wages and salaries at competitive levels. Yet there are experts in the field who cite bonuses of 20 and even 50 percent of the profits gained in formulas they have helped develop. Gain sharing then truly becomes extra compensation and more motivating to the work force.

Measurement Issues

One of the critical issue areas of gain sharing plans has to do with establishing meaningful measurements. There are two experts in the field of gain sharing who offer advice that is invaluable to the HR profession. Let me address the concepts of Timothy L. Ross first. He and Ruth Ann Ross differentiate between control and reward systems. They define two polarities in productivity performance: (1) pure productivity and (2) financial productivity. Pure productivity measures are considered to be of a control orientation, while financial productivity reflects a reward orientation. The Rosses contend that managers have attitudes that lead them to support one orientation or the other.

For example, a control-oriented manager would say to employees, "You did a great job this month even though we didn't make much profit." A reward-oriented manager, who is focused on the larger world of profits, would say, "You did a great job this month, and since we also were able to raise prices, we made a nice profit." You can see that one manager can and will draw the relationship to worker performance and increased productivity despite the profit picture. The Rosses believe that gain sharing formulas generally make a distinction that matters to the company based on these orientations.[9]

Gain sharing plans focused on pure productivity use measurements like direct labor costs, direct labor hours, and physical counts such as outputs. Common inputs include labor costs (direct to indirect) and labor hours (direct to indirect). Gain sharing plans that focus on financial productivity consider measurements like sales and inventories on the output side and labor and other costs, such as materials, on the input side. (In some formulas, all variable costs are included as inputs, but these formulas are more complex not only to administer but also to communicate effectively.)

Since customization has become the name of the game in developing gain sharing plans in the 1990s, many more measurements are now being considered and used. Besides those above, pure financial measures such as margins, profits, and various returns can now be found in some formulas. John G. Belcher, the second expert I want to discuss, cites numerous examples such as manufacturing cost, delivery performance, inventories, safety, reductions in scrap loss, and conservation of energy. In his opinion, there are no "right" answers to the numerous design questions facing a company when developing its gain sharing plan.[10] It's inevitable that creative measures such as number of suggestions or innovations implemented may soon be seen in some gain sharing formulas as companies design plans to fit their specific cultures.

One of the challenges that will face compensation professionals is the selection process used to determine which of the many measures should actually make their way into the gain sharing formula. A technique that is commonly used to develop measures lends itself well to the complexity of American business. This technique, called the Family of Measures, works well with multiple independent performance criteria. Critical performance variables can be merged into a final outcome for payout by calculating the gain (or loss) for each factor, then aggregating them to determine the size of the bonus pool. The advantages of using this technique are inclusion of a broader range of performance variables and a greater opportunity to focus on improved performance than is possible with a cost or financial measure.[11]

Case Examples

Before you become disillusioned with the many decisions that need to be made when installing a gain sharing plan, let me provide some wonderfully motivating examples. Vickers AMD in Jackson, Mississippi, again proves to be successful with its plan, which emphasizes quality. Rejected parts were displayed on the shop floor with dollar values attached, not for just the part itself, but also for the entire contract. As employees became aware of the cost of "nonquality" and gains were shared with them, more and more employees have become committed. Gains as high as 8 percent of wages have been paid since the gain sharing plan's inception.[12]

All gain sharing plans do not exist in manufacturing concerns, so an example using a nonprofit hospital, St. Luke's in Kansas City, Missouri, seems appropriate. Its plan, called SHARE (for Sharing Helps Accumulate Rewards for Efficiency), is a modified Scanlon plan that focuses on cost reduction. Only controllable costs are included, bonus distributions are based on cost savings only (not net profits), and adjustments are made for inflationary increases. Since salaries at hospitals typically lag behind other industries, the extra compensation helps attract and retain top candidates.

St. Luke's piloted its program in 1979. During the pilot phase, the program weighed department performance but has since moved to total organization results. The percentage of savings that is shared with employees is 50 percent, with departments showing savings earning a higher percentage bonus. This plan also includes a "maintenance" bonus once an operation reaches peak efficiency in order to reinforce the high level of performance. Everyone from the CEO on down receives the bonus.[13]

Another early entry to the gain sharing arena is Trans-Matic Manufacturing Company in Holland, Michigan, whose program began in 1977. After one false start, this company established a bonus based on production cost. The first 12 percent pretax profit is retained as an investment for growth. Profit above 12 percent becomes the bonus pool and is split 50/50 between employees and the company. Bonuses are paid quarterly, with 25 percent retained in a reserve account and paid out as a fifth bonus at the end of the year if the company has operated at the 12 percent level or above during the year. Even though the company faced some very tough years, the plan was considered to operate effectively. The plan, plus the serious commitment made to employee involvement, resulted in decreased absenteeism and tardiness at Trans-Matic, with very little turnover.[14]

Even a large corporation like McDonnell Douglas Electronics in St. Charles, Missouri, reviewed its gain sharing ideas with employees and told them that 75 percent had to approve it or it would not be put into operation. In July 1985, 80 percent of the employees voted for the plan, which used earnings divided by investment as its simple formula. Some of the productivity gains are shared proportionately with McDonnell Aircraft, to whom MDEC is a subcontractor. The rest is split 60/40 between employees and the company. All full-time employees are participants and are asked to propose improvements. If the steering committee views the proposed change as worthy of consideration, the change is submitted to the work force for a vote. A typical quarterly bonus is $200, an amount that is not uncommon in organizations of any size.[15]

Hopefully, these illustrations of gain sharing plans will encourage their consideration as you seek to improve the link between pay and performance in your company.

Design Checklist

This segment would not be complete without a short section on key design issues that need addressing when installing a gain sharing plan. The following checklist will help ensure your plan's success:

- ☐ Make sure that historical records exist to establish baselines. If not, determine how to use rolling averages correctly.
- ☐ Use overall corporate indicators only if there are no other measures that are more clearly tied to job performance.
- ☐ Monitor and record performance regularly and accurately.
- ☐ Time the installation for when revenue exists so that payouts will be made.
- ☐ Ensure that top management commitment exists.
- ☐ Involve employees in plan design and direction from the start.
- ☐ Develop a communications strategy that shares business information regularly and broadly.
- ☐ Reinforce the connection between the desired work output and the company's success.
- ☐ Research and benchmark successful plans prior to designing your company's.
- ☐ Consider hiring a consultant to assist in the design and installation.

☐ Bring the final design to your employees for their concurrence.
☐ Plan for periodic reviews and potential adjustment to the formula.

Last, it is important to reiterate that professionals should not make the plan too complicated. Gain sharing is a unique approach that people may not be familiar with, so it is wise to construct a plan that can be easily understood.

Pay-for-Knowledge Systems

Pay-for-knowledge, also known as multiskill compensation or skill-based pay, is another type of variable pay that is projected to grow dramatically in the 1990s and into the next decade. This newer compensation plan saw its roots on the factory floor and is an outgrowth of the organizational redesign associated with semiautonomous or self-directed work teams. However, it is finding its way into the service sector and is expected to grow dramatically there as well. These systems, which look like the technical ladders of the past, are found in skilled trades, law offices, and R&D labs.

The purpose of a pay-for-knowledge plan is to build flexibility into the workplace so that employees can perform several different or increasingly in-depth responsibilities. The structure often ties pay to the number of different jobs an employee can perform within or beyond the work group. This goes hand-in-hand with participative cultures that encourage team problem solving and employee ownership of the work process.

While flexibility and better use of staff are clear advantages of this pay system, there is an increase in administrative and training costs. Increases in productivity will offset these costs as team members become multiskilled, but initially a company would be wise to look at this effort as an investment. Another consideration important to pay-for-knowledge programs is the ability they offer to pay employees for skills they bring to the workplace, rather than for seniority, position, or status. These are not bonus programs. Rather, they encourage employees to learn more about the business and to develop a wider range of skills than ever before.

The keys to designing these systems are similar to some of those given for gain sharing. Employees need to be involved from the start, preferably in the design stage. A thorough communications strategy must be built so that all employees will understand the program. Supervisors have to be prepared to receive pressure for training for employees and must plan when and how they will rotate people through identifiable and learnable skill levels. Management must be committed and must reinforce continuing growth and decision making at the lowest levels in order to reap the productivity benefits this system promises.

Often a design task force is created well in advance of the installation to wrestle with the issues of which employees will be covered, how the skill levels will be determined, and where the pay-for-knowledge system will be implemented in the organization. This necessitates detailed analysis. Then, of course, this team could be used to develop the actual implementation plan. This plan describes how people will be informed, trained, and evaluated. It also includes developing the actual pay progression and deciding what to do once employees reach the highest level. This team might also look at how the pay-for-knowledge system integrates with other forms of compensation in existence. And finally, if not this task force, some mechanism needs to be in place to monitor and review the program's effectiveness.

Pay-for-knowledge reinforces attainment of technical skills by individuals and therefore can act as an effective supplement to gain sharing programs that make rewards according to financially based organization-wide measures. It can also be an appropriate supplement to incentives for groups or entire organizations when the measures are purely productivity-based.

This is how it works. A worker generally enters a work group at the entry level of pay. (Occasionally, someone brings skills to the job that would support a higher step in the pay ladder.) Then, as the employee learns new skills, he or she receives incremental pay increases. A typical pay-for-knowledge ladder follows:

Skills Acquired	Pay Rate Per Hour
Entry Level	$5.00
Team Skill 1	5.50
Team Skill 2	6.00
Team Skill 3	6.50
Team Skill 4	7.00
Team Skill 5	7.50
Team Skill 6	8.00

Team members often have the option of learning skills outside of their natural work team. Generally, there is another pay ladder for this advancement of skills above the level of Team Skill 6. In some plans, there is also a plantwide rate that reflects a person who can be moved throughout the facility. It would take quite a long time before anyone could master all the skills needed in his or her facility.

You can see the benefit this has on motivating the worker. This type of pay system leads to increased satisfaction, greater feelings of self-worth, greater commitment, and increased job security. In an era when upward advancement is not always an option, horizontal learning adds breadth that can enrich a person's job. On the other hand, people are people, and they will want to advance from one level to another. If the organization does not require a period of time during which the employee agrees to perform the newly acquired skill, it may not benefit fully from the employee's new capabilities.

Case Example

Before moving on to other forms of variable pay, it always helps to give an example. I will share one that I saw in action thanks to my colleague, Richard L. Bunning, when he was with Sola Ophthalmics in Phoenix.

Sola Ophthalmics, a contact lens manufacturer, was under financial pressure in the mid-1980s. After a move that vertically reorganized the manufacturing process so that work groups would be responsible for the complete production of a finished contact lens, it became apparent that the reward system also needed realignment. Work groups were large, often as many as twenty-five members. These employees were responsible for completing up to thirty different processes that resulted in a marketable lens. Since work group members needed to be able to move throughout the unit to assist in production wherever needed, a pay-for-knowledge system was devised.

Luckily, the employees at the plant were familiar with the concept of skill-based pay, so support was high and initial educational efforts minimal. A task force was created to develop the initial proposal. (This task force was made up primarily of supervisors. I would encourage broader participation.) Small group meetings were also held with all employees to answer questions and gain input. Another task force was brought together to rank and then cluster jobs. Once this was completed, appropriate pay grade levels were assigned. I talked with employees in one of the work groups, and they were quite pleased with the system and proud of their work. Bunning's article on Sola in *Personnel Administrator* cited benefits of increased flexibility, productivity gains, reasonable costs, and employee acceptance.[16] He also talked of broader implementation to the point where skill-based pay is now the norm in the organization.

Other Variable Pay Systems

Many other forms of variable pay exist. They range from simple to complex and show that much creativity is being used in the compensation field. I will list just some of the other avenues that are being used in order to compile as complete a list as possible for you to research further.

• *Lump-sum bonus*. This pay method was created to contain costs. The reward does not get added to the employee's base pay. Lump-sum bonuses are being used in as many as one-third of the companies responding to national surveys. They are given only mixed acceptance by employees since the base pay rate does not change. They are welcomed by employees who still receive their annual merit increases.

• *Instant incentive*. These one-time bonuses are presented within reasonable time frames following exceptional performance. They are generally cash but can be in the form of material rewards ranging from trips to sporting event tickets. Usage is relatively common.

• *Earned time off*. As a reward for exceptional service, employees are given earned time off that is not recorded against either vacation or sick leave. This is not being used that extensively, yet from my own management experience, I found it to be an effective reward and a positive motivator.

• *Equity bonus*. Shares of stock, especially to those employees who do not have access to stock option plans, can be a solid motivator. Not commonly used, it has potential beyond the highly technical key contributors to whom most equity shares have been awarded.

• *Budgetary discretion*. Another less widely used reward, primarily for technical key contributors, is to be given discretion over special budgets outside of normal accounting controls. An even more unusual expansion of this reward is to give key contributors the authority to grant salary increases or bonuses to support staff or colleagues who contributed to their success.

• *Two-tier pay*. This type of pay system arose out of the need to contain costs and retain employees. It is often implemented in unionized companies. New hires are paid at a lower rate than current employees doing the same job. Over time these pay differences tend to decrease. These programs are not popular with employees and do create equity issues, even if they are part of the union contract.

• *Profit sharing*. The traditional profit-sharing plans continue in common use as a compensation incentive. The steady growth of these plans over several decades is expected to continue. This uniform payment based on organizational profitability is motivating but may be difficult for individual employees to link with their job performance. Another motivational concern is that often these payments are deferred for a long period of time, and therefore are not a means of immediate feedback for employees.

• *Recognition programs*. Since Chapter 4 discusses recognition, I will briefly list some of the noncash type of rewards being given to employees across the nation. These include verbal and written thank you's, praise, certificates, trophies, flexible work schedules, breakfasts, lunches, dinners, pens, caps, jackets, pins, special assignments, and time for personal projects. There are many other rewards that are given either formally or informally, at banquets or in the office. While not always considered part of the pay system, recognition programs do cost time and money and are generally held to be part of a company's overall reward system.

Critical Considerations in Compensation Systems

It is clear that an evolution in employee rewards is in progress. When taking into account the importance of the labor force in any company's success, the compensation arena is a crucial one. No matter what motivational survey is cited to show that variables beside pay are important, it remains clear that what a person earns or how he or she is rewarded is a top priority to every individual in the work force.

Since the cost of living has squeezed people to do more with less, there is all the more reason to reevaluate our reward systems and look for creative alternatives. There are a few key design issues that must always be considered, regardless of the type of system that may be selected. It seems logical to close this chapter with a reminder of these critical considerations.

- *The objectives to be fulfilled by the new reward system must be clear.* HR professionals need to know what the new plan is expected to accomplish. Whether the objective is cost containment, motivation, competitive advantage, teamwork, or increased risk taking, the professional charged with the task of creating a new plan must see that it fits with the vision and the objectives of the company.

- *The performance criteria must be measurable and must relate directly to the business objectives.* The more quantifiable, the better. The more customized to the company, the better.

- *The target of the reward system must be determined.* By *target*, I am referring to the employees who will be eligible to receive the reward. Plan participants who can see the relationship between their performance and the rewards are more likely to exhibit the desired behaviors and produce the desired results.

- *How much should be paid or awarded must be determined*, once the measurements are established and the eligibility clarified. Gaining information about competitors' practices in these early stages is important, but not always easy. But if that information is available, it does help to determine what the award levels might optimally be.

• *The funding formula for the plan must be developed.* Various decisions must be made about the formula used. One has to do with leverage. If only a small amount of additional earnings are available for improved performance, then the motivation to perform exceptionally well is decreased and vice versa. Remember the old maxim, "the more risk, the more reward."

• *At what point rewards kick in must be determined.* If incentives are awarded at low performance levels, what is the impact? If a minimum return is expected, as with the company cited in this chapter that rewarded only after 12 percent improvement was reached, would this change the formula?

• *Whether or not to place a ceiling on earnings from the plan must be determined.* The decision about capping the rewards paid relates to the values-driven issue of distance between boss/subordinate pay. It may also have to do with certain business realities.

• *The method and timing of payment must be determined.* Is the reward a cash award? If so, is it paid monthly or quarterly? Is any of it held in reserve? Is any of it deferred? If the reward is noncash, should it be stock, trips, or what?

Doing good planning and involving others will help to ensure a smoother implementation, but making the right decisions in the first place is paramount.

Conclusion

This chapter in no way is meant to be the textbook for change in your organization's compensation system. As it scratched the surface, it was meant to be a catalyst for thinking about how effective your present reward system is in light of the many new variable pay systems and the change TQM is bringing to the workplace. Hopefully, it also posed many of the critical questions and considerations that need to be addressed if you should choose to join this "quiet" revolution.

Besides seeing that the appropriate reward system is in place, another important challenge for the HR professional is to improve human resources planning at all levels so that there are openings available for qualified employees who have worked hard to develop new skills. Hopefully, the benefits of experimenting with these various approaches to compensation will be worth the time and effort for everyone. These pay systems are only a part, albeit an integral part, of an overall human resources development system.

Chapter 7

Organization Development: The Role of Internal and External Consultants in TQM

Large-scale systems change is not only complex, it is fragile. It is imperative that top management be committed to the change because of the challenges the move to a new vision will bring. This holds true for Total Quality implementations, too, since the word *total* in front of *quality* means a comprehensive initiative that will bring large-scale change to the organization. Rosabeth Moss Kantor coined the term *change masters* in the 1980s. It will be used throughout this chapter to describe the internal or external organization development (OD) consultants so necessary to successfully coaching top management and the organization through the phases of change and all that ensues.

This chapter discusses the skills and competencies needed by internal or external consultants implementing TQM in the hopes of helping HR executives to discern how these skills and competencies differ from others needed by HR professionals. The chapter discusses the differences between using internal and/or external resources and also addresses how to work with outside consultants. A model of effective change management is offered along with discussion of what to expect from the different phases of a large-scale change effort. A detailed elaboration of the phases in a consulting process is also addressed in order to draw relationships between the phases of change efforts and what can be expected of consultants as the consultation progresses. Finally, the chapter closes by showing the role of consultation in a TQM implementation.

Consulting Skills and Competencies

The role of the consultant is multifaceted and complex. It takes a flexible, creative, and honest relationship builder and problem solver to make a good consultant, whether internal or external. It also takes many other forms of knowledge, skill, and ability. To understand the many dimensions of the consultant's role, it is helpful to consider the different ways a consultant works. At times, a consultant is not helping to lead an initiative but is a nondirective observer or process counselor. At other times, the consultant may be viewed as a content expert and advocate, as well as a guide. Figure 7-1 shows the different roles of the consultant.

In a TQM effort, the role of the consultant varies according to how much knowledge the organization already has and the level of need. In my experience, the TQM consultant is generally a proactive partner in the process and plays a role tending to the right side of Figure 7-1. This, of course, does not mean that the consultant does not act as a fact finder. On the contrary, it just implies that all skills and competencies required of a consultant must be in place to ensure success.

Gordon and Ronald Lippitt are well-known names to OD professionals everywhere. They have summarized responses from more than thirty experienced consultants regarding the competencies and skills needed for success as a change master. They are categorized into knowledge, skills, and attitudes. Here is their list, supplemented with knowledge, skills, and attitudes needed for TQM implementation.

Knowledge

1. Thorough grounding in the behavioral sciences.
2. Thorough foundation in the administrative philosophies, policies, and practices of organization systems and larger social systems.
3. Knowledge of educational and training methodologies, especially laboratory methods, problem-solving exercises, and role plays.
4. Understanding of stages in the growth of individuals, groups, organizations, and communities and how they function at different stages.
5. Knowledge of how to design and facilitate a change process.
6. Knowledge and understanding of human personality, attitude formation, and change.
7. Knowledge of oneself: motivation, strengths, weaknesses, and biases.

Figure 7-1. The multiple roles of the consultant and levels of consultant activity in problem solving.

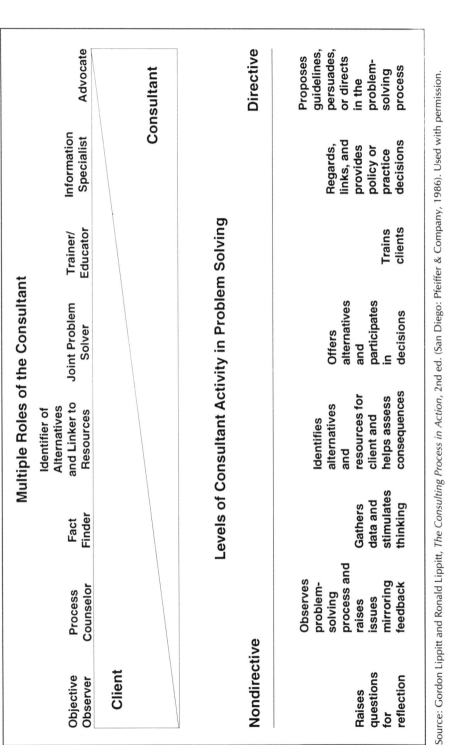

Multiple Roles of the Consultant

Levels of Consultant Activity in Problem Solving

	Objective Observer	Process Counselor	Fact Finder	Identifier of Alternatives and Linker to Resources	Joint Problem Solver	Trainer/ Educator	Information Specialist	Advocate
Nondirective	Raises questions for reflection	Observes problem-solving process and raises issues mirroring feedback	Gathers data and stimulates thinking	Identifies alternatives and resources for client and helps assess consequences	Offers alternatives and participates in decisions	Trains clients	Regards, links, and provides policy or practice decisions	Proposes guidelines, persuades, or directs in the problem-solving process	Directive

Client

Consultant

Source: Gordon Lippitt and Ronald Lippitt, *The Consulting Process in Action*, 2nd ed. (San Diego: Pfeiffer & Company, 1986). Used with permission.

8. Understanding of the leading philosophical systems as a framework for thought and a foundation for value systems.

Skills

1. Communications skills: listening, observing, identifying, and reporting.
2. Teaching and persuasive skills: ability to impart new ideas and insights effectively and to design learning experiences that contribute to growth and change.
3. Counseling skills to help others reach meaningful decisions of their own accord.
4. Ability to form relationships based on trust and to work with a great variety of persons of different backgrounds and personalities; sensitivities to the feelings of others; ability to develop and share one's own charisma.
5. Ability to work with groups and teams in planning and implementing change; skill in using group dynamics techniques and laboratory training methods.
6. Ability to use a variety of intervention methods; ability to determine which method is most appropriate at a given time.
7. Skill in designing surveys, interviewing, and other data collection techniques.
8. Ability to diagnose problems with a client; to locate sources of help, power, and influence; to understand a client's values and culture; to determine readiness for change.
9. Ability to be flexible in dealing with all types of situations.
10. Skill in using problem-solving techniques and in assisting others in solving problems.

Attitudes

1. Professional attitude: competence, integrity, feeling of responsibility for helping clients cope with and solve their problems.
2. Maturity: self-confidence; courage to stand by one's views; willingness to take necessary risks; ability to cope with rejection, hostility, and suspicion.
3. Open-mindedness, honesty, and intelligence.
4. Possession of a humanistic value system: belief in the importance of the individual; belief in technology and efficiency as a means and not an end; trust in people and the democratic process in economic activities.

A few important areas that are not on this list need mention. A knowledge of systems theory is an important aid to a consultant, as is having a grasp of coaching, feedback, negotiation, and conflict resolution skills. In addition, planning and project management skills and boundary spanning skills are very helpful to consultants. In regard to TQM, there is a body of technical and teaming knowledge that is important. Included are:

1. *Knowledge of work process.* Customer/supplier relationships, inputs and outputs, and value-added work activities.
2. *Strategic planning tools.* SWOT (strengths, weaknesses, opportunities, threats) analysis, critical success factors, criteria matrix, and other decision tools.
3. *Employee involvement techniques.* Quality circles, idea generation, semiautonomous and self-directed work team concepts.
4. *The basic quality tools.* Process flow analysis and charting, Pareto diagraming, cause-and-effect analysis, scatter diagraming, histograms, run charts, and control charts.
5. *Teaming knowledge.* Chartering teams, roles in effective quality teams, effective meeting techniques.
6. *Direction setting techniques.* Developing mission, vision, and value statements.
7. *Measurement techniques.* Family of Measures, customer satisfaction measures, supplier measures, process and outcome measures, and organization effectiveness measures.
8. *Organization improvement strategies/tactics.* Communication, rewards and recognition, integration of quality planning with strategic planning, training needs assessment, and leadership styles and characteristics.

The Role of the Internal Change Master

As this list shows, many competencies are needed to consult effectively in an organization. This reality may make it seem impossible that internal staff can accomplish the job. Not true! There are many organizations that have exception OD consultants as full-time employees. (Two that come to mind are Digital Equipment and Levi Strauss. These companies hire people well-grounded in the field and have talented internal leaders for their OD teams.)

The role of the internal consultant varies with the issue at hand and the organization's willingness to accept help from internal resources. The internal consultant is not usually expected to be a technical expert, but rather a fact-finding, problem-solving, and change process expert. After providing feedback from the data collection and making recommendations, the internal consultant continues working through the action planning phase, supporting the implementation of the change and assisting in its evaluation. The only time that internal consultants tend to leave change projects is if they are brought in to consult as a technical expert and then complete that task. An example might be asking a compensation professional to assist with changing a reward system when moving a work unit toward self-direction. The compensation expert would be needed when planning the design of the new reward system, but not needed to help the work group implement the change to self-management (although another internal or external consultant with teaming experience might well be an ongoing member of the team).

There are other internal models besides general organization development consultants. Some companies have consultants who specialize in certain types of change implementation. This is true of the Total Quality movement. Many enterprises have created quality departments whose members are expected to assist in implementing TQM as it is deployed across the organization. These staff members, again, generally stick with the change effort from the planning and design phases through implementation. Their initial lack of expertise may well be supported by outside consultants who are brought in with the expectation to transfer their knowledge and skills to the internal staff.

The Role of the External Change Master

External consultants play various types of roles in organizations. Two common roles are (1) the expert role and (2) the partner role.

The Expert Role

The contracting manager may not only lack the expertise to deal with the problem, he/she may not have the time to address the issue well. This is when a specialist or expert is called upon to diagnose the problem and recommend changes. The contracting manager tends, in this case, to open lines of communication for the consultant, but remains quite inactive. He/she is waiting for the feedback report. Many external consultants are hired for this type of engagement. Often, once the findings are presented and recommendations made, that is the end of the external consulting relationship.

The Partner Role

Here, a larger change is often called for and the external consultant is brought in from planning through implementation. This consultation is more of a 50/50 proposition in that the responsibility is shared more equally between the internal and external players. In this type of consulting role, the outside expert joins his/her special expertise with that of the internal players to address the issue at hand collaboratively. The internal players are more involved with all phases of the consulting project than when an external consultant is retained as an expert. They plan with the external person or team and are actively involved in the data collection phase (or some of their staff are). They help set the action plan once the findings are presented, and they often play key roles in the implementation of the change. Throughout the engagement, responsibilities are continually negotiated and agreed upon. This is often the nature of TQM consulting engagements.

In TQM engagements, there is often a clear deliverable for the external consultant to transfer technologies, methodologies, and skills to the internal staff. This direct coaching differs from the issue/problem to be solved and needs its own clarity between the players. The role played by the consultant delivering this type of service is often a highly collaborative one between the parties involved even though the expertise initially rests with the external consultant. Peter Block, a highly regarded management consultant, considers the core transaction of any consulting contract to be the transfer of expertise from the consultant to the client.[2]

Working Well With an External Consultant

OD consultants are facilitators, helpers in making organizations better for the good of the company and its people. They are motivated by influencing others to improve and reap the benefits of positive change. They work through others and, as such, find satisfaction in aiding others to better solve their problems or create and implement new visions. There is an element of bravery in OD: the consultant must (1) make authentic responses to individual or organizational needs in order to solve problems so they stay solved or (2) create new visions that are reachable, realistic, yet significantly better than the existing situation. HR professionals can therefore count on OD professionals generally to own the objectives and goals of their clients in any consulting engagement. And they can expect honesty from them.

These truths lend toward effective partnerships between OD consultants and their clients. But any initiative can go awry if there is a lack of clarity between the consultant and the client from the start of the effort. The entry and contracting phase of the project is important in that ground rules, roles, boundaries, chemistry of the players, identification of the customer/client, project resources, customer/client needs and wants, and agreement on approach must all be determined in order to build alignment between the contracting organization and the consultant. (This holds true for internal consultants as well.) Yet upfront planning and meeting time is not always built in or well used. This is a mistake. At one point or another, there will be a need to clarify the above expectations and requirements, and the beginning of the engagement is the optimal time for this discussion.

It also goes a long way toward establishing positive interpersonal relationships among the team members seeking to solve the problem or create the new reality. Another benefit of this upfront interaction is that a great deal of information critical to the project will come out in the discussions, increasing the chances of success.

Peter Block outlines the elements of an effective contract. They include:

• **The boundaries of the consultation**. Beginning with a clear statement/understanding of the problem that is the focus, there is a need to identify what the consultant will *not* get involved in. For example, a consultant in a TQM implementation may be involved with providing a methodology, but not expected or wanted to be involved with any personnel decisions that arise, whether they affect the TQM implementation or not.

• **The objectives of the project**. These identify the organizational improvements expected if the consultation is successful. This helps the client and consultant to be realistic about the potential and the limitations of the project.

• **The kind of information needed**. Access to people and information are the key needs of the consultant. Often, it is not easy for the internal contracting principal to decide how far into the bowels of the organization the consultant should go. The external consultant has the responsibility to be as explicit as possible about the kind of information and the type of people he/she will need to work with.

• **The roles of the players**. This is where the parties state *how* they want to work together. This does not have to be very detailed. (That might be difficult to foresee at this early stage.) But if the contracting principal wants the consultant to operate somewhat autonomously and the consultant's natural style is to involve his/her clients, a lack of clarity about this could end up with the contracting principal feeling "bothered" by the consultant. Also, this element can help the consultant understand who is calling the shots regarding the engagement. A self-starting consultant may overstep boundaries with a contracting principal who wants or needs to be in control. It is at this time, also, that the educational role the consultant is to play should be agreed upon.

• **The product/service to be delivered**. This is a critical dimension of the consulting relationship. The specificity and nature of the deliverable needs to be discussed early on in order to establish realistic expectations between the consultant and the client. For example, will interim reports be required? Will they be oral or written? How specific do these reports need to be? How long are they to be? Are general recommendations expected or should the consultant make step-by-step recommendations?

• **The support and involvement needed from the client**. To project forward at this early stage is not always simple, but this element of the contracting agreement is critical to success. The consultant needs to specify what he/she desires from the client. For example, if the consultant will need lines of communication opened with the top executives of the company, this is the time to say so. Resources are another important topic at this time. If the consultant needs a certain number of people to assist in any segment of the project, this should be made known early on so that these people's time can be planned and allocated.

• **The timeline**. Starting time, interim mileposts, and estimated completion dates are key components of this element. Sometimes, clients will want cost estimates to accompany the timeline. Since it is difficult to schedule meetings with a group of busy executives, it is wise to forecast dates at this point and schedule important meeting times early on.

I like to work with Gantt charts on TQM implementation since they usually cover twelve to eighteen months of activity. A big-picture Gantt chart can act as an overall roadmap and a communications device. Figure 7-2 depicts the major activities needed to implement TQM. A more detailed Gantt chart can be developed if the client desires, but this overall chart is a minimum requirement.

• **The confidentiality issue**. This element is important to discuss since who gets what report or who hears what feedback is generally part of the political reality of an organization. Even if the consultant's values and desires are for open communication, it is the internal client who needs to make the final call.

• **The need for follow-up**. This element of the contract is often an optional issue. Yet many consultants are interested in following up with their clients to see how successful the project really was. Whether this was discussed or not, I often phone my client to see where things stand at this stage. It reinforces that the relationship had meaning and it allows for any final or unfinished business to be discussed.[3]

This contracting method did not address all of the elements cited in the introductory portion of this segment on external consultant working relationships, such as ground rules or identification of customers. Yet it

Figure 7-2. Gantt chart depicting TQM implementation.

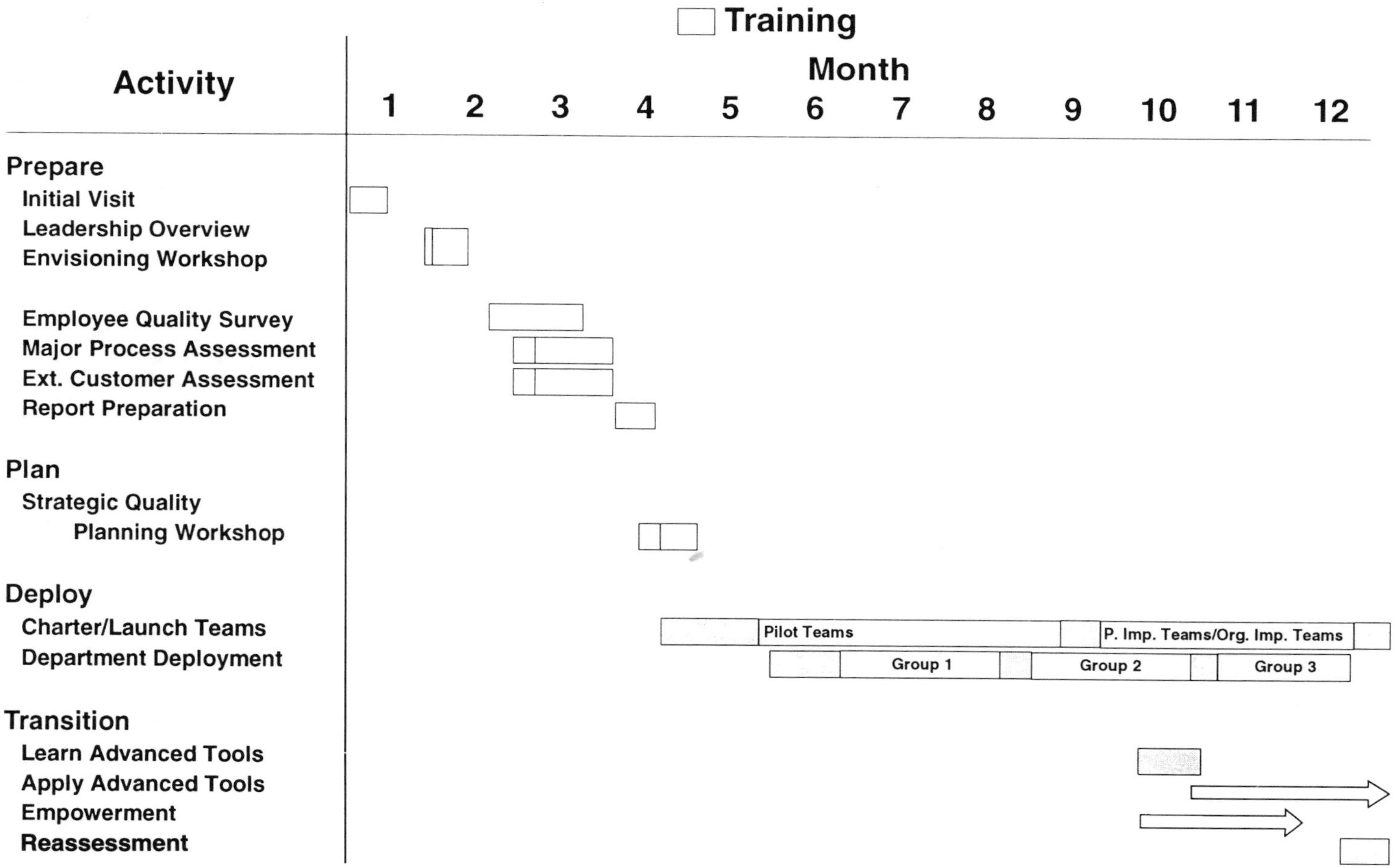

is an excellent benchmark to work from in developing the early project plans and interpersonal relationships. Following these steps will improve your project's chances of success.

Large-Scale Change

To think about change, it is helpful to think of present and future states— that is, of the status quo and the vision. Since I am a hiker, it always helps me to picture change in terms of a hill. Figure 7-3 depicts the nature of change.

"The climb" begins by understanding the starting point, the present state. Knowing that large-scale change is an uphill climb is critical to ensuring continuing commitment through the early phase of the climb, when the realization dawns that no matter how wonderful the vision, the journey is a challenge. Remember, it is hard to see the other side of the hill when you first look up to the crest. In addition, once the top of the hill is reached, the organization must still manage its way down the backside before reaching the new equilibrium—the stable, balanced, level vision that is the quest of the change.

The climb, therefore, has two parts: the upward side of the hill and the downward side. Hikers know that climbing uphill is rough, but many blisters are born on the downhill side as well. Managing the transformation through all phases of the change is crucial. Figure 7-4 divides the hill into four phases. Let's look at them one at a time.

Phase I

In Phase I there is excitement about the future state. Sometimes in launching the change effort, communications are extensive and expectations are lifted to a level that cannot be achieved in the short term. Yet if the communications paint a realistic picture and continually reinforce it, then building excitement for the change can set the stage well. The caution in TQM efforts is that the transformation takes years, not months.

HR professionals who are part of the steering team need to let people know "what's in it for them." Otherwise, you might hear comments like, "Why should I get all excited? I'll be retired in five years." Tom Peters's concept of building in small wins comes into play here. If successive celebrations of progress can be made visible to the work force, they will hang in there. The shifts in the culture or improvements in various work units need exposure. But all the hoopla in the world will only lead to disappointment if the progress of the change effort is closely held. To

(Text continues on page 120)

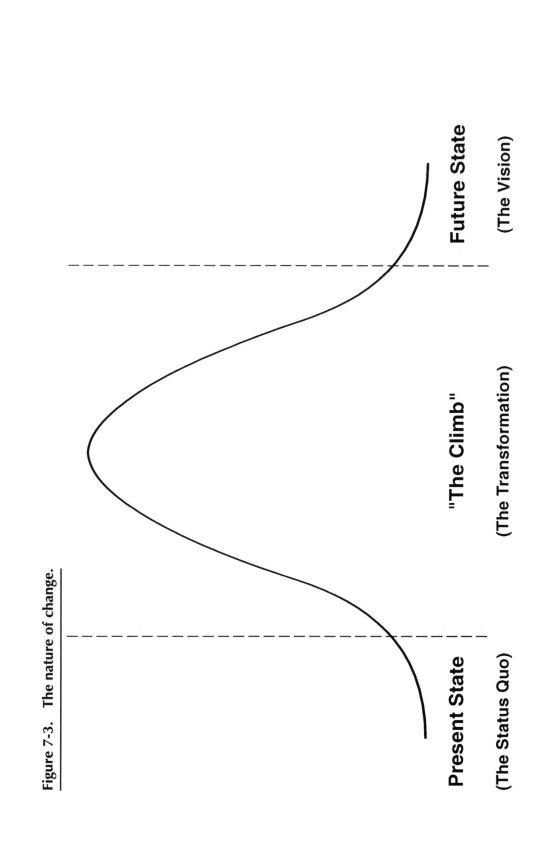

Figure 7-3. The nature of change.

Present State
(The Status Quo)

"The Climb"
(The Transformation)

Future State
(The Vision)

Figure 7-4. The four phases of the hill of change.

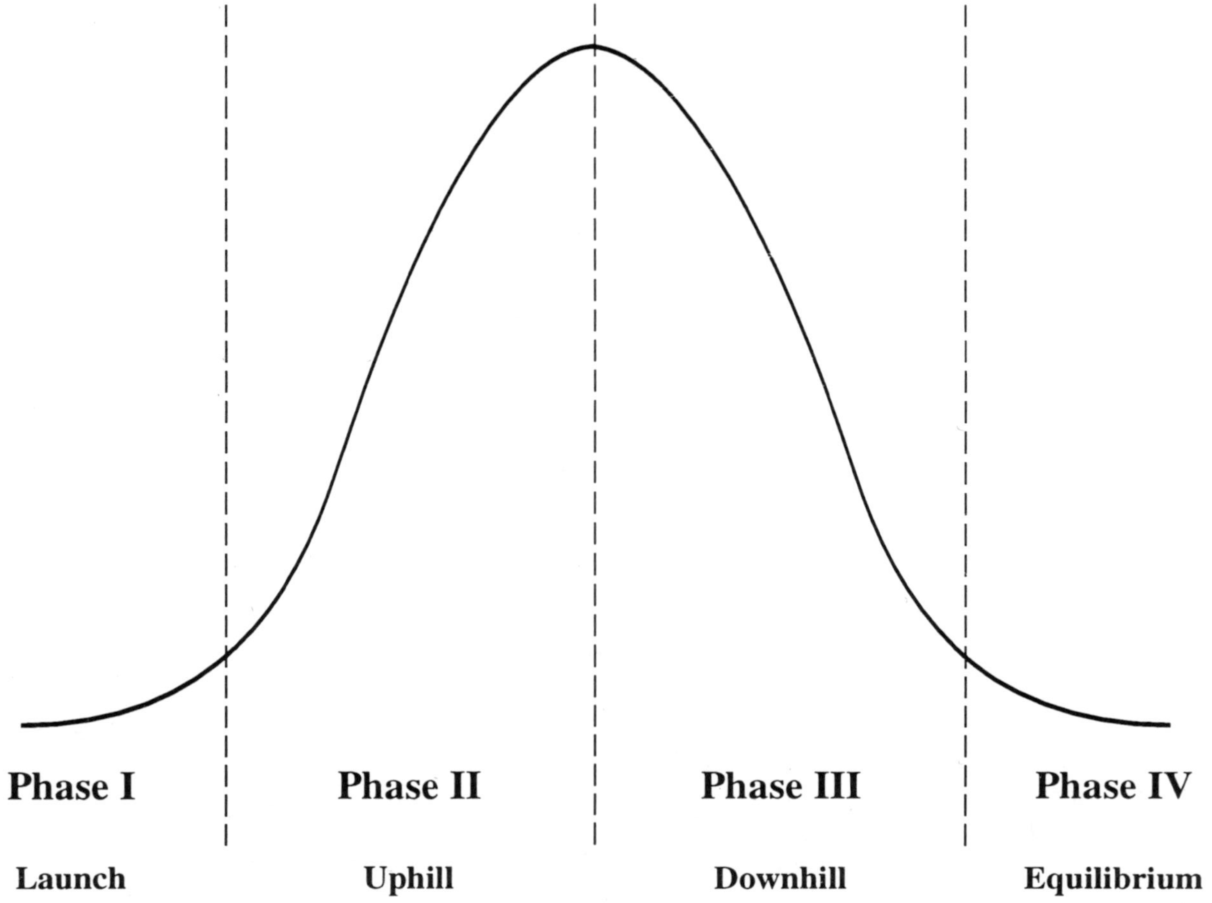

Phase I	Phase II	Phase III	Phase IV
Launch	Uphill	Downhill	Equilibrium

the work force, the effort will seem to have gone into another one of those "black holes."

Phase II

After the effort is kicked off, the real work begins. People are completing tasks often related to discovery, such as data collection needed for assessment and direction setting. Problems begin to surface, like time pressures or confusion among personnel. The natural resistance to change begins to raise its head, and solutions to problems are still in the development stages. This is the phase when you face the greatest danger of losing commitment to the effort. Skeptics abound, and keeping the vision in sight is of prime importance.

Those sponsoring the change can begin to feel like a broken record, especially when the external consultant keeps asking them again and again to visibly continue showing their support. It is also important to keep people involved, so that as many people as possible who have a stake in the new vision are actively working on it. The continued education of the work force is also important since one of the goals of this phase is to build a critical mass of people who will support the new direction. The external consultant really earns his/her money at this time since it is an awesome task to keep the project on track and instill belief in its benefits.

Phase III

By the time the organization reaches the top of the hill of change, there usually has been some progress made, small wins have begun to be celebrated, potential solutions are being discussed, and the skepticism or pessimism that may have been growing begins to diminish. In short order, the final recommendations will be in and a renewed hopefulness is felt among the players. The consultant and the internal team now have to take advantage of keeping the effort's champions visible, of reinforcing the change. But the train is generally moving steadily down the track, and the real challenge is in keeping it from moving too fast.

This brings me back to the hiker analogy. Here in Phase III, the downhill climb must be managed just as carefully as the uphill, but since there are more facts leading the considerations and decisions being made, this part of the journey is less dangerous. However, there are often those who now want to take what has been learned to reinforce and support their ideas, regardless of the facts.

During the downhill climb, the recommendations that have been made must be supported by evidence and include at least an initial implementation action plan. This may or may not be the time to terminate the consultant relationship. If the recommendation marks the end of the consultant engagement, then the internal team needs to understand that it is responsible for managing the rest of the change process. Since this is the time to deploy the initial implementation, a disciplined approach is still the best bet. If the external consultant is to remain through the implementation, he/she will be able to help with this challenge.

Phase IV

After the implementation, an evaluation of the change is generally completed. The external consultant may be part of the evaluation team and may help to develop the plan to institutionalize the change. Or the internal team may feel that there is no need to continue the consulting relationship; the team may have been enabled by now to institutionalize the change without the consultant's help. Two things are important to remember in this phase. One is the need to reward and/or recognize successful achievement. The other is to document and communicate expectations about the new state to everyone involved in the change.

This overview of the phases of change provides a grounding for what to expect during a large-scale change effort. You can probably see that managing commitment is an integral part of the consultant's job. An excellent model of the stages of commitment to change is provided in Figure 7-5. You can use it as you move along the hill of change with others in your organization.

The Phases of a Consulting Project

It is time to move the focus from change efforts themselves to the phases of the consultation process. As we go about discussing a typical consultation, the relationship with the phases of large-scale change will be drawn. I will also integrate some observations about internal and external consultancy as appropriate. The six phases of consulting we will address are:

1. Engaging in initial contact and entry
2. Formulating a contract and establishing a helping relationship
3. Identifying problems through diagnostic analysis
4. Setting goals and planning for action
5. Taking action and cycling feedback
6. Completing the contract[4]

Figure 7-5. The stages of commitment to change.

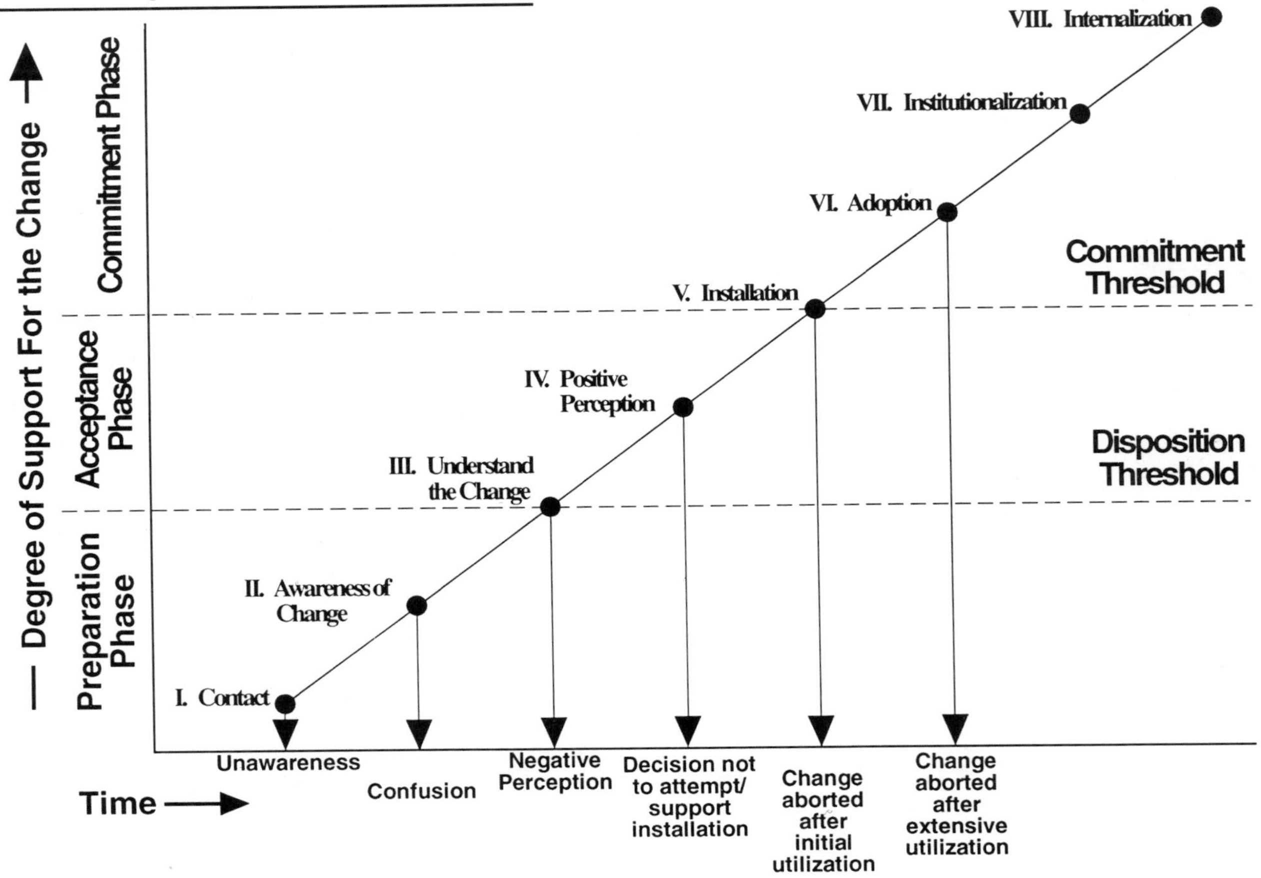

Degree of Support For the Change

Commitment Phase
- VIII. Internalization
- VII. Institutionalization
- VI. Adoption

Commitment Threshold

Acceptance Phase
- V. Installation
- IV. Positive Perception

Disposition Threshold

Preparation Phase
- III. Understand the Change
- II. Awareness of Change
- I. Contact

Unawareness Confusion Negative Perception Decision not to attempt/support installation Change aborted after initial utilization Change aborted after extensive utilization

Time →

Source: Daryl R. Conner, *Managing at the Speed of Change* (New York: Villard Books, 1993).

Engaging in Initial Contact and Entry

Opening the potential relationship includes identifying and clarifying the need for change, exploring the readiness for change, and exploring the possibility of the client and consultant working together. It is during this time that the contracting principal tends to decide whether or not to work with internal or external consultants. It is also during this phase that chemistry is judged to be positive or not. Certain considerations, such as whether it would be difficult to withdraw from a working relationship with an internal consultant, are usually made at this time. Also, this can be a time of self-education for the contracting principal, resulting in a go/ no go decision to move to the next phase.

In a TQM implementation, this phase often occurs because the CEO or another senior management person has read, heard, or otherwise been exposed to the basic concepts underpinning Total Quality and sees value in exploring it further. This is an excellent time for you to advocate change.

Formulating a Contract and Establishing a Helping Relationship

Once a tentative decision is made to make the effort formal, the consultant and the client identify the desired essential outcomes. Getting as concrete as possible is important since it is this tangible vision that will be communicated to the larger organization. It is very important at this time to identify all customers or stakeholders so that they can be involved in establishing this initial vision. This will begin to build commitment to the project or unveil potential obstacles.

Once these building blocks are in place, it is time to determine who should do what, clarify the time and cost expectations (including milestones), and clarify accountability of all parties. When these tasks are completed, the kick-off activities can be planned. Remember to take into consideration the need to build belief about the future state/vision into the events that are planned to launch the project. (This is Phase I of the hill of change shown in Figure 7-4.)

Identifying Problems Through Diagnostic Analysis

An assessment led by the consultant is usually the first step in this phase of a consulting project. Whether there is a need to solve an existing problem, to improve a current situation, or to create something entirely new, an intensive diagnostic journey generally commences. An internal consultant may not need as much education as an external consultant at this stage, but the external consultant may have an easier time getting data since he/she is not a member of the organization. Getting the facts straight at the onset lays important groundwork for the project.

It is helpful to begin to identify the forces that will help or hinder the project at this time. Since this phase dovetails with Phase II of large-scale change (in Figure 7-4), the uphill climb, the consultant and the contracting principal can expect to see the surfacing of problems or resistance.

Setting Goals and Planning for Action

As the uphill climb continues and nears the top, the consulting process has moved to action planning. Here, the imperative questions are who needs to be involved and how to involve them. Answering them sets up an improved plan and increases the project's probability of success. Specific steps should be outlined and shared as part of the formal recommendation.

Internal consultants often have great knowledge of the potential value of organizational players at this stage of the consulting process. Whether or not they have the influence to involve the needed power players is another story. Sometimes the external consultant has more influence over such situations; otherwise, the contracting principal will need to get sponsorship for the involvement of important players.

Taking Action and Cycling Feedback

Whether small steps toward the goal or complete pilot implementations are planned, the consultant has started the downhill climb in this phase of the project (Phase III of Figure 7-4). Assuming the consultant is still on board, he/she usually needs to develop some skills in the people who will be piloting the implementation. It is during this phase that enabling the client to continue without consultant support must become a full-blown endeavor. It is also important to plan celebrations for small wins. They show that the roadmap is being followed and is working.

Progress reviews are in order. The internal consultant may be able to monitor the actions better than an external consultant, but the external consultant may have more leverage in getting meetings called to review progress or in garnering resources for skill development. Continually assessing the effort and eliciting ongoing feedback can save more dollars, time, and effort than you might think. This interim evaluation can help the consultant guide the contracting principal or team toward valuable midcourse corrections.

There are benefits to having either internal or external consultants. The internal consultant may have more knowledge of unused internal resources. The external consultant may be more willing to confront the blockages and resistance to effective action. Depending on their experience levels, either internal or external consultants may bring broad perspectives to the table from which alternative courses of action can be determined. The ideas brought up in this phase of the consulting process show that the downhill climb needs management and discipline even though there is increased support for the change.

Completing the Contract

If the consultant has not been engaged to evaluate the final results of the implementation, then the internal parties must design plans to institutionalize the change. This is not easy since changes can sometimes be short-term if not cemented well. Counterreactions can also occur when a new order is established; they must be addressed in order to guarantee continuity of the change. Even at this phase—Phase IV of Figure 7-4—change is fragile and must be managed well.

Equilibrium is reached because the change has become a new constant. If an internal consultant is still on the job, he/she can observe when additional support is needed to maintain the new state. If an external consultant is present, he/she may feel more comfortable about negotiating around difficult issues than internal staff still pressing for return to the old status quo. Remember, the new state is still not in people's comfort zone, and until it is, it needs nourishment and support before it can be considered internalized.

Transferring all responsibility to internal parties is a necessary step in completing the consulting contract. Once this is complete, the parties need to assess whether any further follow-up is needed. If so, it will likely only be periodic, but it should be planned for at this time. Otherwise, the transfer is finalized.

The TQM Implementation and the OD Consultant's Role

It is a tall order to pull together all of the steps, activities, and phases cited above into their relationship with a TQM implementation. Refer again to Figure 7-2, the comprehensive TQM implementation timeline.

There are four activity categories labeled Prepare, Plan, Deploy, and Transition. Let's look at each of them.

Prepare

The Prepare phase corresponds to Phase I in the large-scale change model depicted in Figure 7-4. This is the time when an initial visit is made by the consultant to determine what obstacles and driving forces exist in the organization for the TQM effort. It is also the time to create the vision for quality that will set the direction. This relates to the contracting stage of the consultation process in that all key players are brought into alignment with the new vision.

The TQM consultant's role is to educate senior management about Total Quality and to facilitate the envisioning workshop for senior management or, at a minimum, the quality leadership team (QLT). This is the beginning of relationship building between the consultant and the sponsors of the change, the QLT members.

A further set of activities, under the umbrella of assessment, takes place. This begins the diagnostic journey. Many people are brought together on assessment teams and charged with the task of gathering information from customers, workers, suppliers, written reports, and documented results. These activities fall under Phase II of the change model in Figure 7-4, where the uphill climb begins. Common problems that surface at this time include time pressures on team members to complete the assessment and still fully perform their jobs, and skeptics about TQM being "just another program" who withhold information that is needed.

Let me digress here to address why I believe initial assessment is worth it. When many organizations begin their TQM effort, they address some obvious opportunities for improvement and launch teams to address them. While some results of the team efforts come in within six to twelve months, results are often spotty, and these TQM implementations lack an effective plan, a strategic focus, and possibly even an organization vision. In addition, little is generally done in these types of kickoffs to change the culture to support the principles and values needed to truly reach Total Quality.

Time and again I have worked with organizations that launched teams and thought that was all there was to it. Then they wondered why the teams were meeting obstacles, why there was inconsistent support, why there wasn't more awareness of TQM and how the team efforts could be integrated into the overall business plan. The plus side of companies that hurried out and launched teams is that the teams acted as pilot projects that reflected the overall needs of the organization in making Total Quality a way of life—that is, if the organization chose to see these initial efforts as pilots, and not the final determinant of whether TQM worked or not.

The consultant must act as a boundary spanner between the teams and the QLT so that barriers and challenges are addressed. In the consulting process stages, this corresponds with the diagnostic analysis where problems ("opportunities," in TQM language) are identified. The TQM consultant plays the role of facilitator, coach, and teacher to these assessment team members at the same time that he/she is educating the QLT further about what is to take place down the TQM road.

Plan

Once the assessment is complete, the QLT receives feedback from the team members and begins planning the focus of the company's TQM deployment. The use of traditional strategic planning tools are integrated into a work session that helps the QLT prioritize the implementation. Key processes are reviewed and prioritized, customer feedback is heard and customer needs prioritized, and employee feedback mechanisms are used in order to get a sense of the culture and work norms that need attention in the overall effort. The outcome of this session is a one- to two-year plan for initial implementation highlighting which cross-functional work processes will be improved, which departments should kick off their own internal effort, what cultural improvement initiatives need to be addressed first, etc. This plan, known as the strategic quality plan, replaces the formal recommendation in a typical consultation. Unlike the implementation stage in a typical consulting project, it is prioritization and focus, not recommendations, that are being decided.

Deploy

The action of chartering teams begins the problem-solving phase. In fact, it is too early in the TQM effort to even know what the possible causes of problems might be. This lengthens the amount of time that the organization will be in Phase II, the most uncomfortable phase of large-scale change efforts. Taking action by chartering teams to address issues is not the same as taking action to make changes. Patience and commitment are necessary and crucial. Yet with what we know already, this is the most dangerous time in the effort. (Perhaps this is another reason for the mixed publicity given to TQM in the early 1990s. Maybe a significant number of organizations did not have the staying power for Phase II.)

The TQM consultant has an obvious challenge in "keeping the faith" candles burning. Education and involvement are needed to keep the leadership team and the people motivated. Although it generally takes quality teams only six months to determine recommendations and begin taking action, it can easily be twelve months or longer since preparation began before teams reach this stage if the Total Quality effort began with a comprehensive assessment, which is best. Yet at about the twelve- to eighteen-month time frame, some results must be realized to supplement "the faith."

The TQM consultant is busy juggling many needs at this stage of the implementation. Specific planning and training is being completed with individual teams and departments. The QLT may well be involved in some of the cultural improvement opportunities or in carrying the TQM banner to teams and work groups. Coaching rules the consultant's day, just as communicating consumes the QLT. In fact, some of the coaching may well be involved with giving feedback to the senior management team or QLT about its own leadership behavior. Yes, there is lots of activity, but it is too early for results, meaning the TQM effort has not yet reached the top of the hill in the large-scale change model. The vision is not in sight. But the job of consulting is ever more challenging at this stage.

By the time initial teams begin to make their formal recommendations, cultural shifts have begun to take place. There may be some skepticism around regarding whether the leadership team really means what it is saying, but change is in the wind. People feel it. The initial recommendations are generally well received and are the first small wins that can be made visible to the larger organization. I like to recommend a rather large event to mark this milestone. For example, a "Quality Progress I" day can be held where teams storyboard their actions to date and share their experiences with other employees who have not yet become quality team members, or who have been filling in for those who have.

The teams whose recommendations are in different stages of pilot implementation can tell their stories to a crowd of employees and be recognized for their efforts. This bit of hoopla would be an apparent sign of support for the effort and may be the first huge sign of success and excitement since the kickoff. Recognition and reinforcement is called for, and a day like the one described is certainly visible and helps people to see over the hump. This is only the beginning of managing down the hill of change (Phase III), though. As the implementation broadens, the areas of the company that are further along will get over the hump before the areas that are just beginning to deploy the effort.

Even if a big event is not held, extensive communications and continual highlighting of successes must now become the norm. The TQM consultant is likely to be pulled into this activity but should keep the team coaching role as his/her priority. (Only because of time. There is likely other talent that can be used to support the celebration/communications effort.) As more and more teams complete their work and cultural initiatives are begun, the role of the consultant begins to move into a transition that will eventually mean the end of the engagement. During this downhill time, people are being enabled to facilitate teams and teach others the problem-solving process. Usually there is internal staff that can now teach assessment workshops and conduct visioning sessions as needed by individual departments. It has been the consultant's role to fulfill these learning objectives.

Transition

Just before moving into the transition state, a planning session for the next major organization initiatives must take place. Not only does the initial one- to two-year plan need updating, but other considerations about the future should be made at this time. It is probably still from twelve to eighteen months into the effort, but the QLT has learned enough to concern itself, for example, with whether or not it sees a move to self-direction in the long-term strategy. The QLT also needs to assess whether any advanced quality tools or other leadership development is needed. For example, the QLT might feel that the organization (or some parts of it) is ready to go out to benchmark with world-class organizations. Or the QLT might want to learn tools to support higher levels of innovation or customer satisfaction inside the organization. It is also common at this time for the QLT to question the traditional functional design of the organization itself.

The TQM consultant's role is to help the QLT foresee the future, but also keep the members on the road to institutionalization of TQM concepts, principles, and practices. An institutionalization plan should be laid out as part of the transition so that all parties can fulfill their responsibilities before terminating the consulting engagement. This also means that a resource question may have to be faced depending on how involved the consultant was on site and how many internal staff members have been trained to what level of development. Obviously, these activities find the enterprise nearing the bottom of the hill (Phase IV) and preparing for completion of the contract.

Conclusion

It is easy to see how large-scale change efforts such as TQM are both complex and fragile. The role of the OD consultant in the change effort has multiple dimensions necessitating the full use of knowledge, skills, and competencies. The HR executive who is faced with developing an internal team of consultants to support a TQM implementation could be facing one of the most exciting and fulfilling leadership challenges of his/her career. If this team of experts does not report to HR, then it might be a great opportunity for one or two members of the HR staff to move into one of these roles for their own development. Certainly, when they return to HR, they bring back valuable knowledge and expertise.

HR executives might be asking what role they play if they do not have the organizational power to sponsor the change themselves. This is a very good question. In any change effort, there are the sponsors of the change, the targets of the change, and the agents of the change. HR professionals have long been advocates of change. Just as staff departments such as human resources were key catalysts for the employee involvement efforts of the 1970s and early 1980s, so too with TQM in the 1990s and beyond.

TQM must not be a "fad," but rather a "movement." The United States needs to move faster and faster toward building Total Quality cultures and practices, and the HR advocacy role is important to the change occurring and to the change lasting. It is a lot of work to advocate for change. It often feels as though it is as much work as making the change happen. The one sure thing about large-scale change is that HR ought to be involved.

Whatever your involvement in the TQM implementation, this chapter has hopefully helped you see that the role of the consultant in the organization is a valuable one.

Chapter 8
Performance Appraisal

HR professionals may have a hard time accepting W. Edwards Deming as a guru, since he denounces one of HR's clearest domains: performance appraisal. Deming actually advises throwing out performance appraisals completely, saying the system doesn't work, hasn't worked, and won't work. The only part of appraisal systems that he contends has any merit is the planning of objectives. Yet he is not an advocate of the once favored MBO (management by objectives) system; he is enamored with aligned planning of results to be achieved by those responsible for the process and its outcomes. And his focus on performance feedback is that it should be given often and continually, not once a year. Deming also contends that salaries should be based on such factors as the market rate, the responsibility and the level of skills possessed by an employee, and the success of the enterprise, as opposed to market competition alone.

Given these beliefs, what is the HR professional's role in relation to improving performance planning and review in a TQM environment? This chapter answers that question and poses an interim solution. Evolution, not revolution, works best with large-scale systems change, and few world-class competitors in the United States are ready to eliminate performance appraisal systems entirely. So HR professionals must be ready to integrate key quality principles into their current systems and processes. This chapter recommends building in a formal recognition of teamwork by taking a team approach to performance appraisal as a first step toward continuously improving the status quo.

Yet that is not enough. HR professionals need to begin thinking about more radically changing such systems. Therefore, Deming's alternatives to performance appraisal must be discussed in order to give a better understanding of his views and to show where many of you may already support some of his thinking. Finally, this chapter briefly addresses Deming's stand against work standards. Once HR professionals begin to see the interdependency of one worker with an entire process, the concept of eliminating standards is easier to swallow.

I am not yet convinced that eliminating either performance appraisal systems or standards is an answer that the United States is ready for, yet thinking and questioning established beliefs (called paradigms in quality language) is part of the Total Quality process. Increased familiarity with Deming's views will help to pave the way. Let's start by looking at traditional systems, identifying some of their constraints, and noting their areas for opportunity in order to establish the need for change.

Traditional Performance Appraisal Systems

As long ago as the late 1800s, performance appraisal systems included assessment of individuals' physical and mental characteristics, personality factors, behaviors, and skills. One hundred years later, performance ratings have changed little, measuring many of the same factors. In the late 1950s, the link between performance and job objectives was made as the MBO system was created. Behaviorially anchored rating scales met with little success in the 1960s, and since the 1970s, multiple rater consensus evaluations have been espoused by some experts as a replacement for supervisory-driven evaluations. The multiple rater methodology has merit for the future since it accepts as given the all-around feedback on performance that fits with the teaming environment of companies instilling Total Quality cultures. Yet the methodology has not been widely adopted to date in the United States.

Since the traditional appraisal system of judging individual performance against certain criteria is still the common method of assessment, a look at its prime purposes and components is in order. Traditional performance appraisal has certain key purposes. These are:

1. Regular appraisal of job performance
2. Salary increases based on merit
3. Recognizing promotability or promotion based on merit
4. Feedback on strengths and developmental needs
5. Assisting employees' training and career planning goal setting
6. Review of fit for job at the end of probationary periods

The question of whether or not performance appraisal achieves these purposes receives mixed reviews in general, and it is commonly thought that performance appraisals are counterproductive in relation to worker motivation. HR professionals know this, yet they have not taken the lead to improve the system. Clearly, it is not the lack of desire that keeps HR folks from creating new systems. More likely, the key obstacle is the vast complexity of making major changes in appraisal systems. It is common to see a task force in place for as long as two years before improvements to existing performance appraisal systems are put into place. And the fear of repercussions in the courts or within the workplace are also deterrents.

For example, the law requires that standards need to be based on an analysis of job requirements, and those standards must be communicated to the employee (*Sledge* v. *J.P. Stevens*, 1978; *Wade* v. *Mississippi Cooperative Extension Service*, 1976; *Donaldson* v. *Pillsbury*, 1977). Objective, observable evidence must support key performance dimensions and should be defined in behavioral terms (*Gilmore* v. *Kansas City Terminal Railway*, 1975; *James* v. *Stocklom Valves*, 1976). One of the most renowned cases, *Griggs* v. *Duke Power Co.*, 1971, denied the efficacy of appraisal systems that on their face appeared neutral if they had an adverse impact on protected minority groups. The list of requirements as now determined by law goes on and on.

How does an HR function begin improvement when case law has determined that certain components of performance appraisal are required? The answer is: carefully, because with the change in corporate culture being achieved through Total Quality and other employee involvement efforts, the need clearly exists to revamp performance planning and feedback systems.

Of course, case law does offer some clues toward appraisal systems that will hold up under scrutiny, and these should be taken into account when the decision to revamp is made. Examples are job-related criteria, specific and written guidelines for evaluation, and inclusion of members of the same groups as those assessed in the review process. As long ago as 1982, the following characteristics were cited as the benchmark for legally defensible performance appraisal systems:

1. Formal, written policies relating to the operation, uses, and communication of the performance appraisal system to all persons covered
2. Standardization of the system, applied consistently to all persons covered, with controlled scoring and administrative procedures
3. Standards, targets, and/or criteria that have been developed through a recognized and correctly applied job analysis technique
4. Performance standards based on the work actually being done and the performance desired
5. Performance measures contained where relative importance is fixed
6. Supervisory, subjective evaluation as only one input

7. Training for raters as the norm
8. Predetermined, written criteria that act as the basis for rewards (e.g., merit pay, promotion)
9. Raters having many opportunities to observe performance ratees
10. Multiple raters for the same ratee used if additional, relevant information can be obtained
11. Procedures for transfer and/or promotion that can be initiated by the ratee without the recommendation of the supervisor
12. Feedback given to raters on their rating behaviors
13. Multiple safeguards built in to ensure fairness to all participants[1]

Fulfilling these requirements is not an easy task, but someone needs to do it. The HR professional is the obvious person to face the challenge.

The Problems With the Single-Rater System

Formalizing policy, establishing standards based on job analysis, determining the importance of performance measures, and developing procedures for transfer/promotion that can be initiated by the ratee are all components that can be built into the design of the performance appraisal system. The need to build in rater objectivity is more difficult because it deals with human nature. The multi-rater concept (being rated by more than one person of more than one organizational level) can eliminate many of the distortion factors that plague current supervisor-based appraisal systems. Those factors are:

1. *The halo effect*. The most recent performance or performance on one performance criterion is commonly known to affect the overall evaluation of the employee. For example, if an employee is performing at high levels because of keen interest in the task at hand, the importance of the task at hand, or any other reason, it is known to bias the supervisor toward a higher rating at performance appraisal time. On the other hand, if high levels of performance are the norm, but the employee has not recently been operating at a normal level of functioning, the recent decrease in level of performance can skew the rating downward. The halo effect can also hold the rating up even if it doesn't deserve to be as high during this performance period.

2. *General perception*. Many employees have a certain reputation among other managers and employees. This perception can bias the supervisor when it comes time to rate the employee. It does not matter if the perception is based on fact or rumor; what is "perceived" is "real" to many. These preconceived perceptions can color a person's rating. In

addition, a supervisor may have a general perception of an employee that has nothing to do with the perception held by others. In fact, perceptions can even be held around types of employees, e.g., those of certain educational levels or certain sexes are categorized as good or bad. These stereotypes are real and can distort the facts.

3. *Central tendency*. Rating someone much above or below average is not the norm due to the need to heavily document or justify the rating. Therefore, it is much easier for supervisors to cluster around the average than to move to an outlying area, regardless of the employee's performance.

4. *Rater self-image*. Some raters like to think of themselves as either generous or tough. This self-image gets in the way of rating by the facts and leads to variation or inconsistency between raters.

5. *Built-in feedback*. Performance appraisal systems that build in one-on-one feedback between supervisor and employee can skew the ratings upward because being a judge and giving constructive feedback make honestly discussing performance deficiencies difficult for many people.

6. *Similarity*. Many people like to work with people who act, think, or look like they do. If "like" people also demonstrate behaviors that the supervisor values, higher ratings may result. This does nothing, of course, to enhance the need for or appreciation of diversity in the workplace.

Multi-Rater Performance Appraisal Systems

Introduced in the 1970s, multi-rater systems may have been ahead of their time. As previously noted, it was during the 1970s that employee involvement efforts increased and during the early 1980s that Total Quality efforts first took hold in the United States. As such, the shift to a multi-rater system of appraising performance may have been thwarted by timing. Considering peer feedback generally occurs at more advanced stages of EI and TQM efforts. And as organizations progress even more toward semiautonomous or self-directed work teams, increasing pressure will be brought to bear on supervisor-only rating systems. How will companies be able to justify supervisory ratings when the role of the supervisor will change from one of direct control of a work group to leading multiple teams of employees?

Let's assess the advantages of using the multi-rater approach. On the dimensions of behavior change, management, perspective, reliability, fairness, and level of observation, the multi-rater approach has some distinct advantages, as shown in Figure 8-1.

Figure 8-1. Supervisor-only approach compared with multi-rater approach.

Dimension	Supervisor-Only Feedback	Multi-Rater Feedback
Behavior Change	Motivational variance (depends on the influence of individual giving feedback; often viewed as biased)	Motivating (credibility higher; motivates behavior change)
Management	Hierarchical (judgments about a person's career made by one who ought to coach: role conflict/position power)	Participative, team-oriented (involves selected employees in decisions that affect careers)
Perspective	Downward view	All-around view
Reliability	Known to be unreliable (assumes each supervisor is accurate)	Shows measure of reliability (inter-rater agreement and score reliability)
Fairness	Unbalanced (unrelated factors can bias the supervisor)	Balanced (ratees select raters from their network, plus supervisor)
Observation	Limited	Daily contact

One of the strongest values associated with multi-rater feedback is that it positions the supervisor in the role of coach rather than judge. In the words of Mark R. Edwards and Ann Ewen, leaders in multi-rater systems, "Instead of having to sit in judgment and defend the supervisor, feedback from the supervisor plus colleagues and others provides feedback that can be used as a springboard for discussion between the supervisor and the associate. The supervisor can serve as a coach or guide to target performance improvement."[2]

Multi-Rater Case Study: The TEAMS Methodology

While many experts have looked into multi-rater performance appraisal systems, Mark R. Edwards has conducted research and incorporated multi-rater enhancements in more than 400 field tests around the country. The Team Evaluation and Management System (TEAMS) methodology is his brainchild and has been implemented in such notable companies as American Airlines, Eastman Kodak, Walt Disney Enterprises, and Westinghouse; more than eighty public and private organizations now use the system. They offer a benchmark for multi-rater processes worthy of use in organizations attempting to change their cultures toward teaming values and Total Quality principles. Since the evaluation and reward systems in place are a most powerful tool in achieving a Total Quality culture, the TEAMS methodology may well be the link in the evolution toward aligned team vision. Dr. Edwards copyrighted the methodology in 1987. Features of the TEAMS approach are:

1. Users customize the process for the organization
2. Users select performance evaluation criteria
3. Multiple-ratee–selected raters are the norm
4. Feedback for every rater is part of the process
5. Safeguards are built in for all users

There are six steps to implementing the TEAMS process. These steps are given in detail below:

Step 1: Select and define feedback criteria.
- Involve appropriate people
- Identify critical behaviors: Individual, work group, team, or organization
- Define each critical behavior/skill

Step 2: Select evaluation team.
- Raters need knowledge of the ratee
- Raters must know their input is guaranteed to be both anonymous and confidential

Step 3: Conduct rating survey.
- Train raters on the content and process
- Design, produce, and distribute survey
- Maintain confidentiality

Step 4: Create reports.
- Ranking
- Profile
- Perspectives
- Importance/performance
- Comments

Step 5: Analyze reports.
- Strengths and development opportunities
- Agreement score
- Different perspectives
- Target improvement area(s)

Step 6: Stage interventions to improve targeted behaviors/skills.
- Communications among appropriate people

- Select the best possible actions
- Action planning
- Initiate the plan
- Monitor the plan

Not unlike many rating factors, the behaviors and skills measured by a multi-rater system vary by the position being evaluated. Some of these include:

- Decision making
- Delegation
- Flexibility
- Initiative
- Interpersonal relations
- Planning
- Organizing
- Problem solving
- Team building
- Presentation skills
- Participation skills
- Goal accomplishment
- Personal accountability
- Budget control
- Creativity
- Customer support
- Technical skills

- Teamwork
- Handling crisis
- Selling skills
- Data collection skills
- Responsiveness
- Courtesy
- Data analysis skills
- Training and teaching
- Coaching/developing
- Use of statistics
- Motivating/influencing
- Building a tangible vision
- Resolving customer complaints
- Leadership
- Facility maintenance
- Safety habits

The beauty of designing specific rating factors for each job or job family is that the key performance factors can be identified and, with multi-raters, reliably measured. The TEAMS approach does eliminate the high and low scores in order to eliminate harsh and lenient raters.[3]

A profile for each ratee is completed that shares the number of people rating, their rating of each criterion on a scale of one to ten, the supervisor's rating as compared with the peer ratings, and the amount of consensus among the members of the rating team. Figure 8-2 is an example of this profile.

Another advantage to such a system is that it is very time efficient. Raters do not need more than ten to fifteen minutes to complete an assessment, since only the key performance factors are rated and seldom does that number exceed ten. A sample of an actual TEAMS rating survey is displayed in Figure 8-3.

Another easy-to-read report shows the person's areas of strength

Figure 8-2. Sample ratee profile.

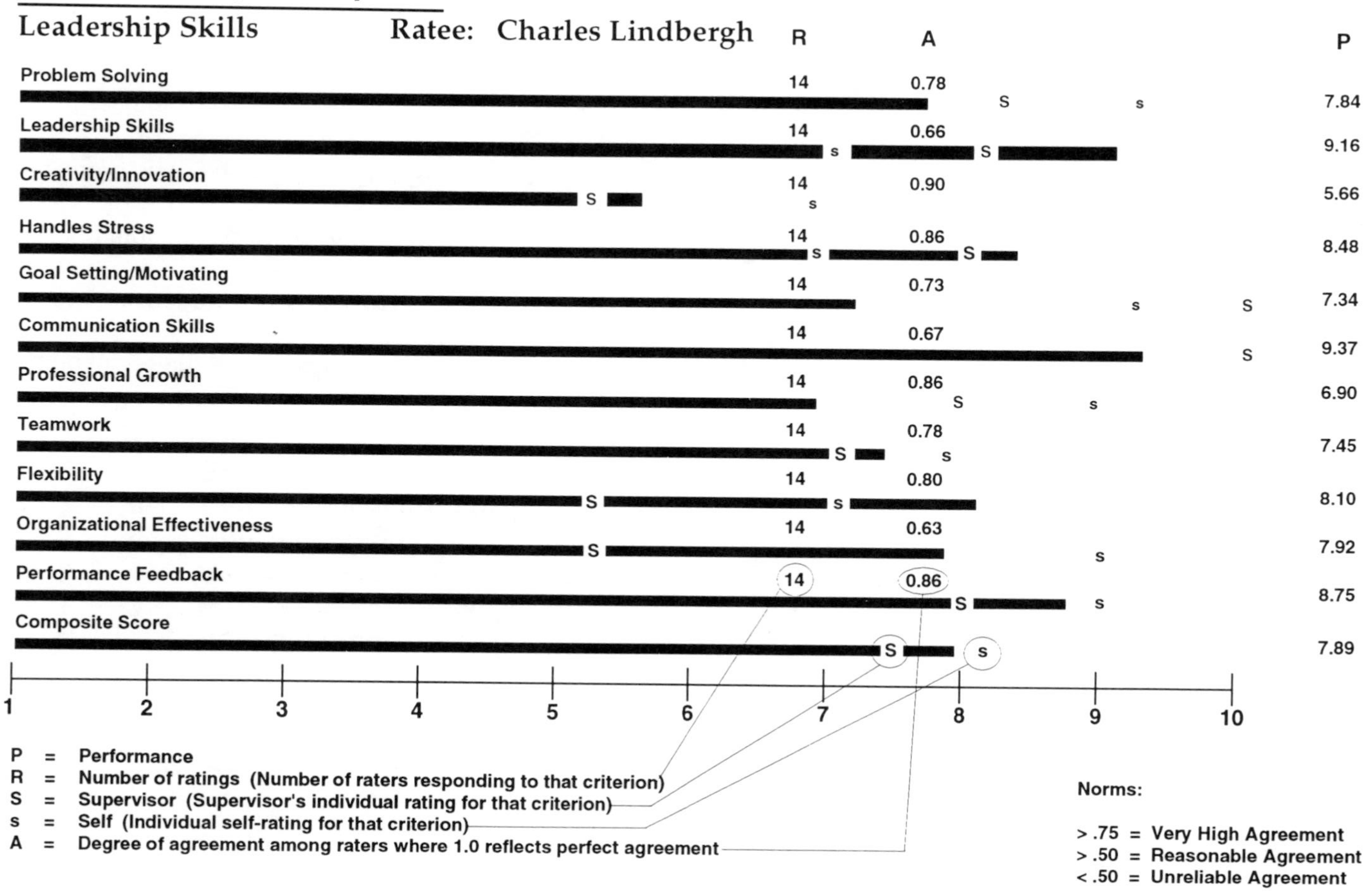

Leadership Skills   Ratee: **Charles Lindbergh**

Criterion	R	A		P
Problem Solving	14	0.78		7.84
Leadership Skills	14	0.66		9.16
Creativity/Innovation	14	0.90		5.66
Handles Stress	14	0.86		8.48
Goal Setting/Motivating	14	0.73		7.34
Communication Skills	14	0.67		9.37
Professional Growth	14	0.86		6.90
Teamwork	14	0.78		7.45
Flexibility	14	0.80		8.10
Organizational Effectiveness	14	0.63		7.92
Performance Feedback	14	0.86		8.75
Composite Score				7.89

Scale: 1 2 3 4 5 6 7 8 9 10

P = Performance
R = Number of ratings (Number of raters responding to that criterion)
S = Supervisor (Supervisor's individual rating for that criterion)
s = Self (Individual self-rating for that criterion)
A = Degree of agreement among raters where 1.0 reflects perfect agreement

Norms:

> .75 = Very High Agreement
> .50 = Reasonable Agreement
< .50 = Unreliable Agreement

Figure 8-3. Sample TEAMS rating survey.

Please check proper rater type:

_____ Supervisor _____ Peer/Colleague _____ Direct Report _____ Other

Rating Key:

N –	Not observed
1 – 2	Low behaviors or skills
3 – 4	Average behaviors or skills
5 – 6	Above average behavior or skills
7 – 8	High behaviors or skills
9 – 10	Exceptional behaviors or skills

Circle "N" if you have not observed the criterion, or you have insufficient information to make a reasonably accurate rating judgment. Your actual ratings are completely anonymous.

Administration and Paperwork	N	1	2	3	4	5	6	7	8	9	10
Communicating Effectively	N	1	2	3	4	5	6	7	8	9	10
Coordinating and Controlling Resources	N	1	2	3	4	5	6	7	8	9	10
Customer Support	N	1	2	3	4	5	6	7	8	9	10
Creativity and Innovation	N	1	2	3	4	5	6	7	8	9	10
Guiding and Motivating	N	1	2	3	4	5	6	7	8	9	10

and areas for development opportunity, as assessed by the rating team. This report is shown in Figure 8-4.

The Team Environment and the Multi-Rater System

In the world of performance appraisal, the move to multiple raters fits the team environment being established by Total Quality efforts. It (1) takes into account that team members know each others' work quite well; (2) facilitates the need to get feedback from team members and team leaders to the supervisor; and (3) keeps the supervisor in place as the final judge/coach of a person's performance, while offering a greater amount of feedback for him/her to work from in fairly assessing the employee. It is a progressive step in the direction that fits the new vision of the organization to build an increased teamwork environment, yet it is not far afield from what people now know and understand.

Finally, the multiple rater concept is a developmental tool for both teams and supervisors in that their ability to give feedback is improved and the supervisor can assume more of a coaching role with his/her employee. Although the technique has been around for almost twenty years, the time may have finally arrived for involving more people in performance appraisal. (In fact, I have recently heard of subordinate input to supervisory performance review being experimented with in the 1990s. I believe this will become quite commonplace in the next ten years. The multi-rater approaches discussed in this section will work for upward feedback as well.)

All of this support of multi-rater systems implies that I support individual performance expectations and feedback. I must state clearly that individual performance does not exclude the need to set expectations and give feedback to teams—not just quality teams, but natural work unit teams as well. In my last operations manager role, in an attempt to build a formal system that reinforced the importance of teamwork, I established an individual and group incentive program for my staff. This integration of personal and group incentives was my way of showing that individual achievement and work group performance *both* mattered.

My advice to HR professionals is to accept the current culture in the United States that supports individual achievement at the same time that you begin to build systems that also recognize and reward teamwork. In that way, you foster the important goal of moving enterprises toward the values of collaboration and cooperation. This progressive instilling of values, and systems that support the new values, will make sense to employees. It will also lend credence to their leaders who are espousing new ideals, since their actions will be reinforcing their message.

Figure 8-4. Report showing person's areas of strength and development opportunity.

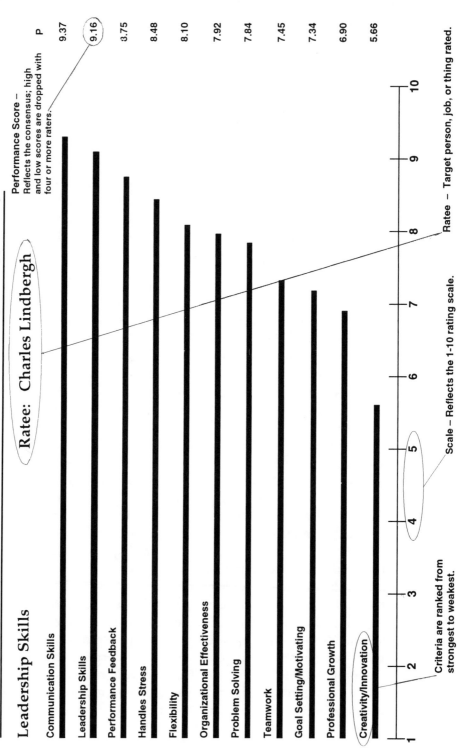

More About Deming

Before moving on to standards and measures, it needs to be made clear that the lack of objectivity and fairness is not the only obstacle Edwards Deming sees to effective appraisal systems. I would be remiss to ignore the other reasons for Deming's true dislike of performance appraisal, and it merits the HR professional's fuller understanding. Perhaps the time to eliminate the annual appraisal is not yet at hand. Nonetheless, HR professionals learning about Total Quality need to be clear about where and how Deming espouses performance feedback. Earlier I said that he does not underestimate the need for continuous feedback; he just contends that performance appraisal systems as we know them today do not work. And two of the key principles of Total Quality are to eliminate non–value-added work and to enlist the hearts and minds of the people of the enterprise. Let's take a fuller look at Deming's views.

• *The individual is part of a larger process/system.* Focusing on the individual is erroneous in Deming's view. Why? Because every individual performing a job is part of a larger process and, therefore, dependent on others in the process over whom they have no control. Yet we continue to ignore this when we appraise individuals, thereby disregarding the many external factors that affect their performance. Peter R. Scholtes cites excellent examples in his treatise on Deming's teachings on performance appraisal.[4] Scholtes talks of the salesperson who is dependent on the state of the economy and the quality of the product or service being sold. He talks of the typist who is dependent on the clarity of someone's penmanship. He talks of the production line worker who is dependent on the state of the machinery or the ability of the machinist to fix it. In each case, it is easy to see that workers are part of a larger process and are affected by factors beyond their control.

Employees are also affected by systems that may or may not be well designed. Since organizations are just beginning to learn how to judge process capability and use statistical process controls to bring predictability and consistency, why would they look to the individual worker and not the process as responsible for results? Deming supports the many quality experts who say, "Quit pointing the finger at people and start asking what is wrong with the process." He believes that 85–90 percent of the problems are with the process and only 10–15 percent are people problems. If this is so, then how can people individually shoulder responsibility for quality output? His advice is to make continuously improving the process part of everyone's job and reward the work team for process/systems improvement.

• *Rewarding individuals discourages teamwork.* I believe focusing rewards on the individual reinforces individual achievement at the expense

of others. It fosters an environment of competition instead of cooperation. When we rank people against one another for the purpose of doling
out merit raises, we negate the reality of the team effort needed for exceptional performance. Even when one or two individuals make a heroic
effort, there are often other players in the background who have been
filling in for them in order to give them time to address the accomplished
feat. When a system rewards individuals, it forces people to choose between being rewarded and being part of the team. The individual must
stand out somehow among his/her peers. Not only does this discourage
the teamwork culture being sown, it also lessens the possibility that the
organization will benefit from the higher level of effectiveness that teams
often bring.

   • *The role of the supervisor is shifting.* As Total Quality efforts progress,
the need becomes clearer for supervisors to play facilitator/coach. In the
"judge" role that is predominant in appraising individual performance,
the supervisor as the "hub of the wheel" is reinforced. Most current performance appraisal systems keep information and control with the supervisor, rather than spreading the data and responsibility more broadly
to the team. As teams are asked to take on more responsibility, supervisors need to forge links with other parts of the organizational system and
act as boundary spanners for their teams. Since the team has assumed
the lead in operating the process and delivering the product or service to
the customer, its members need to be more involved with giving feedback. They now have more of the information.

   • *Continuous improvement is everyone's job.* When individual standards
are developed, people will often work around the current system to complete work. This undermines the need to take time to continuously improve the current process. "Making the numbers" is what is reinforced
and rewarded. It doesn't matter if those numbers are sales figures, units
produced, or loans approved. It fosters volume-driven rather than volume and quality-driven performance. It also fosters what Deming calls
"tampering with the system." This means pressuring the system to produce by tweaking it this way and that in order to meet goal. This does
not reinforce going after the root cause in order to make a lasting improvement that will increase both productivity and quality. It also may
not reduce the rework in the system needed to fix errors made in the
rush to make the numbers.

Deming's Alternatives

If we review the purposes of performance appraisal and consider the
above views, the road that Deming leads us down becomes clearer. Earlier, six reasons were given for performance appraisal. They were:

1. Regular appraisal of job performance
2. Salary increases based on merit
3. Recognizing promotability or promotion based on merit
4. Feedback on strengths and developmental needs
5. Assisting employees' training and career planning goal setting
6. Review of fit for job at the end of probationary periods

Let's look at some of the key concepts inherent in these purposes—feedback, developmental planning, recognition of promotability, and financial reward justification—and what Deming proposes as alternatives.

Feedback

Employees answering various survey instruments often say that they receive very little feedback from their supervisor. Many agree that much of the feedback is negative, and some even say that the only real feedback discussion they have with their supervisors is during the annual performance review. HR professionals know that organized feedback is a powerful reinforcing technique for positive behaviors, but they also know that praise, walking around to chat, and generally engaging in more open, ongoing communication occur too seldom in the workplace. Studies also show that pieces of business information, such as customer satisfaction reports and profitability comparisons, are not shared with employees to a great degree. Feedback, obviously, is a scarce commodity. Deming challenges American management to open the doors of communication, to identify the key processes that work teams have responsibility for, to talk with employees, and to provide them with feedback on a continual basis.[5]

At this point in America's history, ongoing information delivery and feedback are so rare that employees see the sharing of business information as a reward. I have found quality improvement teams totally appreciative of receiving and completely capable of dealing with the business information needed to effectively assess customer needs and determine the root causes of problems. Total Quality efforts can begin to show how sharing feedback with work teams can increase their performance, both because of expanded knowledge and the motivation this feedback provides the workers.

Developmental Planning

In *The Fifth Dimension*, Peter Senge coined the term *the learning organization*. Growth is an admirable value for any company. Yet when we think of growth in relation to organizations, we generally think of something like market share. To value the human resources of the company to the extent that constant learning becomes a precept of operations is a worthwhile endeavor in our ever changing world. Deming encourages on-the-job training for all employees. If this value/principle were truly to guide our organizations, then continual feedback regarding strengths and developmental opportunities would be a norm. Casual conversation between supervisors and employees would address these subjects. Clearly, every person should be enabled by the company to carry out his/her assigned job fully.

Many U.S. companies do not spend the money that those in other countries do in developing their work force. An MIT report in the mid-1980s surveyed 150 companies and found that the median company spent .6 percent of payroll on training, with a cost per trainee of $250. The top 25 percent of responding corporations averaged spending 7.3 percent of payroll on training and $845 per trainee. Dollars were invested more toward white collar and managerial employees and were not evenly distributed.[6] And according to an APQC white paper, the percentage of payroll spent on training by highly regarded companies such as IBM, Xerox, Texas Instruments, and Motorola does not top 5 percent.[7]

How does this compare with Japan and Europe? In the MIT paper cited above, data on productivity, quality, manufacturing practices, human resources policies, and the amount of training were compared from fifty-six auto assembly plants in several countries. The most important results showed that those plants with transformed human resources management systems (rather than traditional HR systems) achieved higher quality and productivity levels. But the point of this section is made by the fact that the distribution of the training effort was deployed at significantly higher levels in Japan and Europe than in the United States. The APQC paper cited above supports this finding in that the number of hours spent by Japanese companies on training new workers was 380; European companies spent 173 hours, while solely owned U.S. companies spent forty-six hours. (The APQC paper also included the results of the World Competitiveness Report, published by the World Economic Forum's Institute for Management Development in Lausanne, Switzerland, in 1992, which placed the United States behind Japan, Germany, Switzerland, and Denmark.)

The HR function can and often does carry the training and career development banner. Ongoing developmental planning and the transformation of U.S. companies to "learning organizations" is a worthy banner indeed; the results prove it.

Recognition of Promotability

While Deming believes that using performance appraisal as a means to promotion will distort the objectivity of the system, his alternatives are not all new. Some have been practiced extensively already. Special assignments, assessment centers, developing a system that is less dependent on promotion, and involving the internal and external customers in selection are avenues that should lead the way. For example, when giving someone a special assignment, it should be not only to test the person at a new level of leadership or ability, but also to develop that person so that he/she will be ensured success. An old standard with a new twist.

Assessment centers have reached new heights of usage in the United States in recent years. They are holding up in the courts as a means of determining promotability. While assessment centers are expensive, what is the cost of continuing to use a performance appraisal system that is not viewed as credible by many employees? This is a good question for the HR professional to ask.

In regard to creating organization cultures that are less dependent on promotion, Total Quality efforts do a good job of increasing the value and contribution of all members of the team. The likely result of such efforts is a natural flattening of the organization. This reality is not new to the HR professional. Career development specialists have long been listening to advocates such as Beverly L. Kaye, whose book *Up Is Not the Only Way* redefined career development from meaning upward mobility to meaning career enrichment through career growth any way one can get it.

The graying of the population and the aging of the baby boomers are demographic realities, yet promotion is still too often the only "carrot" held out by companies to their employees. Even the downsizing of the 1980s, which saw middle managers exit in larger numbers than ever before, has not acted as the catalyst for shifting many organizational cultures. Perhaps this is because the value of teamwork was not an integral part of these events. It is a very integral part of Total Quality efforts, so perhaps the culture shift needed is easier to achieve through this route. In a quality culture, leaders and influencers exist at all levels, and power is redefined so that shared power is valued and seen as having the potential for continual expansion.

Increasing participation by work unit members in the selection process of peers is now common, but how often are work unit members and customers involved in the design of job criteria and in the selection of who gets promoted? Not often enough, yet these people will be directly affected by the selection. Including the key stakeholders in the promotion selection process is a wise strategy. Stakeholders will want the people they recommend to succeed. And they may know more about the capabilities and attributes of the people they work closely with than the upper managers do.

Financial Reward Justification

This section will be brief since the need to pay people based on the market rate, their skills, their responsibilities, and the company's performance has already been alluded to. Deming also supports pay linked to seniority because of the know-how more senior people bring to the table. Salary increases would, therefore, become a function of the above variables and not necessarily be tied to annual performance feedback, since in Deming's world, the annual system would not exist. If this reality were commonplace, I would venture to say that some variable pay system of gain sharing or incentives would replace the annual salary increase.

Standards and Measures

In closing this chapter, it is important to spend a little time discussing standards and measures of performance and showing how TQM can improve common practice. Chapters 6 and 13 use standards and measures as means of achieving important organizational objectives. Yet Deming says that work standards need to be eliminated. He says that MBO systems should also be replaced. His reasons are simple and profound.

Deming says that numbers are crutches of poor supervision and that MBO supports managing by numerical goals. Too often, standards and goals are arbitrary. You can probably tell a story about some whimsical objective that was someone's "good idea." Too often, these objectives are not based on any data and are not achievable. Yet the American worker is too often reluctant to challenge the process and accepts the numbers.

This reminds me of a story that is worth telling here. I was new in an organization and position and had to set objectives. My boss had some numbers that had to do with one of the key processes in one of my operations. I asked him the basis of the numbers. (They had to do with turnaround time of requests.) He told me there was no basis for them—they were "the best guess" the prior manager had come up with.

I requested the chance to determine the facts before I agreed to objectives being set for me that were based on gut instinct alone. He agreed. We found out that the numbers were inaccurate and that the goal he would have set for the work unit based on them would have been impossible to achieve. Instead, we set a more realistic figure, achieved it, and made improving the process a priority for the year. The following year the goal was the continued decrease in turnaround time, and everyone accepted it willingly and eagerly; it was based on facts, and improvement had become a way of life. It is only through knowledge of the process that people can begin to understand its capabilities and, therefore, its potential. Perhaps if management experienced this, then Deming would cease to be so critical of numerical goals. If this were to happen, the numerical goals or standards would be much more fact-based than they are now.

Since TQM is so customer- and process-driven and grounded in managing by facts, there are a couple of obvious hints at arriving at successful measures of performance. Customer-driven priorities and process defect or cycle time improvements are measures that are easy to develop. Going right to the customer for information about what is important and how he/she measures the work in relation to the delivery of products or services is a sound approach. Companies across the nation are gathering these types of data from their customers in increasing numbers as customer satisfaction measurement is gaining sophistication. Why not use this information with employees as part of their performance expectations? Seventy-eight companies were recently questioned about this very area. An impressive 92 percent said they are beginning to measure and base remuneration on quality satisfaction from the customer's perspective.[8]

In regard to process data, employees' work processes produce data that do not necessarily reflect the end product or service, yet there are many ways to measure process performance midstream. For example, you can observably measure quality as a part moves from one operator to the next in the process, and observable measurement is the best and most honest type of information to use in judging the performance of either the process or the person. Endeavoring to build performance review systems on these types of data is relevant and specific. While Deming says that the employee is not in control of his/her process because of the interdependencies, it appears likely that individual performance measurement will continue. Therefore, evolving to basing the performance on specific, related data that reflect the process or its outcome makes sense and can be used to reward both individuals and teams as appropriate.

Conclusion

As HR professionals become more knowledgeable about TQM, they might still try to find ways to set performance standards and measures; at least moving more and more toward observable, customer-driven measures will help. Yet Deming says it is time to eliminate performance standards and measures. What does he suggest we substitute? Leadership. How? By instilling a focus on the customer and on continuous improvement, by controlling processes, by rewarding improvement, by breaking down barriers between departments, by driving out fear, by instituting training, by building quality into the system, by empowering workers, by eliminating waste, by reducing complexity, by encouraging pride in workmanship, and by putting everybody to work to transform the organization.

This is what Deming recommends. This is the road to Total Quality. It can begin in small ways, like the turnaround time story shared above. By becoming obsessed with the customer, making improvement a priority, giving the people the skills they need to ensure success, and rewarding and recognizing both the team and the key individuals for their accomplishment, turnaround time eventually exceeded the "wishful" goal initially cited as a desire by management. But it took time and the team's commitment to improvement. Evolution, not revolution: In small steps, doing the right things right in regard to performance appraisal will lead to new vistas for both employees and the HR profession.

Chapter 9
Staffing and Related HR Functions

One of the often overlooked areas affected by TQM efforts are the staffing-related functions of human resources. This chapter defines staffing broadly and discusses issues ranging from hiring to job descriptions to HR planning. Five areas that will need change and refinement are discussed. Although little has been written on the subject, progressive HR professionals who operate in these varying arenas have already begun to respond to the challenges that TQM brings. Those five areas are:

1. Hiring/Discipline
2. Job descriptions
3. HR planning
4. Career development
5. Employee relations

Hiring/Discipline

Hiring

The impact of TQM on hiring begins with a change in the paradigm that the hiring manager has the final say and is the recruiter's main customer. Teams of people have now begun to hire people. As a result, recruiters in TQM companies often look at the work team as the customer since the people in the unit often provide hiring specifications, interview potential coworkers, and decide together who will be asked to join the team. Supervisors and even team leaders generally support the group hiring process in TQM companies and train their work unit in the legalities and diversity needs of the organization.

Hiring Workers

In those work units that are designed to have workers cross-trained in all basic work tasks, the concept of the multiskilled worker comes into play. Some sort of prioritization of baseline skills needs to be defined for the recruiter. The recruiter and the work team may not be able to find individuals with all of the capabilities or experience needed, but an individual's potential ability and interest in learning the various tasks could be tested for or assessed in some way.

Also, new concern exists for whether the applicant can operate comfortably in a work team environment. Generally, if the applicant has not worked in a TQM environment before, the recruiter must carefully question attitudes, values, and work orientation during the screening part of the hiring process.

New and different interview questions must be developed to determine if the applicant will succeed. Some of those questions could include:

- What kind of background do you have in working on task forces, quality circles, employee problem-solving teams, or quality improvement teams? What did you find most exciting or most frustrating about the team experience?
- Have you ever worked in an organization where your performance was evaluated by your work team members? If so, what did you think of the experience? If not, how do you think you would react to such a practice?
- What roles have your past supervisors played in other organizations? What do you want and expect from your supervisor? (Depending on the answer, the recruiter would likely follow up with explanations of the company's TQM environment and ask the applicant's opinion of it.)
- Have you ever worked in an organization where your work team had responsibility for an entire work process? (The concept of *process* may have to be explained. A flowchart of the work unit's key processes could be used as an aid.)
- Have you ever been expected to cross-train and perform work assigned to others? What was the experience like? How were you recognized for pitching in?
- What are the things that motivate and inspire you to perform at your best? What kinds of behaviors or working environments demotivate you?
- Have you ever had to work with other employees to achieve consensus about what might need to be done to solve a problem?

As you can see, some of the questions have similarities with typical, traditional assessments of "fit with the environment," such as the third and fifth questions, but the answers being sought would likely differ. For example, having a supervisor who trains you and gives you clear directions might be an expected answer to the third question, but in a TQM enterprise, those responsibilities might be work team responsibilities. If so, the recruiter would need to probe for the applicant's willingness to take direction from a peer.

Since new skills and competencies are needed in TQM companies—such as the ability to work in a team environment, to participate in group problem-solving activities, or to master the basic quality tools—recruiters need not only new questions and new answers, but also the means to assess an individual's current competencies and potential capabilities in these new areas. Eventually, these new requirements will become common, but HR executives need to be concerned with the development of their own staffs to meet these challenges. I have thus far been unable to discover any completed, validated selection instruments that assist recruiters in determining which workers will succeed in the new workplace environment.

As I researched this area, I discovered that Murro Consulting, a small consulting firm in Phoenix, had as of early 1993 completed its first round of research with forty TQM companies in its quest to provide an instrument that can be used for hiring and career development purposes. Murro was willing to share its preliminary findings, which point to five characteristics that appear to be requirements for success in TQM companies. The Continuous Improvement Success Profile™ highlights the following categories of needed skills and abilities:

1. Innovation
   - Open to nontraditional suggestions
   - Experiments with new ideas
   - Thinks of imaginative and creative ideas
   - Applies novel ideas to current problems
2. Supportiveness
   - Shares information with other people
   - Praises others for their good work even when not involved in the effort
3. Team orientation
   - Effective in collaborating with others in a team effort
   - Demonstrates honesty in dealing with team members
   - Cooperates with others to reach shared goals
   - Shows flexibility by adapting to different personalities and behavior styles

4. Reliability
   • Responsible, conscientious, and thorough both in the completion of work tasks and in interpersonal interactions
5. Work orientation
   • Shows enthusiasm and active involvement in work
   • Takes the initiative when something needs to be done
   • Places a high emphasis on quality
   • Has high expectations for both themselves and others

While this instrument is still in the development stage, it offers hope that HR professionals will soon have a reliable base from which to work with applicants and current employees to build a TQM work force.

Some companies have not waited for such an instrument to be available. Chapter 14 discusses a "best practice" organization, Diamond Star Motors, which has instituted its own special screening process. Another company, Lake Superior Paper Industries, has had teams assessing "fit" for years. Let's take a moment to look more closely at Lake Superior's process.

Lake Superior Paper has a rigorous selection process focused on getting the right people into the right environment. After taking a battery of general aptitude tests, the candidate is interviewed by his/her prospective peers. Team members, who are aware that they must have defensible, legitimate reasons for turning an applicant down, ask such questions as how the candidate has handled conflict, when he/she has used arithmetic, and how the person feels about working in the team environment. If one team member casts a negative vote, then the candidate is not hired. One Lake Superior worker is quoted as saying, "I like this hiring system better than the traditional system. In the interview, we ask social questions to find out what makes a person mad or upset. We probably turned away some superior craftsmen because they wouldn't fit."[1]

Hiring Managers

Recruiters who have responsibility for hiring managers must also look for people who will fit into the new workplace environment. Since the managerial role is changing, new traits, skills, and abilities must be sought as recruiters attempt to sort out competencies that will help the organization achieve its TQM vision. There has been much said about the changing role of the manager as the year 2000 nears. Based on my experience, some of the common needs appear to be:

• Managers who gain satisfaction from enabling others to solve problems. This is in contrast to the manager who is the "hero" and has to solve the problem himself/herself.

• Managers who are capable of developing and coaching both groups and individuals to their fullest potential. This implies the knowledge and ability to grow teams through the various stages of development, not just the traditional task of developing individuals.

• Managers who are able to build information systems that focus on the right data and who cascade that information throughout their operations as information facilitators. This implies the willingness to be less hands-on and let the work force manage its own processes, since there is appropriate and continual information flow about process performance. It also implies letting go of the traditional paradigm "knowledge is power."

• Managers who value shared decision making and view power not as a zero-sum game, but rather as continually expanding properties that benefit from the expansion of every member's influence. This is in contrast to the manager who, once reaching the managerial ranks, looks at his/her area of responsibility as a domain to be protected.

• Managers who have the ability to create and communicate a shared vision that motivates people toward exceptional performance. This conceptual and motivational ability is necessary as structures are designed that are more decentralized and lower the level of decision making and quick response.

• Managers who have cross-cultural knowledge and value the diversity of people, who are interested in capitalizing on the benefits that come from many perspectives and cultures. This is as opposed to managers who like to have employees who agree with their ideas most of the time.

• Managers who have a secure sense of self, who are able to share the visibility of success with others. This is as opposed to managers who need to take individual credit for any success inside the operation.

There is another way to look at the evolution of management style, and a fine model has been offered by the newsletter of the Quality and Productivity Management Association. Figure 9-1 exhibits its simplicity in graphic form.

I was unable to find any assessment tool currently on the market that would aid organizational recruiters seeking the type of managers described above. The astute HR professional should be proactive in scanning the environment for such a tool. You should also network with colleagues in other organizations since there are a growing number of enterprises that consider their managerial competency profiles a competitive strategic advantage and will not broadly share the information.

Figure 9-1. The evolution of management style.

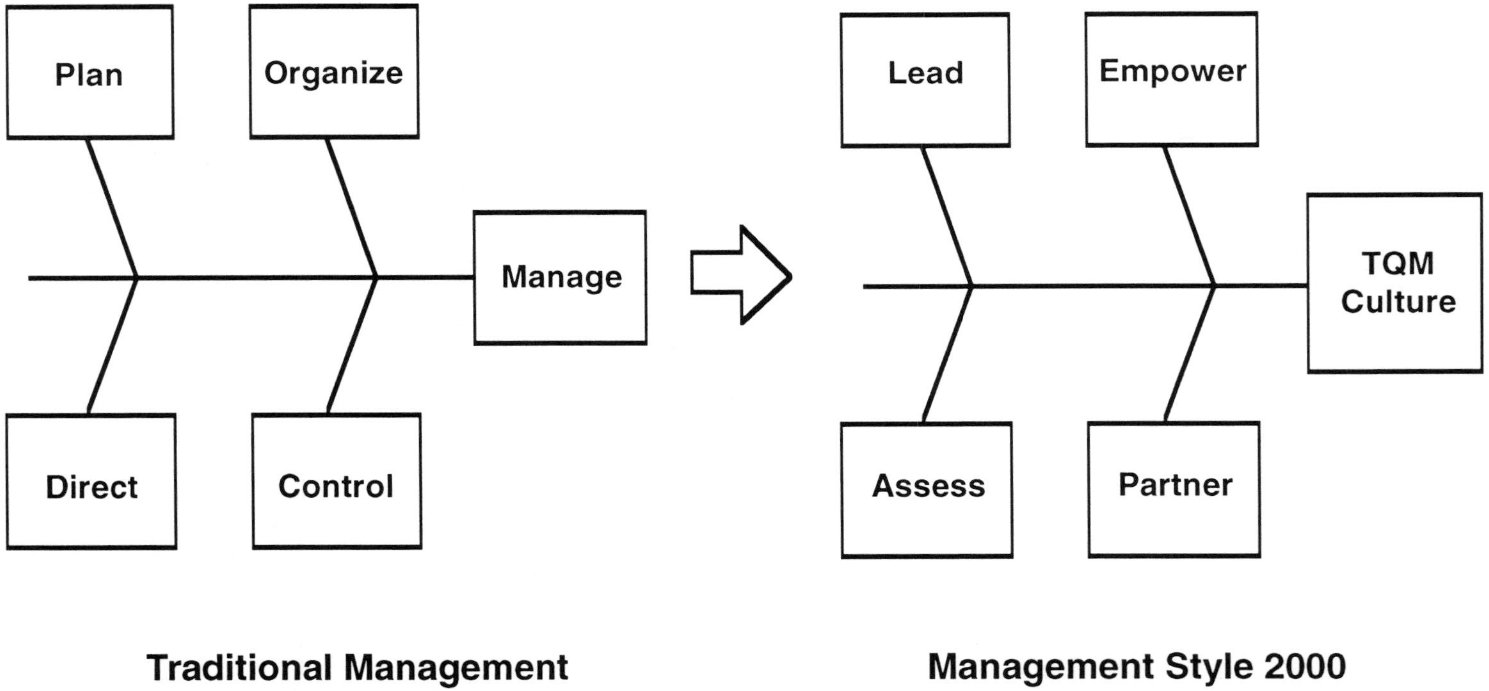

Traditional Management

Plan | Organize | Manage | Control | Direct

Lead | Empower | TQM Culture | Partner | Assess

Management Style 2000

Source: "The Heart of TQM," *Commitment Plus Newsletter* 6, no. 12, October 1991.

Discipline

As work teams mature, they move beyond assuming responsibilities such as scheduling to assuming responsibility for hiring and eventually discipline and even firing. This poses special challenges for the HR professional who is used to working with one person's perspective (the supervisor) on an employee's performance. Since only the most sophisticated organizations have moved work team responsibility to this level, there are few stories yet to tell. But as HR professionals look into the future to be ready for continued adaptation to the way teams work, they may likely see the difficult area of discipline and firing as a shared one between workers, supervisors, and HR. Even in union organizations, this peer review process is becoming more common with disciplinary matters considered by a team of coworkers.

When there is general consensus among work team members that a particular member is not pulling his/her own weight, many creative and correct practices can be applied. This should not cause the HR professional many undue problems. But if a work team is not in agreement, the HR professional could be called on to play an advisory role. For example, if there is dissension among team members about the expected level of performance, the HR professional could be asked to consult with the team about developing realistic, fair work expectations or approaches to take with members who are viewed as not contributing appropriately.

Since the supervisor or team leader would be pulled in to try to address such issues, there might be a low level of dependence on HR. However, when the issues get complex, line management often turns to HR for additional advice and counsel. These issues are sensitive when being addressed by the supervisor, the employee, and HR, let alone when they are being addressed with a team that cannot reach consensus. HR professionals need to be ready to respond.

Job Descriptions

With the changing role of supervisors and the enhancement of workers' jobs to include expanded skills and responsibilities, changes in job descriptions can be expected. Some companies have significantly reduced the number of job descriptions in effect by moving toward families of skills needed by the multiskilled work force, offering much more flexibility in actual job expectations. As or more common is the need to create new descriptions reflecting team leader or facilitator responsibilities. Often, these changes are made to the supervisor's position in the earlier

Figure 9-2. Job description for the new supervisor.

Title: Team Leader   *Department:* Special Orders

Position Reports To: Special Orders Coach   *Date:* 6/10/9X

Summary of Position Responsibilities: Team leader acts as coach and facilitator to work units responsible for input inspection, assembly, and packaging of specialized customer orders for the Northwest Region.

POSITION DUTIES

1. *Coordinating and Managing.* The team leader will work with the team members to develop plans for fulfilling special orders according to customer requirements. Working with the team, a schedule for each order will be developed and concurrence with the customer reached. Interface with Sales and Service will be completed in order to provide reasonable expectations on the part of all stakeholders and to continually update the work teams on information pertinent to successful delivery of the order. Ensures that documentation and minutes are maintained. Ensures that personnel-related and safety needs are met. Ensures that the work unit has necessary resources to complete requirements.

2. *Group Leadership.* The team leader will guide the work teams' group problem-solving process toward continuous improvement of quality and productivity measures and expediently advise the teams of any organizational changes that may affect their processes. Orients new members. Ensures that team goals are pertinent and clear to all. Helps the teams reach consensus on key issues.

3. *Training and Facilitating.* The team leader will develop individual team members and the entire team in group process, team dynamics, the basic quality tools, and problem-solving models and techniques. Assists in identifying training needs and will provide technical assistance and training when necessary. Helps facilitate the group process both in meetings and in daily operations. Provides feedback and coaching for teams.

4. *Participation and Contribution.* The team leader will identify, analyze, and generate ideas on work-related issues. Assists with implementation of changes. Identifies any expertise or information needed by teams to fulfill their goals. Builds rapport with other organizational units and individuals critical to the teams' success. Leads any benchmarking endeavor. Collects data and monitors the progress of the teams.

SCOPE OF RESPONSIBILITY

The team leader is expected to guide efforts of up to four work teams fulfilling special orders. Decisions are to be made at the lowest level possible in order to ensure quick response times to problems or opportunities. Errors in judgment will result in loss of orders and goodwill with customers. Continuous improvement in team and individual performance is expected and will be measured against baselines. Interface with other internal work units, management, and customers is usual and customary.

WORKING CONDITIONS

Clean, safe physical environment and efficient, effective layout of working area is expected. Involvement of employees in maintaining and designing the work area is expected.

EQUIPMENT

Maintenance and smooth operations of high-tech equipment valued at approximately $6 million per work unit is expected.

EXPERIENCE/SKILLS

Team leader position requires technical knowledge of special order activities and process. Two or more years of group dynamics and team problem-solving experience required. Excellent communications skills and knowledge necessary. Knowledge of TQM and teaming principles mandatory. Prior training and facilitation experience a plus.

---

stages of a TQM effort. These new responsibilities have a great impact on the people who are hired or promoted.

A typical, traditional supervisor's job description includes the need for technical expertise. It also lays out accountability for scheduling, budget control, production control, service levels, and various personnel functions for the work unit. The new supervisor's job description is quite different. Figure 9-2 is an example. This job description may or may not look like the supervisory descriptions currently in place in your organization. However, as an enterprise matures in its TQM effort, this type of job description will likely be common for frontline supervisors as they make the transition to the role of team leader and coach.

HR Planning

Forecasting the future of the work force used to deal with numbers relating to the estimated growth or downsizing of the organization. Today in TQM companies, variables such as planned cessation of supervisory positions or at least expanded spans of control are being taken into account. In fact, the actual design of organizations may change from a hierarchical structure to one that is more horizontally process-managed. Figure 9-3

Figure 9-3. The accomplishment of work through horizontal processes.

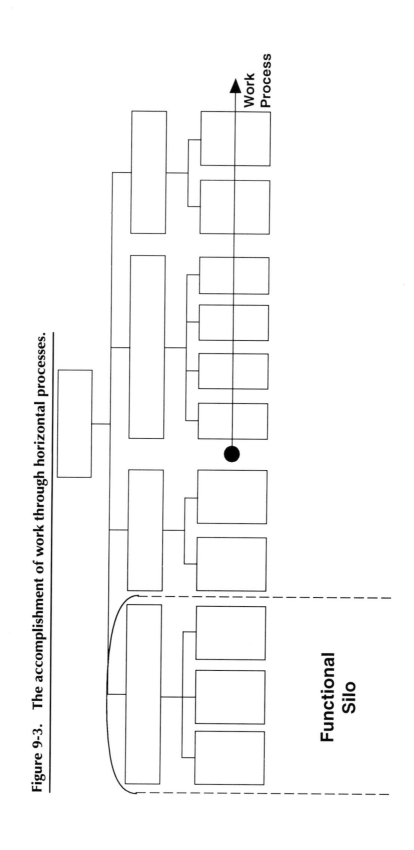

depicts the newly forming concept that, while organizations still tend to be structured in functional "silos," the work really gets accomplished across the company through horizontal processes.

A new structure for the company may take shape that focuses on process management instead of functional silos. For instance, the organization chart shown in Figure 9-4 concentrates on a particular process: relating external customer expectations to the entire business process. When all organization charts take similar focuses, the role of the human resources planner will become more complex with the need to find players with the mix of skills to fulfill roles in process-based structures. In addition, someone in the HR function may be asked to assist with organizational redesign or reengineering around key processes.

As expectations of people's jobs and job skills change and as organizational structures are redesigned to reflect this new reality, the variables in HR planning models will need to be flexible to take the changing dynamics and needs of the workplace into account.

Seeing the work force changes in a five- to ten-year time span may be viewed as the job of the HR planner in some organizations. But the need for HR to play a pivotal role in creating the vision of the future is exactly the strategic role that HR professionals have been striving for throughout the last quarter of the twentieth century. Other changing variables, such as job sharing, compressed workweeks, flex-time, and contracted work forces, have already made the HR planner's job more challenging. TQM, and its potential impact on organizational design, will add another dimension to the job. In fact, there are those who believe that organizational redesign and reengineering efforts will greatly affect not only the HR planner's role, but also put new expectations on the HR function itself to act as the company's organizational designer.

Succession Planning

Even in the most sophisticated companies that have already invested in well-developed competency models of management, the characteristics, behaviors, skills, and abilities attributed to the "high potential" players in the work force have undergone change. As stated in the Hiring section of this chapter, I have not yet run across a competency model that can be shared with you that incorporates such changes. Yet the literature is replete with articles about the changing nature of effective management. New management models can be found not only in management journals; even airplane magazines run features on new styles of leadership. John Naisbitt and Patricia Aburdene began to articulate these new competencies as early as 1985 in *Reinventing the Corporation* and more recently

Figure 9-4. Diagram showing relation of external customer expectations to the business process.

Customer Expectation = On-time shipment
Quantified Expectation = Shipment within 72 hours of order

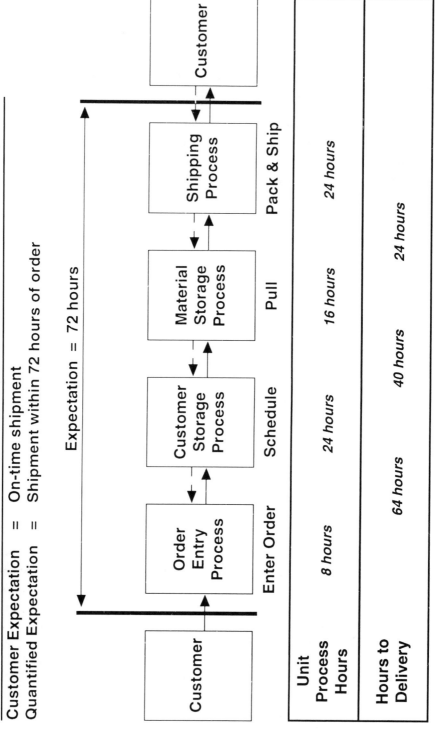

	Enter Order	Schedule	Pull	Pack & Ship
Unit Process Hours	8 hours	24 hours	16 hours	24 hours
Hours to Delivery	64 hours	40 hours	24 hours	

Source: H. James Harrington, *Business Process Improvement: The Breakthrough Strategy for Total Quality, Productivity and Competitiveness* (New York: McGraw-Hill, 1991).

offered a comparison of traditional management with effective leadership that supports many of the new models being touted by management gurus such as Peter Drucker, Warren Bennis, and Jim Kouzes. Naisbitt and Aburdene cite the following differences[2]:

Management	*vs.*	*Leadership*
Objective: Control		Objective: Change
Relies on giving orders		Facilitates/teaches
Rank		Connections
Knows all the answers		Asks the right questions
Limits and defines		Empowers
Issues orders		Acts as a role model
Imposes discipline		Values creativity
Hierarchy		Networking/web
Demands respect		Wants people to speak up
Performance review		Mutual contract for results
Automatic annual raises		Pay for performance
Military archetype		Teaching archetype
Keeps people on their toes		Nourishing, growth environment
Punishment		Reward
Reach up/down		Reach out
Here's what we will do!		How can I serve you?
Bottomline		Vision
Closed: Info = power		Openness
Drill sergeant		Master motivator
Command and control		Empowerment
Little time for people		Infinite time for people
Rigid		Flexible
At the top		In the center
Mechanistic		Wholistic
Impersonal		Personal

This list is not meant to be authoritative, but it is an excellent base. There are other challenges facing management as the paradigm of the effective model unfolds, such as the need to move from being *the* problem solver to solving problems through others, from encouraging through financial reward alone to encouraging the heart and spirit, and from valuing competition to collaboration. Those HR professionals responsible for succession planning in their firms would be wise to begin benchmarking with more advanced TQM firms to see what types of high potential competencies have arisen since TQM and how TQM has impacted the succession planning process. It is the HR professional's job to keep the basis for good succession planning decisions current and timely. And since most large firms invest both time and money in developing the next generation of managers, succession planners need to have an understanding of and even help to forge the role of the company's future leaders.

Career Development

Career planning and development has been a common concern among both employees and HR professionals for a long time now, but there have been too few resources offered in most companies to truly staff and foster career planning and development. Some companies offer training programs for employees to assess their own interests and skills. Some offer career libraries where resources about the enterprise or general career manuals, books, etc., are housed for employees' use on their own time. Others merely know where to refer employees if they raise questions. Most of the time, HR professionals spend a certain amount of time with employees on career-related matters, but too seldom are these conversations formal responsibilities of the HR professionals, and too seldom does the HR person receive any significant credit for this informal counseling.

With the advent of the baby boomers, the increase in retirement age, and the tightening economy, the upward advancement that was taken for granted and pointed to as the road all people should follow has become quite bumpy. There are too many people for too few spots at the top of organizations. Yet the hierarchical model is still the norm, so it is the natural inclination of people to want to strive for the top. TQM offers several alternative leadership opportunities and through them, a much broader perspective of one's potential career path.

The people who end up coordinating the Total Quality efforts at the corporate or division levels have a wonderful opportunity to be involved in establishing strategic priorities, to work with senior management steering teams, and to support cross-functional assessment and improvement teams. These positions are generally full-time jobs and offer skill development and visibility. The payback is there, often for upward mobility from the position. For example, two Total Quality managers I have worked with in the past two years have already moved to or begun development for general management slots. But all TQM efforts offer opportunities to many employees, not just the key coordinators.

A good example is the role of the team facilitator. This role offers a way for employees to grow and stretch while in their current jobs. The skills being learned and applied and the exposure to new people in the organization are often enough to keep any TQM facilitator happy for a long while. Yet, the ironic twist that many organizations find happening is that the people who choose to facilitate quality teams are often the ones who get the promotions because of the enriched skills and knowledge they can bring, let alone the visibility they have received.

Members of steering teams and team leaders also gain new skills and exposure through their involvement in the quality effort. Unless the role is played out on a cross-functional team, the exposure may not be quite as broad. For example, if you are on a department steering team or are leading an intradepartmental improvement team, the visibility may be within the boundaries of your current work environment. However, depending on the size of the department, this could lead to exposure to department heads who would not have other opportunities to work with individual contributors or even frontline supervisors.

But before I mislead you to think that exposure to the top is the only reason that employees volunteer for these roles, let me state that both the personal development and the challenge of being a part of the effort are often described as the true satisfaction by many employees I've talked with over the last several years. Employees who are actively involved in any significant role, whether it be as part of a steering team or as a member of an improvement team, are stretching their boundaries and current skills. They are learning much more about their organizations, and they are making an impact. They are being looked to as the experts and listened to when they make their recommendations. They experience their involvement as the personal career development opportunity it is.

Knowing that a TQM company needs different kinds of employees, organizations now need to develop or refine their current career development programs for employees and identify the career opportunities imbedded in TQM roles. Beverly L. Kaye, a renowned career development expert, has long viewed career development as more than a personal roadmap for individuals in the organization. She says, "Not only does it aid the individual in confronting and coping with a rapidly evolving working world, but it can also be a vital link between individual and organizational goals and objectives. It can become the vehicle for implementing the human resource aspects of a company's strategic plan."[3]

Kaye's six-stage career model cites three key players—the organization (as represented by top management), the individual (as represented by selected employees), and the practitioner (as represented by the HR professional)—as necessary for a successful career development effort. Her model, in brief, follows:

- *Stage 1: Preparation.* Analysis of needs and demands, formulating objectives, assigning responsibility, determining evaluation criteria, outlining actions, charting new activities, and readying resources is the job of the organization and the practitioner in this initial stage.

• *Stage 2: Profiling.* Identifying individual capacities; evaluating personal skills as perceived by others; verifying participant's knowledge about his/her interests, abilities, attitudes, values, and desired work contexts; and reality-testing feasibility is the primary responsibility of the employee, supported by the practitioner.

• *Stage 3: Targeting.* Selecting suitable career goals, exploring options for movement, understanding the organization's future plans, and converting the goal into action statements are the employee's next steps, assisted by the practitioner. The organization is responsible for providing important information about its short- and long-range business plans.

• *Stage 4: Strategizing.* Understanding the system, synthesizing information, formulating a specific course of action, and planning for contingencies is accomplished by the employee with the aid of the practitioner.

• *Stage 5: Execution.* Acquiring specific resources (e.g., new skills, visibility, contacts), gaining new experiences, and demonstrating new abilities to the organization rests mainly with the employee, but the organization must support development in the form of resources and dollars.

• *Stage 6: Integration.* Evaluating the efficacy of the career development effort from both organizational and individual perspectives, reporting results, assessing integration and impact on other organizational systems, and refining the effort is often HR's responsibility.[4]

As TQM ushers in more and more commitment to training, perhaps the commitment to career development will follow. If not TQM, perhaps the changing demographics will support increased internal career development. Either way, the HR professional who wants to remain state-of-the-art will enhance his/her career development practitioner skills.

Employee Relations

This section will be brief since there are but a few key hints or warnings that can be shared with HR professionals. But to skip the fact that employee expectations change with TQM would be remiss. The main employee laments that I hear in TQM companies have to do with:

• Perceived poor hiring decisions, e.g., "He's not a TQM guy. He'll never let us get involved in making decisions. Why did he get the job?"

- Perceived mishandling of disciplinary matters, e.g., "The manager is after Steve. TQM says point the finger at the process, not the person." Or, "Why doesn't she help develop Steve instead of punishing him? Isn't that the TQM way?"
- Perceived recognition of the wrong or not enough people, e.g., "Kathy only got that award because she brownnoses the director. So much for TQM." Or, "Why is Sheila getting that award? Doesn't the selection committee know that she had at least eight people helping her? So much for recognizing teamwork."

Employee relations professionals can expect to hear a rise in TQM-related complaints. There may also be allegations of favoritism as to which employees are appointed as team leaders, facilitators, and members. The new workplace is evolving, and many practices remain status quo for some time before transitioning. This is a very delicate balance for the employee relations staff. The other players walking a tightrope as the company changes are the leaders and the staff actively involved in the effort. The symbolism of TQM is strong and powerful, and employees take note of the gap between the vision and what exists. Employee relations professionals can easily be called upon to help discuss this gap with employees.

Conclusion

This chapter, more than any other, helps us to see how pervasive and important the TQM effort actually is to the human resources profession. Even in HR arenas where little has been published, there is a new future. There are few employment professionals or HR planners out there who know through formal preparation that TQM will affect the way they do their jobs on a daily basis. Yet many intrinsically know that just as TQM has a major impact on the organization, so too will it affect their day-to-day jobs.

Chapter 10
Communications

The human resources function is constantly involved in activities that are important to all employees. Special communications are often a part of these initiatives. Even if a topic is not specific to HR issues, if it involves employees, management often calls upon the HR function to develop the strategies and vehicles needed to communicate important information. Total Quality efforts need clear, consistent messages sent to employees on an ongoing basis. There is so much activity and such a need for reinforcement of management's commitment to TQM principles and promises that an extensive communications strategy must be part of the Total Quality effort.

Organizations that attempt to implement Total Quality without the support of a comprehensive communications strategy are making their implementations more difficult because the level of trust and belief will not be as high, continual momentum will not be being built, and information may not be communicated accurately or consistently. This chapter helps the HR professional shift the organizational culture toward the characteristics of TQM companies by offering the framework for creating a comprehensive communications plan and discussing the types of communications vehicles that can help.

This chapter also includes examples of communications strategies and tools used by both large and small organizations to set the stage and keep the effort in the forefront over time. Finally, an example is given of a typical communications team charter that will ready your organization to commit resources to effectively communicating your Total Quality effort.

The Communications Plan

There are many ways to develop a communications plan. The model offered here is tested and works for TQM. There are several components of the plan that take reflection and involvement of the quality leadership team (QLT); it is not a plan that can be developed solely in the communications expert's office, even if your company has one. The key segments are:

1. Background
2. Lessons learned
3. Goal
4. Objectives
5. Key audiences
6. Key messages
7. Strategies
8. Tactics
9. Timelines
10. Measurements

Background

This segment merely outlines the communications vehicles that the company currently uses most to send information to employees, as well as the company's communications capabilities. It includes readership or other effectiveness measures available. It discusses the results of any survey or interview information gathered about Total Quality communications. It is brief and merely an introductory overview.

Lessons Learned

This segment of the plan offers the developers an opportunity to reflect on past communications efforts by focusing on what worked well and what didn't. Specific techniques need review. For example, a small hospital discovered that the use of their "cascade info through managers" tactic had brought only mixed results in the past. Therefore, in a break from the past, they did not rely solely on this technique but rather considered it an important supplemental tactic in the overall Total Quality communications plan. When setting expectations for each department's quality steering team, the hospital's quality leadership team determined that, as each department deployed the effort inside its own boundaries, its steering team would also develop its own communications plan.

Goal

This segment is self-explanatory. A typical goal of a communications plan includes words like "to increase awareness," "to update," "to reinforce," and "to communicate to internal and/or external audiences." It is important that the QLT knows what it intends the communications strategy to achieve. For example, there are some organizations that decide to focus on the internal/employee aspects of the quality information flow and not to communicate to the outside world what is happening as the effort unfolds. Others choose to distribute information about their quality effort widely to both their internal and external audiences.

Objectives

Specificity is important in helping to turn goals into items that can be acted upon. Objectives such as "To produce a monthly Total Quality newsletter" help the organization to integrate quality activities into the current workload and assist in identifying the resources needed to accomplish the objective. Other objectives are common, such as "To establish awareness of the Malcolm Baldrige National Quality Award."

The objective "To develop tactics that actively involve the steering team in one-on-one communications about quality" was easily achieved by the Dietetics Service Steering Team at the VA Medical Center in Prescott, Arizona, through its informal but effective "grapevine." The creative tactic developed was an "employee word-of-mouth" process to communicate messages about the department's quality effort throughout the work force. The employee word-of-mouth tactic was for each steering team member "to discuss current events and values of the quality effort on a biweekly basis." Each steering team member was assigned to talk with one to two informal leaders in the workplace in order to capitalize on the organization's natural communications channel, the grapevine.

Key Audiences

The audiences for communicating the quality effort are as diverse as with any other communications plan. For example, it seems obvious to identify employees and customers as potential audiences. But what about suppliers? What about the press? What about contract workers? What about congressional or regulatory bodies? These questions point out the potential extent of the communications effort.

Clearly, an organization does not want to overplay the quality effort with many audiences unless there is value in doing so. Careful consideration must be given to which audience or audiences will be targeted. If there is a clear payoff in targeting numerous audiences and the organization is staffed to support such an effort, then making the right decision is easy. If resources are scarce or the company wants to learn through experience first, it might be best to begin with one or two key audiences.

Key Messages

What is said about TQM is as important as what vehicles or tactics are selected. This is true because the communications plan must support the large-scale change that is occurring in the organization's culture. As in any major change effort, there will be as many people who are skeptical of the shift as there are those willing to jump on the bandwagon or who will remain neutral until they are convinced this is not "just another program." The QLT needs to work out consistent and crisp messages that are believable and can be reinforced on an ongoing basis with actions as well as words. "Measuring customer satisfaction in everything we do" is an example. Later in this chapter is a complete series of one team's key messages.

At least some of the key messages will appear in every written, verbal, or pictorial tactic used and will become part of every QLT member's daily, informal communications. The time it will take different organizational cultures to believe that the messages are real varies, but the more the messages are sent, the more they are reinforced and the more meaning they will take on for employees. Remember that there are many major programs that have lasted two to three years. It is likely that it could take eighteen to twenty-four months for a critical mass of employees to become believers; the true skeptics will take longer or may never "join the faith."

Strategies

Strategies support the goal of the communications plan and target creative and critical pathways that help achieve the organization's mission. For example, the goal of increasing employee awareness of TQM principles can be supported very well by the strategy "Use existing communications vehicles as a means of recognizing those teams that are actively involved in continuous improvement efforts." Other strategies might be "Solicit ongoing employee feedback in every way possible" and "Use team members to assist management in visibly showing commitment." Strategies are deployed through the tactics or means determined to support them effectively.

Tactics

There are many vehicles for sending communications messages. A major point to keep in mind when choosing which tactics to use is their degree of effectiveness. This would be measured by historical experience or by developing indicators of the various tactics' effectiveness once implemented. What matters is not the volume of tactics selected but the quality of those tactics.

Another important point to keep in mind is that different communications work differently on different people. For example, most organizations that have worked on a TQM initiative suggest and approve a newsletter as a primary tactic, but the truth is that not all people like to learn by reading. So if past written communications in your company have been only marginally successful or if people don't like to take much time reading, even if the newsletter is excellent, it still won't work with all of the target audiences. Multiple channels and vehicles must be used to communicate TQM efforts successfully.

Brochures, electronic mail, press releases, internal publications, electronic bulletin boards, training classes, an information hot line, and regular business update meetings round out Intel's quality communications tactics for establishing awareness.[1] (The company has other tactics to achieve other objectives.) This is an excellent mix of multiple channels and vehicles.

Timelines

Just as in any deployment, the actual actions to be taken, by whom, and by when are spelled out in an action timeline. This type of implementation tool goes a long way toward clarifying the responsibility and accountability of various key players in the communications endeavor. An action timeline can also serve its own communications purpose in that people have a document that they can discuss and refer to in assessing progress.

Measurements

Modeling the way by developing quality measures for the communications strategies and tactics employed is an essential step for the QLT or department steering team. "Plan, Do, Check, Act" is a basic quality principle, and measuring the effectiveness of communications is an excellent way to show by example that checking what we do to determine its value is truly how everyone lives in the new culture. And it is automatic TQM behavior to continuously improve communications as you collect data about what is fulfilling the target audience's need. Measurements also help the organization to continue to learn about what works for it in this realm.

As in other quality initiatives, communications measures are focused on both process and outcomes. A good example of process measures comes from Exxon, where the number of business units with quality strategies, press targets, and spokespersons is measured on an ongoing basis. A natural outcome measure counts the number of press mentions and articles versus those of key competitors.[2]

Summary: Communications Plan Segments

The above elements of the communications plan are not etched in stone. People modify the plan segments to suit their purposes. What is critical for success is to develop a comprehensive plan supported by a timeline and clear responsibilities. The framework offered above works well and is a solid model. The quality and variety of the tactics selected will determine how many people in each given audience are reached.

There are many top quality organizations that can be looked to for advice in building the above plan. The International Association of Business Communicators and the Public Relations Society of America are two excellent professional associations that can be of assistance. But let's look at what I consider a benchmark communications effort—that of Texas Instruments. Perhaps its lead will be all the help you need.

Case Study: Texas Instruments

At a recent conference on communicating quality, Texas Instruments (TI) shared its 1990 Total Quality communications strategy.[3] While not covered here in its entirety, the strategy holds many lessons, and its various components are well done. Here are some of them: One of TI's goals is to "achieve management buy-in for Total Quality." TI's target audience is identified as all employees. A strategy supporting the TQM communications plan is to "use the global network to spread the gospel." The major tactic selected to reinforce messages is current, internal publications, which are expected to deliver quality communications. Some of the past lessons learned include "use telling examples instead of philosophy" and "steer stories to appropriate media." It begins to be clear why I consider this company's communications strategy as world-class.

The TI endeavor has high expectations. They are:

1. Demystify quality by presenting it as a process that has universal application and is a manageable task.
2. Raise visibility on need to satisfy internal and external customers by showcasing approaches that are getting results.
3. Build common language and understanding of quality issues through communicating common synergy of diverse programs.
4. Be a critical path for aligning individual efforts with organiza-

tional goals such that open communications has bottom-line impact on productivity.[4]

One of the objectives leading to an implementation step includes planning integrated communications across existing internal news and information channels. The outcome of this objective was an action item to develop a series on quality to change employee mindset and behavior, timing topics to TI's quality council agenda. The specifics are:

1. Four quarterly communication efforts with local examples.
2. Articles in between the quarterly campaigns to communicate key messages.
3. Use of electronic bulletin boards to elaborate the messages.
4. Integration of the quality thrust with other communication themes set for the year.

Again, the TI team developed specific key messages oriented toward the objectives of changing mindset and changing behavior. These messages were developed to change mindset:

1. We're working in a continually changing environment. Companies accepting this fact will be winners.
2. Customer satisfaction has surfaced in industry as the key differentiator. It is the key to a successful future.
3. Customer satisfaction is:
   • A true understanding of the customer's needs/wants
   • Meeting and exceeding those needs/wants
   • Doing it in a way that is better than everyone else
   • A moving target
4. TI will achieve customer satisfaction through Total Quality.
5. The guiding fundamentals of Total Quality are:
   • Customer focus
   • Continuous improvement
   • People involvement
6. Total Quality begins with—in fact, requires—individual commitment.

These messages were developed to change behavior:

1. To instill total quality, managers must provide leadership, communication, and education.
2. To install total quality, individuals must:
   • Learn the techniques and tools

- Adapt the techniques/tools to their own work tasks/environment
- Practice what's been learned
- Become an activist for Total Quality
3. The best movement toward Total Quality will come through managers and individuals working together to create a feeling of empowerment.

Finally, a yearlong timeline was developed for the plan, including the monthly themes as well as the vehicles and responsible parties. Execution of the plan was part of performance expectations and included target completion dates. A survey feedback instrument, focus groups, and readership statistics acted as some of TI's communications measures.[5]

Quality Communications Criteria

Establishing specific criteria to act as a framework against which all communications are developed and measured is a worthwhile step for any professional asked to own the communications process. Federal Express is an excellent benchmark for establishing measurement criteria. Ed Robertson, manager of management and quality communications, spoke about measuring customer satisfaction in employee communications campaigns at the 1992 Communicating Quality Symposium.[6] Four levels of criteria were outlined, with the easiest criteria to achieve related to logistics and the most difficult related to influencing behavior. The four levels are (1) logistics criteria, (2) attention criteria, (3) relevance criteria, and (4) influence criteria. Let's move through these four levels.

Logistics Criteria

This originates from the communications professional's need to ensure that messages are received by the audience so that higher level criteria can be achieved.

- *Delivery.* Did the communication arrive at the intended point of contact with the audience?
- *Timeliness.* Did the communication arrive when the sender and receiver needed it?
- *Input.* Was the communication read/viewed/heard by the receiver?

Attention Criteria

This originates from the need to measure a communications professional's technical expertise and competence.

- *Compelling.* Did the communication get and keep the receiver's attention?
- *Understandable.* Did the receiver understand the key information about the topic?
- *Credible.* Did the receiver believe the communication?

Relevance Criteria

This originates from the audience's need to receive information that will allow them to perform effectively as organizational members.

- *Relevance.* Did the communication relate to what was happening in the receiver's environment?
- *Useful.* Did the communication help the receiver to perform better?

Influence Criteria

This originates from the client customer's need to influence the audience's behavior.

- *Attitudinally affective.* Did the communication affect the receiver's attitude or opinion on the topic?
- *Commitment affective.* Did the communication generate a desire in the receiver to focus energy on the topic?
- *Behaviorally affective.* Did the communication affect the receiver's behavior on the topic?[7]

The communication is measured against these criteria using survey methodology. Many lessons can be learned by asking the questions given relating to the criteria of the intended audience. As you can see, it is a simple matter to develop a measurement tool against the above criteria.

To Team or Not to Team?

Examples in this chapter imply that communications professionals have the primary responsibility for the Total Quality effort's communications plan. But not all organizations have or even want their communications professionals to be the only players in the quality effort's communications game plan. For example, the quality leadership team takes a look at many organizational improvements that need to occur under the Total Quality banner. Communications is often addressed in the first year. As such, the QLT often decides to create a cross-functional team of people from various levels to develop and execute the Total Quality communications plan.

In this case, it is important to include the communications "process owner" on the team if there is formal responsibility inside the company. Yet in many cases, there is no functional responsibility for communications. Whether or not functional accountability exists, there are many obvious benefits to chartering a diverse team to lead the quality communications initiative, and the human resources function should be represented.

Figure 10-1 is a typical communications team charter. One of the real benefits of specifically chartering a team to develop the organization's Total Quality communications plan is the opportunity to use this large-scale change initiative to experiment with the company's current methods of communications. As the Total Quality effort progresses, much will be learned about how to communicate well throughout the organization, and this will benefit all communications that follow. It is highly likely that the QLT will support innovative methods of communications along with placing a high priority on them. This increased understanding of how to communicate the Total Quality effort effectively will be a learning experience for the entire QLT.

Potential Tactics

Many tactics exist for communicating quality. While several have been discussed thus far, it seems reasonable that a list of ideas be offered for consideration. This list is not exhaustive, yet it offers many potential vehicles for use in achieving the goals and objectives of a diverse, multifocused approach. It includes, in alphabetical order, the following:

Potential Quality Communications Tactics

- Advertising campaigns
- Annual stockholders' meetings
- Articles in business/ professional publications
- Bulletin board campaigns
- Conferences/symposiums
- Electronic bulletin boards
- Electronic mail
- Features in existing publications
- Flyers

Figure 10-1.   Quality communications team charter.

Team Leader: Ms. Ima Communicator, QLT Member

Process Owner: Mr. Iva Message, Communications Department Head

Goal: To create awareness among employees of the strategic quality plan and to communicate ongoing progress of the plan.

Process Boundaries:

- The communications plan actions can be widely distributed to all employees on all shifts.
- The execution of the plan can be achieved with existing personnel.
- Minimal budgetary impact should be felt as a result of the plan's approval.
- The plan will be coordinated and overseen by the formal communications team until such time that it is institutionalized automatically into ongoing responsibilities of current staff.
- The team will report directly to the QLT.

Strategies to Define the Plan:

- Assess/review current communications policies/procedures related to em-ployeewide communications; recommend improvements where advisable.
- Identify any and all employee audiences that are to be targets of the commu-nications.
- Determine the current resources that will be needed to execute the plan.
- Seek input from all levels of employees as to the effectiveness of existing com-munications vehicles before submitting the recommended plan.
- Identify both process and outcome measures that will assist in clarifying com-munications effectiveness.

Desired Outcomes:

- An action plan that will use a variety of vehicles and channels to spread the quality gospel.
- An increased awareness on the part of all employees as to the mission/vision of the organization and the quality effort's part in achieving the vision.
- Target audience's satisfaction with the communications regarding the Total Quality effort as evidenced by a measurement tool.
- Increased management buy-in to the effort as evidenced by behavior change in assigned areas of responsibility as evidenced by a measurement tool.

Preliminary Timeframe:

Report to the QLT within ninety days, with communications plan to be formally recommended within 120 days.

- Focus groups
- Grapevine
- Management by walking around visits
- Mission/vision statements
- Networks (formal or informal)
- Newsletters
- Orientation
- Participation groups
- Partnership activities (customer and supplier)
- Posters

- Presentations/briefings
- Press releases
- Professional journals
- Recognition programs
- Site events
- Special reports
- Staff meetings
- Storyboarding
- Success stories
- Surveys/findings
- Television
- Training classes
- Videotapes

Conclusion

Communication—there can hardly be enough of it in organizations. Yet it is the exceptional leadership team that fully understands the payoff of developing a systematic, comprehensive plan to communicate a changing vision. TQM offers an organization the opportunity to experiment and improve its communications systematically. It offers the HR function the opportunity to hone skills and abilities often learned through trial and error. The result of both opportunities will likely be more successful communications efforts for your organization.

While short in pages, this chapter is packed with ideas for action that will assist both experienced or inexperienced communicators to develop a world-class communications plan for your organization's Total Quality effort.

Chapter 11

Labor-Management Partnerships

Cooperative labor-management efforts in the United States are not new, but there has been much more publicity about them since the 1970s, when the quality circle, quality of work life, and employee involvement movements began. There is evidence that in the 1920s, the railroad industry had labor-management cooperation committees to improve both performance and working conditions. Also, negotiated compensation plans can be traced from the turn of the last century into the early 1900s. One of the more recent and well-known examples of successful labor-management agreements in the United States is the 1985 UAW-GM contract for the Saturn plant. It makes the union a strategic partner with management in the successful operation of the plant and states that consensus decision making from top to bottom is standard operating procedure.

No matter how wide-ranging cooperative agreements are, they have a profound impact on everyone. That makes labor-management partnerships a cornerstone of the human resources professional's job and a must to look at as we consider TQM implementation.

TQM itself has ushered in its own success stories and its own challenges with regard to labor-management partnerships. This chapter highlights some of the real issues as well as opportunities linked to effective TQM implementation by highlighting both the payoffs and barriers facing U.S. organizations. It also shares success stories of organizations evolving toward cooperation.

Finally, the chapter closes with a list of implementation issues that need to be addressed before a union company kicks off a TQM effort, as well as several ways that unions add special value.

The Payoffs of Labor-Management Cooperation

Labor-management partnerships have payoffs from both the organization's and the worker's perspective. Let's look at the organization first.

A landmark study was conducted in 1992 by the Industrial Technology Institute of Ann Arbor, Michigan, for the Federal Mediation and Conciliation Service. The goal of the study was to develop guidelines for implementing labor-management problem-solving teams in manufacturing. The report's most significant finding about problem-solving teams was the effect they had on employees' perceptions of TQM. The employees noted increased commitment to quality in their plant and stated that the company had become better at involving workers in setting quality goals, rewarding people for quality work, and focusing on quality as a major priority. Three key quantitative findings supported the qualitative research. They were:

1. Improvement in production time and costs
2. Increases in quality seen by customers, resulting in decreases in customer complaints, decreases in rework, increased quickness in response time, and problem elimination
3. Direct improvement in safety measures such as cost of prevention over cost of injury or repairs[1]

Another productivity and quality program, implemented at Dayton Power and Light Company, was showcased at a recent Ecology of Work Conference. The program not only increased employee awareness of opportunity for productive staff utilization, but also improved actual productivity as measured by union members and supervisors using work sampling techniques.[2]

When Xerox began its TQM movement in the early 1980s, a cooperative program was part of the strategy. Bob Landsman, director of corporate industrial relations, stated at a recent Department of Labor symposium, "As a result of our cooperative program, we've been able to get our product out to market faster. Without those changes, there's no doubt that Japan, Inc. would be able to increase its market share to our detriment. Our top management has taken the position that it's absolutely essential to our future to continue down this path."[3] Xerox had taken a beating in the marketplace and committed significant resources to their TQM process as a key component of their competitive strategy.

Consultants and their firms have been working with and studying the impact of employee problem-solving teams since TQM came into its own. Consistently, they cite averages of 30–40 percent improvements in operating results in both union and nonunion companies. Statistics show TQM increases in market share, customer satisfaction, and employee relations.

Many of the payoffs of labor-management participation efforts are less quantifiable. Again and again, the literature shows that shared responsibility is making positive changes in the culture of organizations. This higher level of collaboration positively affects management in that it can seek assistance from union officials with initiatives at early planning stages; management and union officials can sit together to draw up plans that will be more easily implemented with fewer challenges. They can work through the problems of large-scale change knowing that a shared vision is in place. There is more control over the organization's destiny than ever before.

From labor's perspective, TQM ensures job security in that the organization's improving performance in the marketplace cements current, let alone future, job growth. And working toward job security is the right thing for the union to do.

Another major advantage of TQM for workers is their increased involvement in decisions made about work and working conditions. Often, TQM problem-solving teams address issues that have long been obstacles to workers' performance. Having the people who perform the jobs on the teams leads to better recommendations that have staying power. In fact, I have worked with union stewards who have said, "This level of involvement is what we have been asking for all along. How can I *not* support TQM?"

Another benefit of TQM and labor-management partnerships is the potential sharing of the gains made by problem-solving initiatives. In some companies, a portion of the gain achieved is shared directly with the team members and/or workers. In fact, TQM is implied to be one of the reasons for the resurgence of gain-sharing programs in the United States. In companies not installing gain-sharing plans, other forms of reward and recognition are being developed. Union involvement and support in developing these reward systems can enhance its credibility with workers, besides being the right thing to do for employees.

The expansion of skills and knowledge of workers is a payoff that cannot be underestimated. Quality efforts include many opportunities for training, and being on a quality team leads to increased visibility for members. These opportunities have both personal and professional benefits. Not only does a person broaden his/her own knowledge and skills, he/she might also be able to advance in the workplace because of them. This outcome of TQM could lead to increased status for the union supporting the implementation.

The Barriers to Cooperation

There are many reasons for moving toward increased labor-management partnerships and agreements, but the adversarial history and years of distrust do act as a major stumbling block. Some union leaders are so distrustful that they have formally gone on record saying that TQM or employee involvement is a union busting technique. As recently as 1992, two cases were even on their way to the Supreme Court. However, the Federal Labor Relations Board has since ruled that employees can be required to participate in TQM activities.

Let's begin by reflecting on the interests of management (in private industry, to maximize profit, and in the public sector, to perform services at lower costs in budget reduction times) as they relate to the interests of unions. Unions came into being to achieve the best wages, benefits, and working conditions for employees. TQM has nothing to do with increasing employee's wages, yet it can affect the way employees are rewarded and the "pie" that is available to workers if the company improves its lot in the marketplace. Unions could say that the gains would go only to the shareholders or back to the organization if they weren't around to rally for the worker. This may too often be true and reinforces the "we versus they" history of unions and management.

Some observers put the responsibility for antiunion sentiment in U.S. industry squarely on the backs of management. It would not surprise you to know that Edwards Deming feels this way. Another knowledgeable person, Stephen Schlossberg, director of the International Labor Office, also addressed the Labor Department's Labor-Management Symposium as early as the late 1980s by stating, "Employers have to make the first move—a move that says that the institution of unionism can add value and improve the quality of a particular organization".[3] Not all management in the United States is ready to make that type of move. Yet I firmly believe that the overture of partnership is up to management because the overall leadership responsibility for the organization's culture rests at the top.

Many managers still see the union as infringing on their right to operate the business and have a difficult time seeing their union stewards and members as partners. The adversarial past inhibits trust. Giving employees the right to be involved in business decision making is part of TQM. Resistance by management can be expected.

These examples of barriers put up by management may be discouraging. Strategies must be formulated to address management's needs, not just those of the union, in order to proactively remove the obstacles facing the Total Quality effort.

There are many union barriers to TQM as well. Let's look first at the threat cited by some unions that TQM builds teams that replace the collective bargaining process. The creation of parallel structures in many companies implementing TQM is seen by some as a threat to the union because shared decision making between management and employees is often the result. Yet many labor officials take a more positive view, maintaining that in this belt-tightening, competitive climate, many organizations do sincerely want to make peace by building collaborative cultures.

The adversarial history of labor-management relations is of paramount concern to union officials. There is also fear of the change that the partnerships will bring. Union leaders must take the attitude that TQM is worth the risk and educate and communicate the positive effects it will bring to the members. Taking risks on the future rather than riding on the past is a must for union officials.

Individual union leaders certainly run the risk of losing upcoming elections if management does a poor job of implementing TQM. In fact, labor leaders who support the implementation of TQM, yet fail to see a marked decrease in grievances because effective management practices do not occur, risk losing credibility with workers.

When a union backs the implementation of a management process such as TQM, it expects management to make a solid commitment to those principles. Yet senior management often has the additional challenge of educating and aligning current management style and practice to these new principles. This takes time; it is an evolution, not a revolution. The transformation period holds built-in inconsistency. This is generally difficult for union leaders, and they need support during the transition.

Implementing cooperative programs takes time—lots of it. Union officials' first priority is to represent workers. Many union leaders feel that there is not enough time in the day to do all the things needed to maintain and support workers' rights, let alone implement a cooperative effort like TQM.

Finally, there is the possibility that as companies shift their cultures to collaboration over competition, there will be less need for the union and due process will not have to be protected as it is today. This is an often unspoken yet real threat to union officials. There is no way a union leader who has gained power and status could easily support an effort that could mean a decrease in that power and status.

In fact, this fear of decreased power and status has already been mentioned as a possible root cause of management's resistance to participatory management, employee involvement, and TQM. The loss of power and status of individuals remains a real barrier to team-oriented movements, whether we are talking about managers or union officials.

Success Stories

Despite all the barriers, there are success stories to tell about labor-management partnerships. Here are some of them.

Crane Division Naval Surface Warfare Center

One of my favorite success stories is one that I personally witnessed. It represented, to me, more of a major cultural change than a productivity or quality improvement even though the cycle time and dollars saved were significant. At Crane Naval Surface Warfare Center in Indiana, the TQM effort involved the union president, who sat on the leadership team. After about six months, the union requested that union officials be added appropriately to ten strategic teams that had been formed to keep the base focused on the future. This was accomplished with a little resistance by the executive members of the strategic teams.

The HR strategic team (which included union representation) was tasked with coming up with a new way to look at and conduct negotiations when a new contract was needed. The team was led by a line manager who had no professional HR background, although the personnel staff was well represented on the team. The team leader and the union president met several times to discuss possible changes in the negotiation process. The idea of developing subteams, called Cluster Teams, to negotiate the major HR issues was conceived and met with everyone's approval. Cluster Team 1 dealt with leave, pay, and benefits issues. Cluster Team 2 addressed performance and development issues. Cluster Team 3 negotiated safety, security, and work environment issues, and Team 4 addressed merit staffing. Each team also took special topics such as the contract's preamble, the fire fighters' special union concerns, and the creation of the Center's resolution committee (a joint grievance resolution team). The formal process to be used in these subteams was created with members of the union who were asked to sit on the subteams with the management staff who were already permanent members of the HR team.[4] The contract agreement process is outlined briefly in Figure 11-1.

The basis for beginning the contract talks was a simple list of HR categories. The team actually threw the old contract out and started from scratch! In a little over two months, a completely new contract had been drawn up. Union officials and management agreed that the process used was a significant improvement over the old one in that it was less adversarial, more liberal toward employees, and was more participatory. Prior to these negotiations, the average length of time that it had taken to settle on a new contract was four to six months. The cost of negotiations had previously run $52,000 and this time it cost approximately $35,000.

Figure 11-1. Contract agreement process at Crane Division Naval Surface Warfare Center.

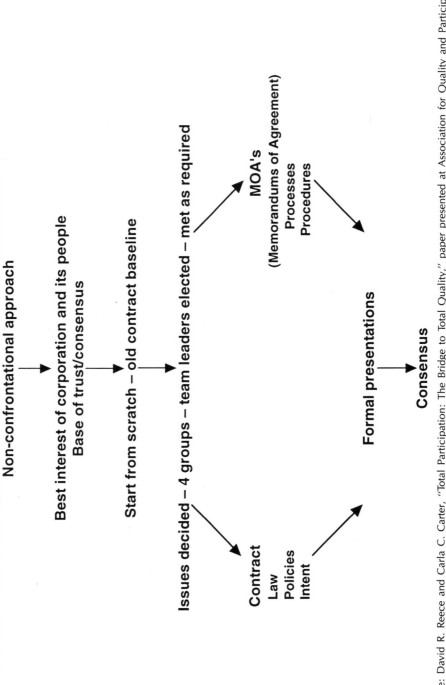

Source: David R. Reece and Carla C. Carter, "Total Participation: The Bridge to Total Quality," paper presented at Association for Quality and Participation National Conference (Seattle: 1992).

The prime reasons for this tremendous improvement were leadership (both union and management), the willingness to risk trusting each other, the joint commitment to develop and then follow the new process, and the dedication of the people involved. Yet, here, too, there was an important lesson learned. The history of poor relations with one of the key process owners of a contract area led the negotiating team to avoid involving that owner. This proved, not surprisingly, to be the only area where resistance to the agreement was met.

TQM encourages differences of opinion to be put on the table in order to encourage resolution. Involving the key players in the process and getting them to address their differences and work toward a win-win solution is part of what quality teams learn. But remember: evolution, not revolution. This team not only had 100 reasons to be proud of its accomplishment, but its members learned a great deal from the process. *And* their management was smart enough to reward the entire team for a job well done.

Cadillac

Perhaps the most inspiring story I have heard about labor-management relations is the Cadillac story, told at a recent conference sponsored by the American Management Association and the American Society for Quality Control. Let's put Cadillac's commitment to quality in perspective. Quality is the driving force at Cadillac and always has been. As far back as the early 1900s, Cadillac was winning quality awards, and pride of craftsmanship was evident. Yet in the mid-1980s, Cadillac's long-standing reputation was in jeopardy.

Cadillac was reorganized and made its quality plan its business plan. One of the objectives is to involve every employee in the running of the business; another seeks to involve everyone in planning. With the UAW as a partner, this has been achieved. That is why Cadillac is such a success story. Detroit has a long history of adversarial union-management positions; if Cadillac could succeed with the UAW, then the turnaround to labor-management partnerships can happen everywhere.

Inherent in Cadillac's cultural change effort are leadership teams whose roles are to nurture and lead the transformation, with more teams responsible for quality, cost, timing, and technology. This movement to a teaming environment broke down long-standing walls between functions. In 1987 management and the union developed the UAW-GM Quality Network, comprised of joint union-management quality councils at the corporate, group, division, and plant levels. Together they oversee improvement efforts and assist in the implementation of the business plan. Customer satisfaction is the core value that they jointly and actively support.

Finally, Cadillac has what it calls a People Strategy that focuses selection and reallocation of employees on the needs of the business. Developing employees, involving them in decisions, well-understood communications, and an effective work environment are also key components. The People Strategy is carried out by a governing body that represents every plant and staff operation. Seven different teams report to this body—the Human Resources Management Operating Committee—and are responsible for researching, designing, implementing, and evaluating Cadillac's people processes.[5] Sure doesn't sound like the old Detroit, does it? The success at Cadillac acts as a bright, shining light of hope.

Xerox

Xerox implemented both TQM and labor-management partnerships as part of its strategy to regain market share from the Japanese. There are two interesting components of Xerox's success. One is the way training was conducted and the other is the guarantee of job security that was put into the union contract back in 1983.

Many companies that do not hold labor as a partner, yet believe that the union needs to be informed about management decisions or strategies that are being implemented, offer special training courses for union officials. This is a positive move with regard to information sharing and, in some companies, a big first step. But in organizations where a true commitment to partnership has been made, such as Xerox, joint training of managers and union officials is the norm. Xerox believed that if the plant managers and the shop stewards had the same educational background and experiences at the same time in training, a common language and a common understanding would result.

The job security guarantee was a calculated risk, in opposition to the trend in the country to let go of no-layoff policies. At Xerox, this pledge was made to back up in action the commitment management said it espoused to the work force. The reality of the payoff of TQM and this high level of partnership has helped the work force to grow. According to Bob Landsman, Xerox's director of corporate industrial relations:

> As long as they know their jobs are not at stake, as long as they know that the company will continue to expand, they're willing to make some difficult decisions, such as telling the company to go ahead and buy parts and components externally when they know we can't make them competitively in our own

plants. They get all the economic data because, as far as the CEO is concerned, they're a true partner and he's not going to withhold any information from them that will impede their ability to make an enlightened decision.[6]

Special TQM Implementation Issues

When a union company begins to consider TQM, management may ask when the union should become involved. In organizations with positive labor relations, the answer is as soon as TQM becomes possible. It is smart to work from the start to forge the understanding of why and how the TQM implementation will unfold. If labor relations are poor, then the decision to implement TQM is generally first made by management alone. Many organizations make a mistake at this point. Instead of bringing the union in to assist in planning the implementation, they go about the task of planning alone and inform the union of their plans when they are completed. This reinforces the union's belief that "something is being done unto them." *And* it is not in keeping with TQM principles that everyone be involved in the transformation.

Let me tell you about an actual situation. A major national organization planned to implement TQM throughout its many sites across the country, but it did not involve the union in the implementation planning or execution. (Labor relations were poor.) The union retaliated by threatening a cease and desist order since TQM had been "mandated" without a cooperative agreement. The TQM implementation was upheld by an arbitrator with some concessions, but it is being appealed by the union. This shows the high price paid for not risking early involvement.

There is an important lesson to be learned here beyond early involvement. When a major organizational change is anticipated, management needs to make improving labor relations a part of its strategy as well. This may take the form of small steps toward rectifying past ill will, as well as conceding that management, not just the union, has allowed relations to be adversarial. A shift toward cooperation is what is sought, and while the going may be slow and sometimes inconsistent, it is imperative that this effort be made. The better labor relations are, the easier the TQM implementation.

Another implementation issue important to union companies is the need to make involvement voluntary. Few people have involvement in continuous improvement efforts as part of their normal job descriptions prior to TQM implementations. This voluntary strategy often goes a long way toward helping workers willingly see the benefit of TQM, rather than feeling it forced upon them. If an enterprise can make the kickoff of TQM exciting and meaningful, many employees will want to be involved.

Another implementation issue is the reality that employees on quality teams may need to work overtime to get their jobs done. Certainly, this is an area that union officials are rightly interested in, especially if a company does not make a provision upfront as to how it will handle the issue. Most organizations that I have dealt with offer comp time or overtime to employees who need it. Some leave it up to the discretion of line management to decide who will accomplish daily tasks, because it may make sense for an employee other than the quality team member to pick up the slack. It is top management's responsibility to address this issue early on in order to best guide middle managers and supervisors in this area.

Whether or not the union president or other union official sits on the QLT is an obvious decision that needs to be made. To expand the possibility of union involvement beyond this one team is another. For example, if an organization is going to set up department steering teams in each function, then a union representative may be considered a necessary member of this type of team. If a team of trainers or facilitators is going to be developed, then management would be wise to consider if it wants union officials in these roles. If the company is highly unionized, then it may have to determine if each quality improvement team needs a union representative.

You might think that having a union representative on every team is going a bit too far, for it is more important to have the right members who can offer a solid contribution to the problem the team is addressing. Yet each organization must consider how and where it wants and needs union representation and involvement. Most companies I deal with have the union president as part of the QLT. Beyond that, they encourage union officials to volunteer for any involvement that piques their interest. I have worked with union officials on steering teams, on assessment teams, and on improvement teams. They have always been interested and made a real contribution.

When developing the initial training plan for a TQM kickoff, the QLT must consider how it will train the union leaders. I do not advise separate training but do advise early training, especially for the union officials. If for some reason union officials have been left out of early training efforts, a special briefing is warranted as soon as possible.

When developing the initial communications plan, the QLT needs to consider the union's role. It makes a great impression on employees if top management and the union president speak to them together.

Other contractual considerations that may come into play and should be considered at the onset include how current HR policies and current union contracts may affect the TQM plan. For example, there may be a clause in the contract already stating that productivity gains made by workers will not result in layoffs, and TQM may raise the issue of layoffs due to improvements. An HR policy that may affect the effort might be that there is no compensatory time. Knowledge of this policy will help the QLT realize that more financial resources may be needed since employees who have to work overtime will be paid in dollars. It is wise for the QLT to understand how the current contract and policy fit with the future vision and to be aware of the issues that TQM might raise.

It is a sound practice to clarify and delineate what commitments and expectations both management and labor have of each other. For example, there may be a need to clarify that workers must be given what may have been confidential business information. Management should not hesitate to help union officials feel secure that employees will have what they need to succeed. I am not suggesting that these expectations necessarily be put into writing, but I do recommend that this type of conversation be held. It not only builds a higher level of trust, but it also ensures understanding of the common goal and allows for early agreement between the parties.

The plans for rewarding employees for the gains achieved do not always come prior to implementation but are generally a QLT priority and addressed in the first year. Since financial matters are of key concern to union officials, involving them in planning the strategy for rewarding teams is important. Bonuses or gain-sharing plans are often considered by companies. If the company seeks training about different methods of pay, union officials ought to be included. If there is expertise inside the system, it should be shared. The design team that works on rewards should have a union official on it to ensure consensus as the new plan evolves.

Finally, management and labor should establish a process to resolve any crises or disputes that may occur because of TQM. Of course, there are probably already grievance-type procedures in place. But the issues surrounding TQM do not necessarily need to go through the same process, since they are not generally part of the standing agreement. A parallel process for discussing issues related to TQM would provide a mechanism that gives both management and labor a way to explain and resolve any serious problems in a constructive, cooperative manner.

I am often asked if I have seen union contract language relating to TQM. There are probably many union contracts that either contain language in the body of the contract itself or in a memorandum of understanding signed by both the chief operating officer and the union president; I have seen both. Unless the union contract is up for negotiation, it is most common to create a memorandum of understanding. Figure 11-2

Figure 11-2. Memorandum of understanding between management and labor.

Commitment to Total Quality Management

1. Local XYZ and the management of ABC Corporation define Total Quality Management as a strategic integrated system for achieving customer satisfaction that involves all managers and employees and uses quantitative methods and improvement teams to increase organizational performance.
2. The management of ABC Corporation and Local XYZ hereby agree on the implementation of Total Quality Management concepts and processes at ABC Corporation and that the TQM process will assist in meeting the following objectives:
   a. Identify and solve workplace and service-related problems by direct involvement of employees.
   b. Increase morale and job fulfillment of employees through the TQM improvement process.
   c. Improve product quality and delivery to our customers.
3. It is further agreed that no understanding arrived at as part of the TQM process shall in any way interfere with the Labor Agreement between the parties.
4. Local XYZ and management encourage all employees to participate actively in the TQM process and recognize that such participation may be the proper subject of recognition.
5. Likewise, an employee's nonparticipation in the TQM process is to have no negative impact.
6. Local XYZ and the management of ABC Corporation agree to work together in an active partnership to achieve the above objectives in securing the organization's and its people's success.

---

is a typical example, based on a real agreement signed by a local union with its local management. Whatever form the language takes, it is usually very positive and underscores, whether stated or not, that a partnership has been forged around TQM and its goals.

The Special Value That Unions Can Bring

Union leaders have seen special programs come and go. They have the pulse of the people and can help management to convince employees that TQM is not just another program. Having union leaders sit on the QLT can sway people from labeling TQM "management's" program. Union officers can help management understand the reality of employees' attitudes from the onset.

It is also feasible that because of their perspective, union leaders can help build better plans that have a higher probability of succeeding by helping management stay pragmatic and reminding management of lessons learned. Labor leaders can keep both management and employees on track and moving toward the future, rather than slipping into old ways. When union officials understand and buy in to the direction that TQM will take the company, they will oppose quick fixes, crisis management, short-term orientation, and the like. They will act as a reminder that participative management and employee involvement are part of TQM.

Union leaders can help employees to understand better what is happening in the work setting and educate them as to what is expected in the new order. Unions have been known to offer training programs for employees and could well choose a TQM-related topic if an implementation has begun.

Union leaders can also raise issues to the QLT that are important to the people but that management may overlook because of their differing perspectives. For example, one union leader I know asked the QLT to consider modifying the company's practice of work scheduling because it was not helpful to TQM or to the employees trying to be a part of the effort.

In another example, membership in a QLT was made up of senior management with a union representative. Employees felt that there should be more than one employee sitting on the QLT. They felt that different work areas and different levels of employees bring important knowledge and concerns to the table. Membership was modified to include three employee representatives because the union let management know that employees perceived a potential problem. Part of the reason for the change was not only that it made sense, but also that it could have ended up part of negotiations anyway.

Involving union leaders as members of the QLT or steering team allows matters that have contract implications to be dealt with swiftly, since the parties are part of the group making decisions.

Critical Success Factors: Labor's Perspective

There are a few key critical success factors that have been outlined by Betty L. Bednarczyk, a labor leader, that bear mention as we come to the close of this chapter. She admits that a certain amount of courage is needed for both labor and management to move toward partnerships, but that as soon as labor recognizes the need to change its relationship with management, selection of appropriate members for a joint team like the QLT is essential. Another critical success factor is the need to educate both management and labor in effective communications and problem solving.

Bednarczyk also suggests that agendas address both sides' issues and concerns. It is important to communicate results that are jointly achieved and reinforce the common goals. Also important are equal representation and paid time to attend TQM meetings. Finally—and clearly her most important critical success factor—is the need for total trust and commitment from top management and top labor leaders. "That trust and commitment must be trickled down through middle management and frontline supervisors in order to reassure union members that management is sincere," she emphasizes.[7]

Conclusion

The concept of furthering labor-management cooperation efforts as part of a TQM implementation is an exciting one. Many HR professionals would love to be a part of increased collaboration rather than a continuation of competition between management and unions. This would mean a shift from the paradigm of win-lose negotiation so common in adversarial labor relations to win-win negotiation, partnership, and facilitation. New attitudes would drive the need for new skills and usher in a more productive period of growth for the organization.

While there would still be a need for the grievance procedure in cases where individual managers fail and gaps need addressing, union officials would find their time being taken up with designing new work systems and creating new strategies that would solidify the company's place in the market. The same would be true for HR professionals. Fewer grievances, disciplinary actions, and arbitrations would free their time for creative, fulfilling work.

There are many reasons to look at the opportunities that labor-management cooperation can bring to a TQM implementation, rather than focus on the problems or barriers. Although a bargaining unit adds a dimension of complexity, there is no reason to believe that a partnership cannot be achieved that will benefit all parties and the enterprise. One of the beauties of TQM is the fact that it makes sense for all the people in the company. Involving them, watching them grow, and seeing the paybacks are all the more rewarding if a transition in labor-management relations is part of the culture change.

Chapter 12
The Malcolm Baldrige National Quality Award

The Malcolm Baldrige National Quality Award was instituted by Congress in 1987 to encourage and recognize U.S. corporations in the quest for global competitiveness. The award criteria consist of seven categories of performance that are broken down into ninety-two areas to address. The categories are:

1. Leadership
2. Information and Analysis
3. Strategic Quality Planning
4. Human Resource Development and Management
5. Management of Process Quality
6. Quality and Operational Results
7. Customer Focus and Satisfaction

The Human Resource Development and Management category deals with how an organization uses its people and how effective it is in developing and realizing the full potential of its work force. The category is also concerned with how the organization maintains an environment conducive to employee participation and personal and organizational growth. The human resources category is a significant one, worth a full 15 percent of the total points awarded.

Applying for the Malcolm Baldrige National Quality Award is done in phases, beginning with the compilation of data in the seven categories and corresponding areas addressed in the application guidelines. These guidelines can be obtained by calling or writing the American Society for Quality Control (ASQC) in Milwaukee. The ASQC is the Baldrige administrator for the National Institute of Standards and Technology of the Department of Commerce in Washington, D.C. Companies synthesize the data collected into a fifty- to seventy-five–page report and send it to Washington for review. A team of examiners prescreens each application and writes a feedback report to the companies that are not selected for the next phase.

Many companies go through the process of applying for the award with no intention of winning. Instead, they do it for objective review of their processes and results in order to improve their operations and competitiveness. Other companies conduct an internal assessment using the award criteria. They write a report for internal information only and either train a cadre of their own employees or hire an outside consulting firm to review the report and provide feedback. Some organizations even have an internal award competition between divisions.

If a company is selected as a finalist after the initial prescreening phase, a team of examiners makes a site visit to take a closer look at the operations and to talk with employees to see how pervasive the quality culture and processes truly are. This team is, in essence, seeking the evidence that supports what was reported in the application. Once this phase is complete, the examiners make recommendations to a prestigious panel of judges who determine which organizations will be honored. Each year, only six organizations can receive the award: two in manufacturing, two in service, and two small businesses. Some of the past award recipients include Motorola; IBM's Rochester, New York, plant; Federal Express; the Ritz-Carlton Hotel Company; AT&T's credit card division; and the defense systems and electronics group of Texas Instruments.

The Seven Baldrige Categories

The first Baldrige category, Leadership, examines how senior executives create and sustain clear and visible quality values along with a management system to guide all activities of the company toward quality excellence. This includes an assessment of how the executives extend their quality leadership into the external community. This category is worth 9.5 percent of the total points awarded.

The next two categories together are worth 13.5 percent of the total points, with Information and Analysis worth slightly more than Strategic Quality Planning. Information and Analysis examines the scope, validity, use, and management of data and information that underlie the company's overall quality management system. In essence, the category addresses whether or not the company manages by fact. The Strategic Quality Planning category examines the process for achieving or retaining quality leadership, how the company integrates quality planning into its overall business planning, and how performance requirements are deployed to all work units.

The fourth category is Human Resource Development and Management, worth 15 percent of the total points. It will be discussed in detail later in this chapter. The fifth category, Management of Process Quality, is worth 14 percent of the total points. This category examines the systematic approaches used to ensure quality of goods and services. This includes how these processes are integrated with continuous quality improvement, R&D, design, and supplier quality practices.

The Quality and Operational Results category is worth 18 percent of the total points awarded. This category examines quality levels and improvement trends based upon objective measures derived from customer requirements and business operations. Also assessed are company operational results and current quality levels in relation to those of competing companies.

The final category, Customer Focus and Satisfaction, is also a significant one, worth 30 percent of the total. It is here that the company's knowledge of the customer, overall customer service systems, responsiveness, and ability to meet requirements and expectations are reviewed. Current levels and trends in customer satisfaction are also examined, and a comparison to competitors is requested.

As you can see, the Malcolm Baldrige National Quality Award is very demanding of those seeking to achieve this high honor. It is significant for human resources professionals to note first that a category was identified to address the people issues of the company, and second, that it carries the third highest point total of the seven categories.

Public Sector Comparison

This is a good place to stop and compare the Baldrige award with its federal counterpart, the Federal Prototype Award. All of the categories in both awards show surprising similarity. For example, the Federal Prototype Award's list of categories is headed by Quality Leadership, with a percentage value that closely resembles that of the Baldrige award's Leadership category. Quality Measurement and Analysis, worth a bit more than in the private industry award, mirrors its counterpart even to the point of asking for data comparing the operation to others.

The public sector award gives 10 percent of its total points to the Human Resources category specifically focusing on Employee Involvement and Employee Training and Recognition. The Baldrige category of strategic planning for quality is matched by the public sector category of Quality Improvement Planning, asking for both short- and long-term goals. Forty percent of total points awarded go to the quality-related categories, Quality Assurance and Results of Quality Improvement Efforts, clearly establishing these areas as the dominant force in the public sector award. Finally, the Customer Focus category is valued at 20 percent of total points.

As you can see, there are great similarities between the two awards. Besides the varying weights, however, the content differs within some of the categories. The human resources-related categories do not cover HR planning or employee well-being and morale. The Leadership category does not measure the key executive's role in the external community. The Customer Focus category does not include the same level of comparative benchmarking. Nonetheless, the similarities far outweigh the differences.

It follows that states are also creating quality awards. They, too, are generally similar to the Baldrige Award. Twelve states have instituted their own award processes thus far.

The Human Resource Development and Management Category

This Baldrige category, as previously stated, examines the effectiveness of the company's efforts to fully achieve the potential of its entire work force and its success in maintaining an environment of employee participation and personal and organizational growth. It has five subcategories:

1. Human Resource Planning and Management
2. Employee Involvement
3. Employee Education and Training
4. Employee Performance and Recognition
5. Employee Well-Being and Satisfaction

Let's look at these one at a time.

1. *Human resource planning and management.* This item asks a company to describe how its overall human resources management effort supports its quality and operational objectives. It seeks to find out how the human resources plan and strategies are driven from the strategic quality goals. Plans and activities that would be considered beneficial include initiatives such as labor/management partnerships, quality-related recognition systems, or mechanisms for increasing or broadening employee responsibilities or skills. There are three areas to address in

this subcategory. The first is the human resources plan itself, including both short-term activities (one to two years) and longer-term activities (three or more years). Of particular interest are plans for training, developing, hiring, involving, empowering, recognizing, and rewarding employees.

The second area is the key quality goals and improvement methods in place for practices in such areas as hiring, career development, morale, and turnover. How improvements are measured falls into this area. Remember, these initiatives must be related to the corporation's quality as well as business goals. The third area to address is how the company analyzes and uses its employee-related data to evaluate and improve the effectiveness of all categories and types of employees. Employee satisfaction is assessed by asking how indicators are used to reduce adverse results in areas such as absenteeism, turnover, grievances, and accidents.

2. *Employee involvement.* This subcategory looks at the means available for all employees to contribute effectively to meeting the company's quality and operational objectives. While the Baldrige criteria are not meant to be prescriptive, there is an inherent value for teamwork, as evidenced by this subcategory. Current levels of involvement and trends over a period of years are positive indicators. For example, if your company has seen a steadily growing number of employee teams addressing quality improvements, this would indicate that the corporate culture is moving toward increased teamwork.

Four areas are specifically addressed in this subcategory. The first has to do with the management practices and specific mechanisms, such as suggestion systems, the company uses to promote employee contributions. How quickly do contributors receive feedback? How many ideas are approved? The second area addresses company actions that increase employees' authority to act, to be responsible, and to innovate. What actions are being taken with different levels and categories of employees? The third area relates to the key indicators used by the company to evaluate the extent and effectiveness of involvement by all categories and types of employees and how involvement initiatives are linked to quality and operational results. The fourth area addresses the effectiveness and extent of involvement by all categories of employees. Results that show increasing numbers of new products designed or patents obtained, or increasing numbers of suggestions submitted and accepted, are considered typical positive indicators.

3. *Employee education and training.* This subcategory reflects what quality education and training are needed by employees and how the organization utilizes the knowledge and skills acquired. It asks for a summary of types of training received by employees at all levels and how

these efforts are improved over time. Four areas are specifically addressed. The first area addresses how needs for quality and related education are assessed, what linkages to short- and long-term plans exist,
what growth and career development opportunities exist, and how employees' input is sought and used. The second area asks for a summary
of how education and training are reinforced, including methods used
for delivery of training and education to all employees, on-the-job application of knowledge and skills, and quality-related orientation for new
employees. Customer satisfaction courses fall within the definition of
quality-related training. The third area addresses key methods and indicators the company uses to evaluate and improve the effectiveness of its
quality education and training for all categories and types of employees.
The fourth area asks for trends in the effectiveness and extent of quality
and related training and education.

4. *Employee performance and recognition.* This subcategory describes
how the company's recognition, performance, compensation, reward,
and feedback approaches support quality plans and goals. Three areas
are specifically addressed. The first area is concerned with how the various approaches above support the company's quality and operational
objectives. This includes how quality is reinforced relative to other business considerations such as schedules and financial results and how employees are involved in the development and improvement of performance and recognition approaches. The second area is about the methods
and indicators used to evaluate performance and recognition approaches. Included are employee satisfaction information and actual results. The third area asks for trends in effectiveness and extent of employee reward and recognition by employee category.

5. *Employee well-being and satisfaction.* This subcategory asks the company to describe how it maintains a work environment conducive to the
well-being and growth of all employees, including summary trends and
current levels in key indicators of well-being and morale. There are four
areas to address here. The first is how well-being and morale factors such
as health, safety, and ergonomics are included in quality improvement
activities. For accidents and work-related health problems, descriptions
of how root causes are determined and how adverse conditions are pre-
vented are asked for. The second area asks what special services, facilities, and opportunities are available to employees. This could include
counseling, employee assistance programs, and recreational or day care
programs. The third area addresses how the company determines employee satisfaction by employee type or category. The fourth area asks
for trends in key indicators of well-being and satisfaction, such as safety,
absenteeism, turnover, and grievances. Adverse results must be ex-

plained and problem resolution activities discussed. Significant indicators are asked to be compared to those of industry averages and industry leaders.

The Baldrige Winners' Human Resources Practices

Researching the literature and hearing the stories of the Baldrige winners reveal six noteworthy trends in the winners' HR practices:

1. Employee involvement in their daily jobs and as team members is evident. Employees are involved with both planning improvements and assessing business and statistical information at all levels.
2. Training permeates the way of life for all levels of employees. (The lowest number of required hours per year that I could find was twenty-eight hours per employee, with forty about average and eighty hours at the high end.) Dollars spent reflected the commitment.
3. Quality performance objectives were built into both the culture and processes of the winning companies.
4. Recognition programs abounded, and suggestion systems results were well above average for the United States.
5. In those corporations with unions, labor-management partnerships were the norm and guarantees of fair treatment could be found.
6. Climate or attitude survey results were assessed and acted upon annually in a significant number of the companies.

There were a few other exceptional practices that appeared either very innovative or spoke to the fact that human resources were at the heart of the companies' cultures. For example, at Westinghouse Commercial Nuclear Fuel Division, a 1988 winner, the four imperatives driving the organization were management leadership, product/process leadership, human resources excellence, and customer satisfaction. The top executives at Westinghouse also visibly credit the work force for the great improvements made.

New ways of organizing both jobs and work groups support the resulting high levels of performance. For example, a 1989 winner, Milliken, has a very flat structure and self-managing work teams. Flexible job assignments are found at Globe Metallurgical and IBM Rochester, and managers at Federal Express are evaluated based upon employee input and annual improvement plans. In fact, at Federal Express if company leadership is rated lower in the annual survey than the prior year, the executives receive no bonuses.

Applications for Human Resources Executives

The criteria above offer HR executives valuable information on new needs and opportunities for growth in the field, as well as growth for the organization and its people. For example, when taking a close look at the areas to address and considering the types of indicators that would be considered appropriate evidence of effectiveness in human resources, it is clear that there are many sources of information that could be used as yardsticks of effectiveness whether applying for the Baldrige or not.

The following checklist will assist you when measuring your organization's HR strategies, practices, and results against the Baldrige award's HR Development and Management category. The key things to remember, if you are actually applying for the Baldrige award, are that the examiners are concerned that your human resources approaches and processes are appropriate for your company and that you have data that demonstrate the effectiveness of your strategies and practices.

While such a checklist may seem extensive, it reflects the extent to which the examiners will delve. If you do not intend to apply for the award, you can peruse this checklist for key indicators you would like to use to begin tracking your own function's potential impact on important quality and operational objectives.

Human Resources Category Checklist

- [ ] Strategic human resources plan is developed
  - Short-term (one or two years)
  - Long-term (three or more years)
- [ ] Strategic training and development plan exists
- [ ] Goals and strategies in place for increasing employee empowerment and involvement
- [ ] Statement or other examples of relationship exist between HR plans and short- and long-term quality goals
- [ ] Goals and strategies are ongoing for recognizing employees based upon achievement
- [ ] Evidence exists that HR plans are part of the overall strategic planning process
- [ ] Job posting shows positive career development trends
- [ ] Career pathing programs/systems are developed
- [ ] Recruiting strategies are designed to attract and hire better employees
- [ ] Amount of teamwork/cooperation efforts are increasing over time (number of teams, percentage of employees involved, etc.)

☐ Level of morale and job satisfaction is known

☐ Absenteeism figures are tracked over time

☐ Turnover figures exist over time; reasons why employees leave the company are known and acted upon

☐ Degree to which compensation is based upon employees' quality-related performance is known

☐ Evidence exists that quality objectives are set for employees

☐ Goals are in place for improving the HR function

☐ HR indicators show relationship to organizational success

☐ Evidence exists that employee data are used to identify causes of problems or deviations from standards

☐ Evidence exists that feedback from employee data is used to evaluate and improve HR strategies/practices

☐ Data show degree to which organizational structure is based on teams versus traditional hierarchy

☐ Number and use of cross-functional teams working on improvement or planning initiatives tracked

☐ Extent to which staff departments are evaluated on internal customer satisfaction measures is evident

☐ Extent of customers on improvement/planning teams tracked

☐ Extent of suppliers on improvement/planning teams known

☐ Objective data demonstrate increased authority/empowerment of employees

☐ Objective data demonstrate increased innovation over time

☐ Scope of evaluation/measurement effort assesses effectiveness in key HR practices related to quality

☐ Trends are available on number of employee suggestions submitted and accepted over time

☐ Evidence exists that a systematic needs analysis was completed to identify quality-related training needs of all functions and levels of employees

☐ Evidence exists that a variety of training methods are used in quality education efforts

☐ Evidence exists of on-the-job reinforcement of employees' use of quality tools and concepts

☐ Evidence exists of executive and upper management reinforcement of middle managers' use of quality tools and concepts

☐ Evidence exists of use of tangible and symbolic rewards to reinforce use of quality tools and techniques by all employees

☐ Total hours spent orienting new employees to quality goals and practices tracked

☐ Total hours of quality education and training per employee, per category/level, tracked over time

☐ Simulation exercises used to evaluate skills of prospective customer-contact employees

☐ Amount of quality education and training delivered to executives and upper management tracked

☐ Percentage known of employees receiving quality education and training

☐ Percentage known of total education and training budget spent on quality-related subjects

☐ Size known of quality-related education and training budget as a percentage of total organization income

☐ Trends over time tracked for expenditures dedicated to quality education and training

☐ Test scores and trends show improvement in quality-related knowledge

☐ Evidence exists of application of quality knowledge and skills demonstrated through behavior change or output measures

☐ Evidence exists of a cause-effect relationship between education and training efforts and improved quality results

☐ A performance measurement system exists that links goals and results from top executives to individual contributors

☐ Evidence exists that employees have control over indices used for performance measurement

☐ Extent to which compensation is based upon achievement of quality goals is known

☐ Degree to which recognition programs are based upon a combination of group and individual performance measures is tracked

☐ Percentage of employees receiving recognition awards based upon quality-related performance measures tracked

☐ Extent to which employees at various levels are involved in developing quality-related performance and recognition approaches is known

☐ Degree to which employee feedback is regularly solicited regarding performance, compensation, and recognition is known

☐ Evidence exists over time of a follow-up system for evaluating and improving performance, compensation, and recognition programs

☐ Trends show that increasing numbers of employees at various levels and functions receive quality-related recognition over time
  • Individual employee trends
  • Employee groups/team trends

☐ Number of health or safety improvement projects completed tracked over time

☐ Results known of safety audits by internal or external organizations

☐ Absence of lawsuits or complaints related to health or safety issues

☐ Results known of employee feedback about the health and safety of their work environment

☐ Systematic process exists for analyzing the causes of accidents

- ☐ Evidence exists that the organization corrects the causes of accidents
- ☐ Number of type of programs in place to promote the health of employees known
- ☐ Macro plan exists for development and cross-training for all levels of employees
- ☐ Individual development plans exist for all employees
- ☐ Amount of employee rotation in various departments, functions, and jobs known over time
- ☐ Indicators available for employee satisfaction about the degree and success of job rotation and cross-training efforts
- ☐ Number and types of employee assistance programs tracked
- ☐ Comparison made of organization's employee assistance programs to major competitors' programs
- ☐ Employee satisfaction indicators exist on assistance programs offered
- ☐ Incidence of stress-related illnesses or disorders of all levels of employees tracked
- ☐ Thorough employee morale/satisfaction surveys conducted on a regular basis
- ☐ Percentage known of employees at all levels and in all functions completing satisfaction surveys
- ☐ Multiple indicators beyond survey data used to measure employee satisfaction
- ☐ Evidence exists that a systematic process is used to evaluate satisfaction data and develop corrective action plans for improvement
- ☐ Trends and key indicators exist of other employee well-being and satisfaction factors such as grievances, strikes, and workers compensation

That's certainly a large enough list for any HR function to assess itself against, and it is quite indicative of the types of HR-related information that will be sought. An important note is required for all the items that ask for results or information over time. Trends generally include three years' worth of data, and that is what should be prepared for the examiners. What do you do, though, if you have less than three years of data? About the only thing that can make up for a lack of documented information is to establish the practice area or result as world-class by comparing it to competitors or benchmark companies. This will make up some of the point loss for not having tracked data over time.

Conclusion

What is the real value in looking at the practices and results of your human resources function against the Baldrige criteria? For one thing, the criteria set a new standard for all HR functions and look to the future needs of HR. There is a clear indication of the types of activities and results being sought in the quest for excellence, and they, in fact, are not yet common practice in many of this country's organizations. Using the Baldrige Human Resource Development and Management category as the yardstick against which you create your initial baseline will give you a roadmap to follow that can take your HR practices into the next century.

As shown in earlier chapters, the improvements cited by companies as they move toward involving employees at all levels as partners in the business validates the areas addressed in this important category. Chapter 14 provides further benchmarks for your goal-setting activities. Your future plans and even future deployment of resources may hinge upon the types of endeavors outlined here as HR's critical success factors.

Chapter 13

Looking Inward: Measuring and Improving the HR Function

The human resources profession is viewed by some experts as having a lack of faith, says noted consultant and author Jac Fitz-enz. His feedback from over 1,200 managers about HR show they think the function is "too costly, doesn't add value, is bureaucratic and unresponsive."[1] Since customers are the drivers of Total Quality, this feedback is critical for HR professionals to accept and improve.

The business strategies of today's organizations reflect global competition and the forces driving for increased productivity and quality. Yet HR professionals continue to fill their busy schedules with responding to employee grievances, processing performance appraisals, updating and administering salaries, and the like. Are these the value-added tasks that managers want to see from the professionals in charge of the organization's people? The answer is *yes* if the company and the HR function are in a reactive, traditional role. But even so, there is a clear need for change. HR professionals can take their own lead in increasing the value of the function and, in doing so, enhance its leadership position.

The first step can be taken by measuring the function's effectiveness. This allows the HR function to develop a realistic baseline from which to improve its own productivity and quality. The HR executive will then be able to identify his/her own opportunities for improvement. Results of focused efforts will not only increase customer satisfaction, but also uncover available capacity to move the function into a more proactive role in developing business strategies and tactics to meet competitive demand. HR will be able to devote itself to the pressing need for change because reduced cycle time in current processes will return a precious resource—time. This chapter is devoted to the "how-tos" of measuring and improving the HR function in order to enlarge HR's ability to focus on the company's strategic issues, such as TQM.

Measuring the Human Resources Function

White collar workers have always contended that their jobs were hard to measure. This has been as true for engineers as it has been for systems analysts, financial planners, and even HR professionals. Since the 1970s there have been several groups that have focused their efforts on tackling the challenge presented by the service industry in this regard. One, the American Productivity and Quality Center, has worked with many types of functions in many different industries. Another, the Saratoga Institute, has made its emphasis human resources research and consulting. Both offer excellent conceptual anchors and examples on measuring HR. But before looking at what to measure and how, an important question to answer is "why?"

Why Measurement Is Important

The importance of measurement is finally becoming clear. Not only do managers want measures to know if a function's productivity is improving, but they also want to be able to identify where to focus energies toward improvement. In addition, they want to know whether or not the customer is being satisfied, and they want better information to use in business decision making. From a selfish viewpoint, managers want to be able to quantify information to use in building justification for garnering additional resources and to increase the relevance of their operation to the organization.

All of these reasons are sound, especially in a world where the creative use of resources and survival are often driving forces. Whether people like it or not, becoming quantitative is a more effective way of "telling the story." Supporting opinions and beliefs with evidence is much more powerful and convincing. And sometimes, the evidence even uncovers facts that show that the opinions and beliefs that have been the premise of decisions have been faulty, and more appropriate courses of action need to be taken.

In a time when "faster, better, cheaper" is the way to customer satisfaction, wouldn't it be helpful to know that the right result was delivered in the fastest time at the highest quality and lowest cost? And in the spirit of continuous improvement, wouldn't it be helpful to know if current performance was outpacing past performance? Perhaps even more important, if the HR function is clear about where it fits into the strategy of the organization, the activities can be monitored to continually provide the most value to the organization. Busy as any HR department is, wouldn't the staff be more motivated if they knew how what they were doing fit into the needs of the company?

What to Measure

From the functional breakdowns of work completed in most HR departments, the first "sort" can be made. Employment, EEO/OSHA compliance, compensation, benefits, training, payroll, and labor relations are some common sectors within the HR function, and measures are available to act as barometers of progress for them. At the next level—what quality experts call the process level—we look at specific products or services delivered to the customer and identify the process that leads to the deliverable (outcome).

For example, inside the employment sector, a qualified candidate is the outcome of the recruitment process. The effectiveness and efficiency of the recruitment process can also be measured. Yet the employment sector includes other processes such as the job posting process, the internal transfer process, the promotion process, and the termination process. Measuring the overall effectiveness of the employment sector and the key processes associated with it are the two payoff areas for measurement of the sector.

Let's walk through key examples of major HR outcomes or processes where measurement is valuable for both HR and the organization. Once we have looked at potential measures for the key sectors within HR, we will review how to develop a Family of Measures for overall effectiveness for specific sectors or for the entire HR department.

The Employment Sector

This is one of the easiest sectors to measure. Common outcome measures already exist and are used by many progressive companies. Some are cost per hire, time to fill, and ratio of offers to acceptance. There are many others, but since recruitment is the key process inside an employment department, this segment focuses there.

Cost Per Hire

One of the best measures of cost per hire comes from the Saratoga Institute.[2] Nine categories of cost are taken into account:

1. Advertising charges (AC)
2. Agency fees (AF)
3. Employee referral bonuses (RB)
4. Staff time, both professional and clerical (ST)
5. Hiring manager time (HMT)
6. Staff benefits (SB)
7. Overhead (OH)
8. Travel/relocation costs (TR)
9. Miscellaneous (Misc)

Putting these into a formula over number of people hired looks like this:

$$\text{Cost per hire} = \frac{AC + AF + RB + ST + HMT + SB + OH + TR + Misc}{\text{total \# hired}}$$

This is a key measure because it reflects a total employment sector's outcome relative to cost-effectiveness.

There are other important measures of process effectiveness:

Time to Fill

$$\text{Time to fill} = \frac{\text{date requisition received}}{\text{date new hire starts}}$$

Job Posting Response Rate

$$\text{Job posting response rate} = \frac{\text{\# of internal jobs applied for}}{\text{total \# of jobs posted}}$$

Job Posting Effectiveness

$$\text{Job posting effectiveness} = \frac{\text{\# of jobs filled internally}}{\text{total \# of jobs posted}}$$

Internal Hiring Effectiveness

$$\text{Internal hiring effectiveness} = \frac{\text{\# of jobs filled internally}}{\text{total \# of jobs filled}}$$

Other measures are as easily computed. HR professionals, support staff, and even internal and external customers ought to be included in determining which measures are most valuable. Outcomes that are important inside the department and outside to the customer should be considered. Customers can be hiring managers, external job applicants, and employees bidding on open positions. Everything from length of time to respond to applicants to quality of hire can be considered.

There are other important measures for the employment manager to consider, such as measures of individual performance. Recruiter effectiveness could be assessed by taking many of the outcome and process measures and developing a formula that integrates and weights them. The same holds true for the employment team; the difference would be distinguished by using only one person's results versus using the entire team's results and averaging them.

The Compensation Sector

The activities inside this sector vary from keeping job descriptions current to tracking salary range exceptions. Here are some measures that pertain to it:

Job Descriptions Current

$$\text{Job descriptions current} = \frac{\text{\# of jobs with current descriptions}}{\text{total \# of jobs}}$$

Job Evaluation Quality

$$\text{Job evaluation quality} = \frac{\text{\# of evaluations accepted by customer on first review}}{\text{total \# of evaluations completed}}$$

Salary Range Exceptions

$$\text{Salary range exceptions} = \frac{\text{\# of jobs over salary grade maximum}}{\text{total \# of employees}}$$

Time to Evaluate Jobs

$$\text{Time to evaluate jobs} = \frac{\text{date evaluation request received}}{\text{date evaluation completed}}$$

Once again, measures of process and outcome effectiveness or efficiency are not difficult to develop, and compensation professionals have been using some excellent measures (e.g., compa-ratios) for years.

The Benefits Sector

The total cost of benefits is of utmost concern to organizations today. Skyrocketing health care costs are the crux of the problem, but other variables in the benefits equation are significant as well. The complete formula recommended by Jac Fitz-enz of the Saratoga Institute is again the benchmark to use.[3] Considered are staff time (ST), overhead (OH), processing costs (PC), plan payments (PP), and miscellaneous benefits (Misc). (Plan payments include both insurance and retirement figures. Miscellaneous benefits include vacation, holidays, sick leave, education, and recreation.) The formula is simple:

Total Benefits Cost

$$\text{Total benefits cost} = \text{ST} + \text{OH} + \text{PC} + \text{PP} + \text{Misc}$$

Benefits Cost Per Employee

$$\text{Benefits cost per employee} = \frac{\text{total cost of benefits}}{\text{average \# of employees}}$$

Benefit to Payroll Ratio

$$\text{Benefit to payroll ratio} = \frac{\text{total cost of benefits}}{\text{total payroll cost}}$$

Benefits professionals might also look to some measures having to do with timeliness or quality (e.g., accuracy) of government reports such as EEO or OSHA reports. As far as customer satisfaction is concerned, both accuracy and timeliness usually rank high in importance to employees. Measures for these could be as follows:

Claim Turnaround Time

$$\text{Claim turnaround time} = \text{date claim is paid} - \text{date claim is filed}$$

Claim Accuracy Rate

$$\text{Claim accuracy rate} = \frac{\text{\# of claims rejected because of error}}{\text{total \# of claims processed}}$$

Other outcome measures easily accumulated are processing cost per transaction and number of claims processed.

The Payroll Sector

The payroll sector holds important financial measures for organizations. Here are some of the common ones:

Average Salary Cost per Employee

$$\text{Average salary cost per employee} = \frac{\text{total payroll cost}}{\text{total \# of employees}}$$

Labor Efficiency

$$\text{Labor efficiency} = \frac{\text{total revenue}}{\text{total \# of employees}}$$

Payroll Errors

$$\text{Payroll errors (percentage)} = \frac{\text{\# of payroll errors}}{\text{total \# of payroll checks processed}}$$

While some of the above measures are financial measures, the third—payroll errors—is a quality measure of the service deliverable itself. Other deliverables, such as timeliness, are also easy to develop. Again, the people who work in the payroll sector know what is important to them and their customers and should be involved in developing the process and outcome measures.

The Employee Relations Sector

Besides number of grievances processed or settled out of court, the employee relations sector deals with less easily measured activities such as counseling sessions. Since productivity measures such as volume indicators seem clear, this section addresses how to measure the more complex activities cited above from a quality perspective as well. Let's begin with counseling.

To overview the company's counseling experience, some simple measures—such as number of sessions held divided by the employee population, or number of sessions per topic divided by the total number of sessions held—give an overview of how much time is spent and what topics are taking the most time. But how do you measure the quality of counseling taking place? Three ways come to mind.

Attitude Change

$$\text{Attitude change} = \frac{\text{number reporting attitude changed after counseling}}{\text{number undergoing counseling}}$$

Behavior Change

$$\text{Behavior change} = \frac{\text{number demonstrating changed behavior after counseling}}{\text{number undergoing counseling}}$$

Problems solved

$$\text{Problems solved} = \frac{\text{\# of problems solved}}{\text{\# of problems presented}}$$

There are other common quantitative statistics regarding counseling that HR professionals should be familiar with. One has to do with the number of sessions held versus company population; the other is session time per topic over total time spent in counseling sessions. These measures are easy to develop and should be customized for each company based on its perspective of what is valued.

Other important employee relations measures that reflect employee satisfaction levels can be quantified as well. They include the traditional measures of absenteeism and turnover, which have long been held to reflect employee satisfaction. Their formulas follow:

Absence Rate

$$\text{Absence rate} = \frac{\text{\# of worker days lost over } X \text{ time period}}{\text{\# of worker days available over } X \text{ time period}}$$

Note: This measurement must take into account the average employee population over time in order to be most accurate.

Turnover Rate

$$\text{Turnover rate} = \frac{\text{\# of employees terminated during } X \text{ time period}}{\text{average employee population during } X \text{ time period}}$$

There are also some accession measures that reflect employee satisfaction. One of the best is related to the loss rate of new hires.

New Hire Loss Rate

$$\text{New hire loss rate} = \frac{\text{\# new hires leaving during } X \text{ time period}}{\text{total \# of new hires during } X \text{ time period}}$$

The Training Sector

The most common measure of training sector effectiveness might well be the evaluation completed by class participants at the end of a class. As resources become scarcer, many training departments are being asked to keep a closer handle on the dollars spent. Costs per trainee or costs per training course have become standard measurement expectations. When looking at training costs, both direct and indirect costs need to be considered.

Direct costs include any outside trainer/consultant fees paid, training room rental, materials and supplies, refreshments, travel and lodging, and desktop publishing fees. Indirect costs include trainer salaries and benefits (for design and/or delivery), trainee salaries and benefits, administrative staff salaries and benefits (for registration and preparation), and department overhead. The measurement is now simple.

Cost per Training Course

$$\text{Cost per training} = \text{direct} + \text{indirect costs}$$

Cost per Trainee

$$\text{Cost per trainee} = \frac{\text{direct} + \text{indirect costs}}{\text{\# of participants trained}}$$

Note: The above measure can be broken down into cost per trainee hour if the company desires by taking total cost of training divided by the number of people trained multiplied by the number of training hours.

Other important measures for training departments to consider relate to the application of skills on the job and the acquisition of knowledge imparted and retained from a course. Pre- and post-testing are common methods of measuring knowledge acquisition, but attitude and behavior change measures are important tools for training practitioners and line managers who want to determine true value.

In the employee relations section, formulas for both attitude and behavior change were given, so they won't be repeated here. However, a few definitions about what one would actually look for seems in order. For attitude changes, actions that reflect the new way of thinking would need to be observed by the person attending training and even by his/ her boss or coworkers. For behavior change, specific skills would need to be described, use of them before training quantified, and then comparisons made with demonstrated use of the skills after training. Methods commonly used include questionnaires, observation, and interviews.

The Organization Development Sector

Modern human resources departments find the need for new competencies today. The organization development (OD) specialists provide many of them. Some are organization, process, and job redesign; consultation; assessment/survey feedback; development of change strategies; and team building. Measuring some of these will be less clear than some of the other activities described previously, but it is totally doable. Let's first take a look at some of the simple measures of the specialty itself and then address measuring the outcomes of organization development interventions.

An obvious measure of customer satisfaction with the OD sector is the number of requests made for assistance. But beginning an OD intervention is not the same as following it through to completion. Therefore, an important measure of effectiveness is the completion rate.

Intervention Completion Rate

$$\text{Intervention completion rate} = \frac{\text{\# of interventions completed}}{\text{\# of interventions assigned}}$$

A productivity measure of the function would be to compare the number of interventions assigned with the number of interventions requested. These numerically quantifiable measures are the easiest to develop. But HR managers need quality measures as well as volume measures. Customers may ask for assistance, but they want to be satisfied with it as well.

Satisfaction Rate

$$\text{Satisfaction rate} = \frac{\text{\# of interventions satisfactorily completed}}{\text{\# of interventions completed}}$$

A satisfaction index could be developed to gauge the customer's response to such factors as diagnosing the root cause of the problem, developing effective action plans for change, and providing timely and meaningful feedback. This way, not only do you measure overall satisfaction, but you can evaluate specific components of the consultation.

Other outcome measures can be developed to tie the intervention directly to criteria such as production volume of the client department or to morale and job satisfaction indicators, such as climate survey results or turnover rate. Linking the intervention to improvement in the work process or environment is easiest if baseline measures are compiled before and after the intervention. A couple of examples might be helpful.

Work Indices

It is useful to have cycle time measures, such as the number of days to process a part or deliver a service before and after the intervention. Percent of waste/rework, unit cost, and on-time deliveries are other useful work indices. It is best to use measures that are important to the customer.

$$\text{Cycle time improvement} = \frac{\text{cycle time before consultation}}{\text{cycle time after consultation}}$$

$$\text{Rework improvement} = \frac{\% \text{ of rework before consultation}}{\% \text{ of rework after consultation}}$$

Satisfaction Indices

Satisfaction measures such as the number of customer complaints, absences, and tardiness and the number of customers retained all provide important information. Notice that both internal measures (inside the client organization) and external measures (focused on the client organization's customers) are considered. Morale indicators can greatly affect an organization's productivity and quality and should be included in before and after measures. Here are examples of such measures:

$$\text{Customer complaint improvement} = \frac{\text{\# of customer complaints before consultation}}{\text{\# of customer complaints after consultation}}$$

$$\text{Tardiness improvement} = \frac{\text{\# of tardiness incidences before consultation per average employee population during } X \text{ time period}}{\text{\# of tardiness incidences after consultation per average employee population during } X \text{ time period}}$$

The more the OD sector can align with its client organizations, the more successful it will be perceived to be. Measuring effectiveness of the sector in the manner outlined above can be of great benefit to OD professionals who truly want to prove the value and worth of the sector to the company.

Other HR Processes

While I have tried systematically to cover the majority of HR processes in the measures recommended above, we all know that certain types of measures are more common than others when HR teams take a good, hard look at themselves. Some actual measures developed by HR teams for their own functions are listed below:

Turnaround times for various processes

Workers compensation costs per X number of employees

Health care costs per X number of employees

$$\frac{\text{\# of misplaced files}}{\text{total \# of files}}$$

$$\frac{\text{\# of redos}}{\text{total \# of requests for work}}$$

$$\frac{\text{hours of training in department}}{\text{total \# of department employees}}$$

$$\frac{\text{allocated time to complete task}}{\text{actual time to complete task}}$$

$$\frac{\text{\# of personnel system terminal users}}{\text{total \# of system terminals available}}$$

$$\frac{\text{\# of corrective actions}}{\text{actual manhours used}}$$

$$\frac{\text{\# of repeat problems}}{\text{total \# of problems}}$$

$$\frac{\text{\# of surplus employees placed}}{\text{total \# of surplus employees}}$$

$$\frac{\text{\# of accidents investigated after seven days}}{\text{total \# of accidents}}$$

Overall Measures of Effectiveness

There are two ways to look at developing an overall measure of effectiveness for the HR function. One is to take the most important measures developed above, ensure a cross-representation of the sectors within the HR function, and use these as an overall measure. The other is to try to combine the major purposes of the HR function into categories and develop measures that combine critical elements.

The first approach is easy once the groundwork described above is complete. What is important in determining the indicators to use in the overall effectiveness measurement is to include the measures that are most important to both the customer and the HR function itself. For example, if the recruitment sector is of primary import to the customer base, then a measure such as quality of hire should surface as a final candidate. Yet inside the function, rework in the payroll department may be a major concern even though customers see only timely and accurate paychecks. If this is the case, then payroll rework would also make the final list. A fictious model of overall measures of HR effectiveness, based on the Family of Measures concept used at the American Productivity & Quality Center, works well as shown in Figure 13-1.

The model allows for a fourth or even fifth type of measure. For example, if the HR function includes upholding safety standards set for the organization, then another set of measures—safety measures—could be added addressing number of accidents, number of OSHA violations, etc. A final note on this model: The measures selected need to be somewhat evenly mixed between internal and external importance and spread across the types of measures available. This provides balance for the organization and prevents such things as concern with only productivity at the expense of quality or concern with external requirements at the expense of internal rework (cost).

The second approach to overall measurement, offered as a model by the Saratoga Institute, is more complex. It is based on five factors critical to managing the human assets of an organization. Those five factors are: (1) acquiring the people, (2) maintaining their needs while employed, (3) developing them, (4) utilizing them to complete the organization's work, and (5) managing them. After considering all the HR activities that support these factors, a final set of measures is offered. Those measures include:

Human Operating Expense

$$\text{Human operating expense} = \frac{\text{compensation} + \text{benefits} + \text{HR department expense}}{\text{organization operating expense}}$$

Cost to Supervise

$$\text{Cost to supervise} = \frac{\text{management compensation}}{\text{total compensation}}$$

Stability Factor

$$\text{Stability factor} = \text{turnover \%} + \text{nonexempt absence \%}$$

Figure 13-1. HR overall measures of effectiveness.

	Internal Importance	External Importance
Productivity Measures	Cost per hire Health care costs per # of employees Cost per trainee	<u>Total revenue</u> Total # of employees
Quality Measures	<u># of qualified candidates</u> # of candidates interviewed % of payroll processing rework	<u># of descriptions redone</u> # of description requests % of correct pay checks
Timeliness Measures		Time to fill jobs Time to process claims
Other Measures	% system downtime	Accidents per 100 employees

Development Factor

$$\text{Development factor} = \frac{\text{training expense}}{\text{operating expense}}$$

Productivity Factor

$$\text{Productivity factor} = \frac{\text{revenue per employee}}{\text{compensation/revenue}^4}$$

Improving the Human Resources Function

There is much work to do beyond measuring the activities within the HR function. Measurement provides the baseline and marks the progress being made to improve. How does an HR executive identify the opportunities for improvement, and how does the HR staff begin to make improvements? These are the questions to be answered in this section.

Once the measures of the function are in place, use the knowledge gained about the importance of various activities to help determine the priority opportunities for improvement. This effort will involve all of the staff of the HR function over time. Quality improvement teams (sometimes called process action teams) are created to follow a systematic approach. There are many problem-solving models available to these teams, but most follow the Plan, Do, Check, and Act cycle originated by Walter Shewhart in the early 1900s.

- *Plan.* This phase ensures that the team understands the current process and its measures. It is during this phase that the root causes of problems are identified. Statistical tools come into play in order to confirm that the team is working on the root cause and not treating symptoms. The seven basic quality tools can easily be used in HR improvements. This is contrary to popular opinion among some service industry professionals that these tools are useful only in manufacturing settings. An example of their use in HR follows the four steps of the problem-solving process.

- *Do.* Once data are collected as evidence of the need for a specific change, the team recommendation is generally approved for implementation. (Some experts say that improvement teams that follow a systematic, statistically based approach achieve an approval rate of around 90 percent, much better than typical task forces, committees, or informal problem-solving teams.) An implementation plan is generated and responsibilities accounted for; then the change is made.

• *Check.* After the change, results of the effort are measured and compared against the baseline. If the objectives of the improvement project have been met, then preparation for institutionalization begins. Many times changes are made to solve problems, but they are never checked or studied to see that the actual intent was achieved. This phase ensures that teams know that their improvement did or didn't work before institutionalizing it.

• *Act.* Documentation, standardization, training for full deployment, etc., round out the problem-solving cycle. This phase also typically includes communication about the new procedures and celebration of the success. Also considered is the need for the improvement team to continue to address other root causes of the problem and make further recommendations for improvement.

Using the Seven Basic Quality Tools: An HR Case Study

One of the common concerns of white collar employees is whether statistical tools that began on the shop floor are transferable to an administrative function. In order to show that the basic quality tools can be used in human resources, *HRMagazine* asked me to display their application in 1992.[5] These and other examples are depicted here to help HR professionals see exactly how these tools can be applied in HR settings. (The tools are described in more detail in Chapter 5.) This case involved the internal recruitment effectiveness of a company.

Process Flowcharts

This tool comes from industrial engineering and often proves to have great payoff for an improvement team. Mapping out the process can lead to eliminating unnecessary steps and creating a smoother flow of work. Reduced cycle time and actual cost savings are common outcomes. This tool often leads to recaptured capacity, a result that meets with great appreciation in busy areas.

The flowchart in Figure 13-2 depicts what happens when a vacancy notice/request to fill is received in HR. This acts as the input that kicks off the recruitment process. Initially, a flowchart of the macro steps of the process is created; that is what is depicted here. An improvement team would take these steps and break them down further to the activity and possibly even the task level in their search for improvement.

Before looking at the causes of problems, the current process should be measured "as is" at this time.

Figure 13-2. Flowchart depicting the macro steps in the internal recruitment process.

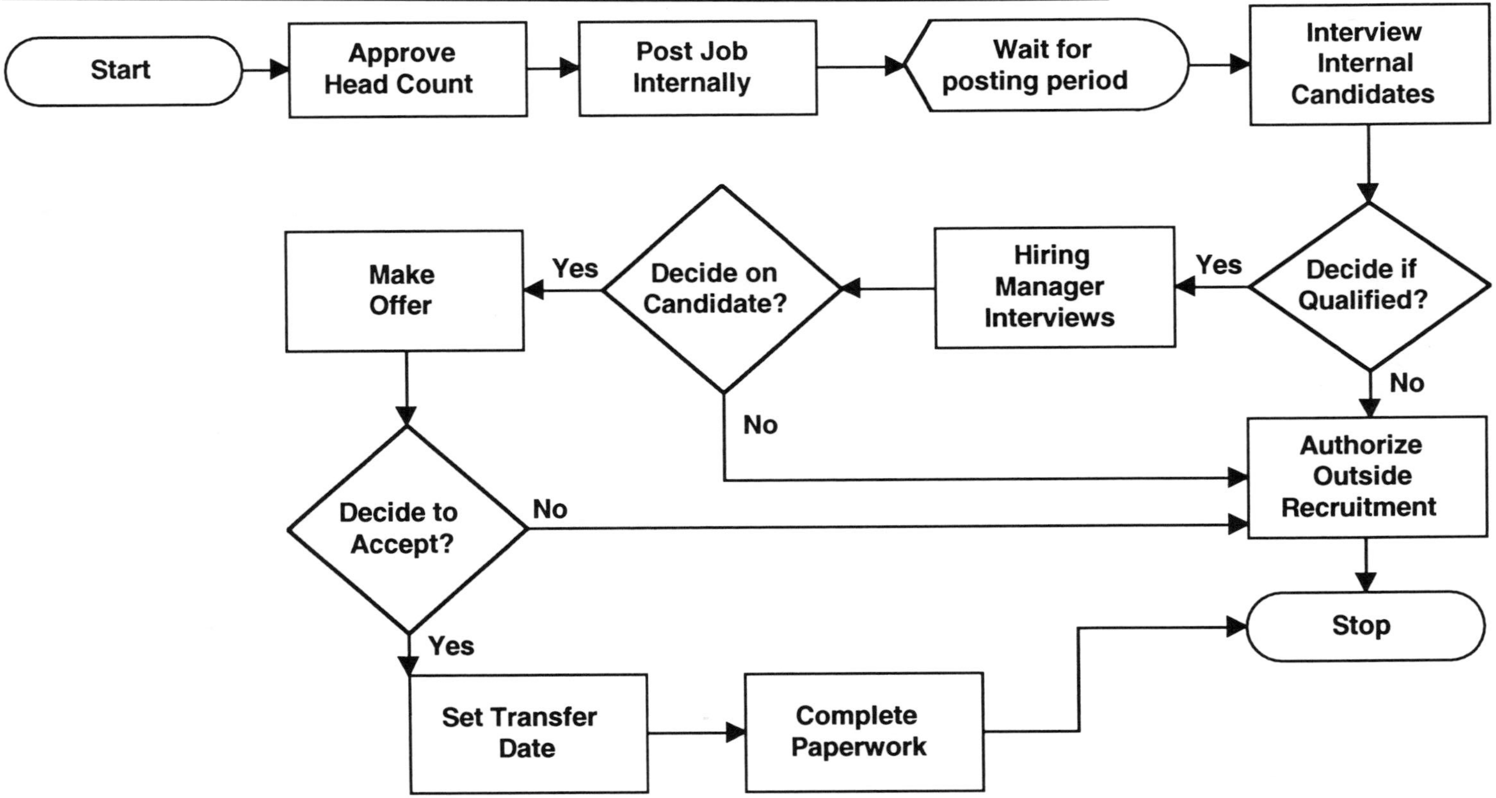

Figure 13-3. Cause-and-effect diagram depicting problems in internal hiring.

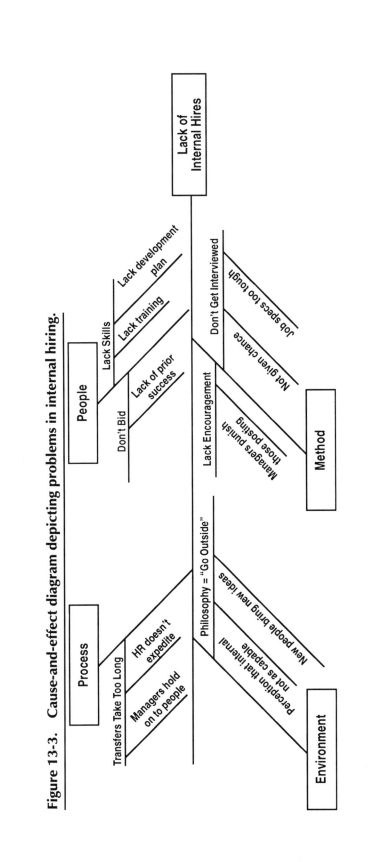

Cause-and-Effect Diagrams

Pinpointing the potential root causes of problems in the process is the next step. Following the above example, several problems exist relating to the internal hiring of current employees for open jobs. Teams brainstorm the potential causes of problems and then categorize them to make a cause-and-effect diagram, shown in Figure 13-3.

It is clear from the figure that the People or Method categories are likely candidates for initial review because of the number of cases cited in this area. The temptation for teams at this early stage is to begin assuming they know the solutions. Without further data collection, this team could easily follow the trial and error method and head down a wrong path. For example, recommending more formal development plans for employees would appear to have merit. Let's use more of the basic tools to see how important lack of developed employees is in this problem of low levels of internal hires.

Pareto Diagrams

Pareto diagrams help us to discern the "vital few" from the "trivial many." Since the well-known 80/20 rule works in process improvement, it can be assumed that 80 percent of the problems come from 20 percent of the causes. It is clear why further data collection is useful: More thorough analysis can lead to a greater payoff. Figure 13-4 shows that the time to transfer takes too long, so most managers don't want to wait for an internal person to fill their opening. If the team studying the problem would have followed its initial opinion of increasing the formal development planning for employees, would the payoff have been there? Would the problem be solved?

Scatter Diagrams

As sometimes happens, some of the reasons for the problem may be related to others. In this example, management discouragement of job bidding was the third most important cause of the problem. The improvement team wondered if a relationship existed between the numbers of employees who bid for jobs and the frequency of management discouragement. The team felt that improving transfer time would need management support, and if the culture of the company was to discourage internal hires, the team might need to work on both increasing management support and the number of employees bidding. The scatter diagram depicted in Figure 13-5 shows a real possibility of a relationship between management discouragement and the number of people bid-

(Text continues on page 228)

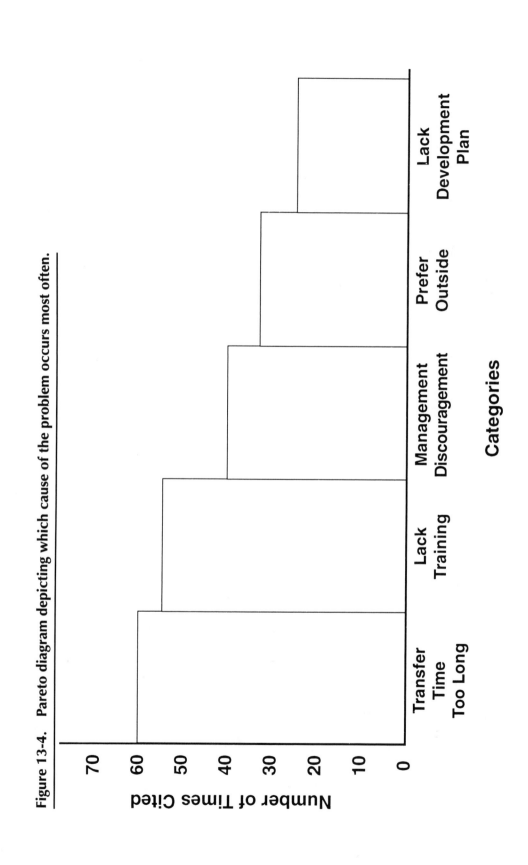

Figure 13-4. Pareto diagram depicting which cause of the problem occurs most often.

Figure 13-5. Scatter diagram depicting correlation between management discouragement and number bidding for jobs.

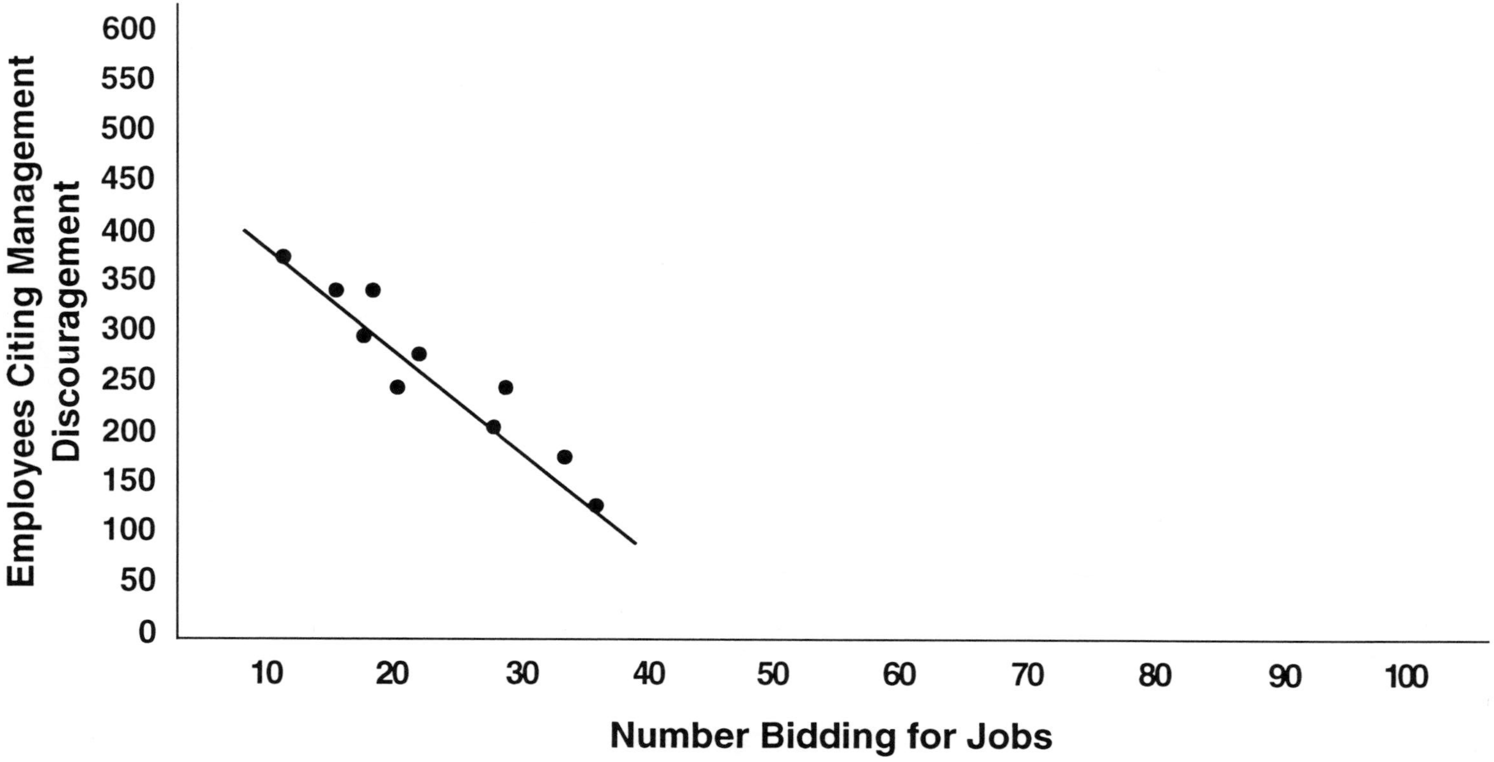

ding. To the team, this meant that there was also a possible tie-in with transfers taking too long. They decided this warranted further research.

Run Charts

Run charts are the most commonly used of the seven basic quality tools. They are used for showing trends and are simple to create. Time is illustrated on the Y axis and frequency is charted on the X axis. In our example, the improvement team wanted to analyze the history of internal hires as it prepared to make its recommendations to management. It was important to the team to know what the rate of internal hires had been over time. They developed a run chart that they believed reflected the approximate internal hire ratio over time. Figure 13-6 shows the team's findings.

Case Study Synopsis

This team determined that a lack of developed employees was not the primary cause that needed attention. They recommended that the organization reduce transfer time on internal hires by establishing a policy of giving two weeks' notice before an employee left his/her current position for a new one.

As evidenced in the case above, the basic statistical tools do help white collar teams to better analyze a process they are improving. The team in this example used five of the seven basic tools; this is typical of many teams' work. Use of the tools shows that much thought and many facts went into the team's recommendation. It is easy to see why management listens to the findings of improvement teams.

Further knowledge of statistical tools could have helped this team even more. For example, using statistical process control would have told the team that the internal recruitment process was stable and that any improvement would need management support in addressing common causes that kept the system from improving. The run chart in Figure 13-6 is further refined into a control chart in the following section.

Other Basic Statistical Tools: HR Applications

The other statistical tools are the histogram and the control chart.

Histograms

HR professionals are familiar with the concept of the bell curve because of its link with performance rating distribution expectations. His-

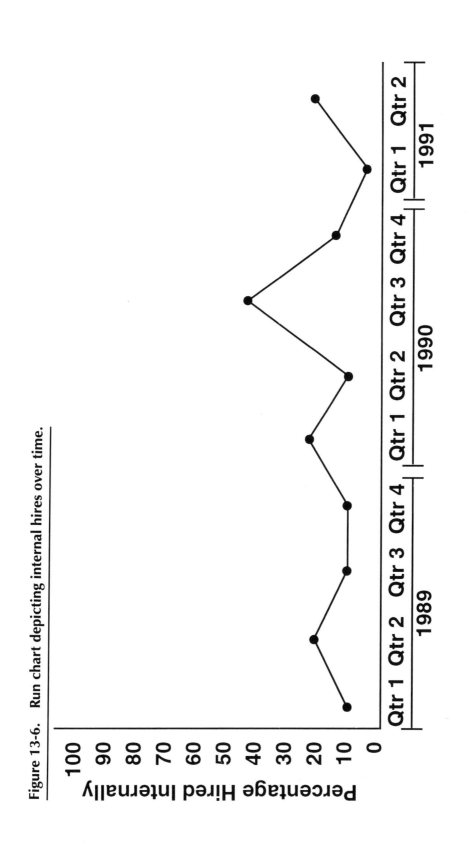

Figure 13-6. Run chart depicting internal hires over time.

tograms show whether a normal distribution from the mean exists, and if not, what the variance might imply. The histogram shown in Figure 13-7 reflects the percentage of nonexempt jobs filled within certain categories (number of days). Thsi tool shows that 26 percent of nonexempt jobs take seventeen to twenty days to fill, with most taking fewer days than that. Using data such as these can assist employment professionals in setting performance standards based on fact, in setting realistic customer expectations, etc.

Control Charts

Control charts incorporate information from both run charts and histograms. They are used to show whether the process depicted is stable and predictable and can aid in determining both common and special causes of variation. In Figure 13-8, there is only one quarter where a special cause was the reason for fluctuation in the normal trend. Special causes can often be solved by the workers themselves, but in some cases, management may need to be involved. Workers generally know when to call in management's help with special causes. For example, in the case study, if recruiters needed to be redeployed to respond to the demand, employees would have cleared that with management if other priorities would be affected. If recruitment load was light and the team somewhat self-directing, team members may just have pitched in to meet increased demand on their own.

It is in the case of common causes of variation, which are process-related, that management must be involved because approval will be needed to change some part of the process itself. In either scenario, having data such as these to use helps both managers and workers to understand when their process is in control and when it is not.

Conclusion

This chapter offers solid evidence that quantifying the HR function and its various activities and improvement efforts is not only doable, but worth doing. But more effective than any other evidence is knowing others who have stretched beyond the norm in developing their own capabilities. There is nothing like a true story to pique interest. In the human resources field, there are many stories told regularly at conferences and in professional publications.

This book cannot end without providing some names of companies that are known to have exceptional HR functions. Comparing with the best is always sound practice. There are many exceptional HR functions

Figure 13-7. Histogram depicting percentage of nonexempt jobs filled within a certain number of days.

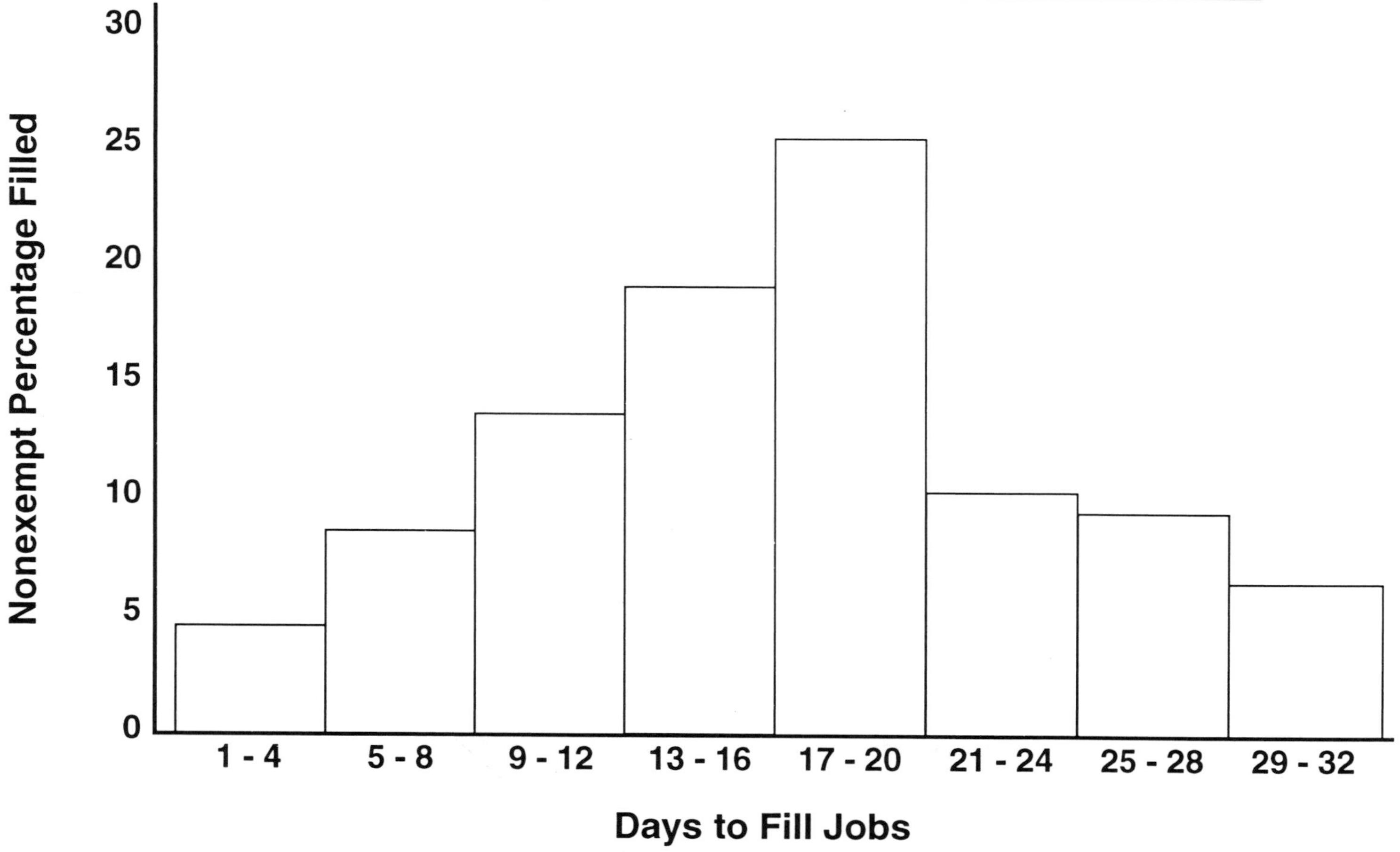

Figure 13-8. Control chart depicting variations in internal hire percentage over time.

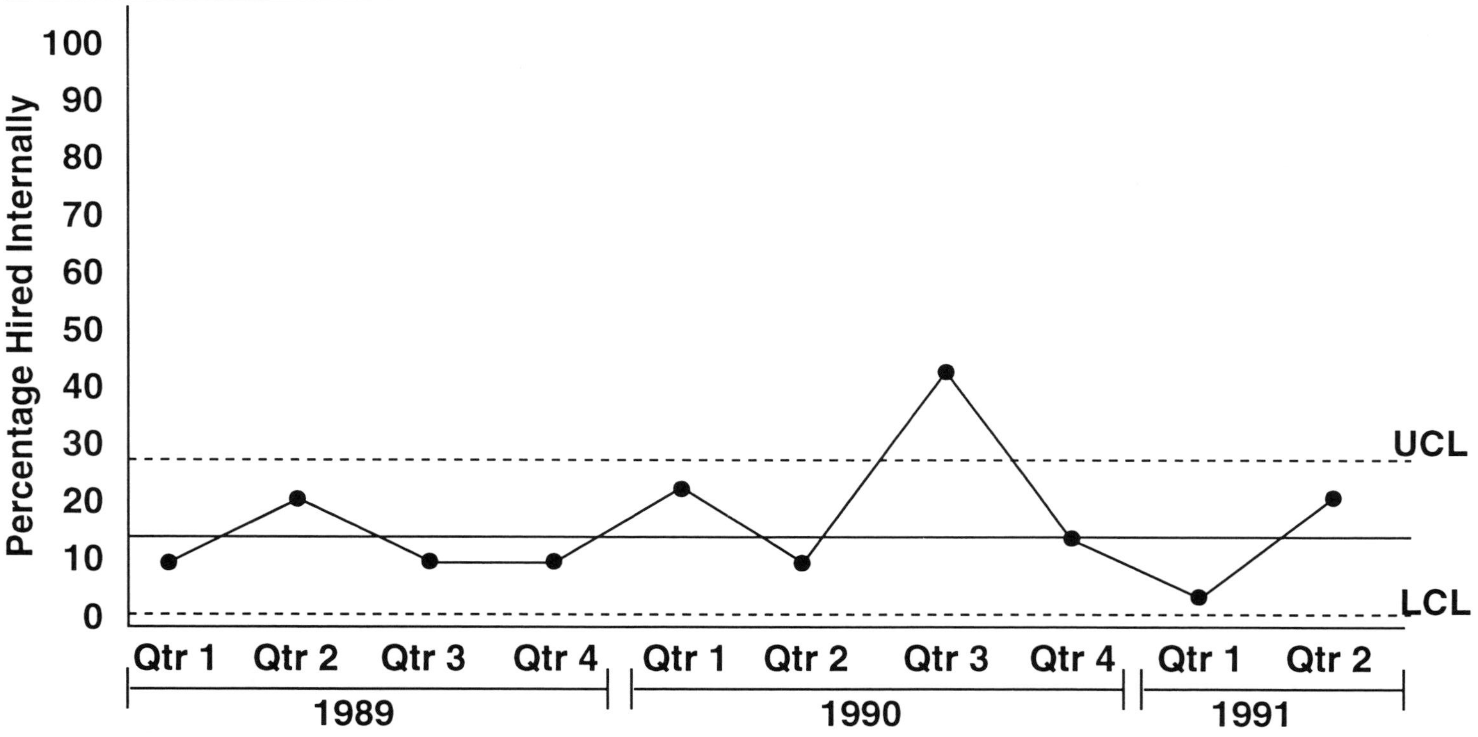

the United States. All of the Malcolm Baldrige National Quality Award winners are a good place to start. Early winners like Milliken & Company, the southeastern carpet manufacturer, and Motorola, the worldwide electronics company, are excellent role models. On the service side, Federal Express and USAA are highly regarded. But excellence in human resources can be found in large and small, successful and not so successful, organizations across the country. There are many exceptional professionals who do well without being in a Baldrige-winning company.

Chapter 14, the final chapter of this book, helps HR professionals look forward to new heights of excellence by citing several of the more recent winners of excellence awards in the profession. It cannot possibly contain the names of all companies that have been cited for quality-related excellence in HR; there are just too many. Instead, the chapter tries to relate the stories of winning HR departments that are working with many of the arenas discussed in this book. Yet there is excellence found in all HR specialties. Whatever arena of human resources you work in, the effort to quantify where you are currently and improve from that baseline is value-added activity.

Measuring current effectiveness and benchmarking with the best will take time if your HR function is starting at the beginning, but being able to show evidence of the function's worth to the organization and to offer better information and service to management and employees than ever before are powerful reasons. Continuously improving inside the function will not only go a long way toward higher levels of customer satisfaction, but it will also increase the likelihood of HR being seen as a leadership role model to follow.

Chapter 14

Looking Forward:
Best Practices

In the early chapters of this book, four arenas of human resources involvement were assessed as necessary for TQM success based on the review of over 100 case studies on quality efforts. These four arenas—compensation, employee recognition, employee involvement, and training—are only the beginning for HR professionals. As TQM becomes better understood at a practical level, more arenas will involve the HR staff. Many functional or programmatic areas are being affected by TQM. The majority of these were addressed in the rest of the book. Perhaps more important, the strategic role of human resources is becoming more understood. I have tried to paint a picture of human resources as it moves into the future and have given state-of-the-art guidelines and success stories in order to assist HR professionals in preparing for this future, regardless of the role they play.

As more and more HR executives move the function to the strategic level of the organization once and for all, major initiatives like Total Quality will become their realm whether they champion the effort or not. HR must be prepared to respond. It is my strong and persistent belief that TQM is part of the solution for America's faltering economy and competitive stance in the global marketplace. As such, it is the HR function's duty to become immersed in any cultural or technological change that will assist the nation in continuing its leadership role. HR has often been the conscience of the organization, and TQM is the right thing to do. It is mandatory for the nation's growth and survival.

On a more global scale, the days when businesses operated within the boundaries of a self-contained national economy are gone. Foreign trade agreements may help us evolve toward a truly global community, not economy—where collaboration for humanity is a prime, driving value. HR executives will be a force in these changing values, just as they focus today on pressing issues brought forth by diversity or demographics or worker values. They *must* find ample room for assuming major responsibility for strategic imperatives such as TQM or the evolving global community.

In addition, as companies continue their experimentation with TQM, HR executives must not be swayed by the mixed messages in the press, some that forewarn of TQM's premature death. Instead, HR leaders must help top management and employees—their major customers—to follow through on their initial commitment to quality and continuous improvement.

HR professionals must exemplify commitment to the customer in their own organizations. They must work to reverse negative polls such as the one conducted in 1990 by Gallup and the American Society for Quality Control. In it, 55 percent of respondents said their company states it is committed to quality, but only 36 percent said their company follows through (with similar results to questions about quality as a priority, support for high-quality products and services, and trust in employees to make good decisions about quality).[1] HR professionals must not succumb to the cynics because HR executives understand large-scale change better than many of their counterparts. There is no more time for complacency on the part of people who care about the effectiveness of their organization and its people.

Yet with results like those highlighted above, how can you address "improving quality," what the August 1992 *HRMagazine* showed as *the* top HR priority for 1992–93?[2] The answer is partly to increase the rate of your personal development to handle the demands that TQM will make on the HR profession in the future. But the answer is also to take a stand now and become a champion for Total Quality as a new or continuing integral strategy in your organization! No one can move an enterprise like the people responsible for "the people." No one (other than the CEO, of course) can influence direction the way HR can, especially if it is a "best practice" HR function. Developing a world-class HR function is another way to improve quality and model by example for the rest of the enterprise. In closing this book, then, it is important to discuss how some of the most successful HR functions operate. Let's take a look.

Best Practices in Human Resources

Several sources attempt to sort out what the term *best practice* really means to human resources. *Personnel Journal* has begun giving the Optimas awards. They are not given for programmatic excellence, such as benefits plan designs or training programs. Instead, they are given to efforts that show imagination and bold initiative in solving business challenges in areas such as competitive advantage, financial impact, innovation, and managing change. The 1992 winner, Levi Strauss, is and has been a model for human resources for many years, and recent business journals have highlighted the company's top management for visionary initiatives involving its people.[3]

Another noted publication, *Human Resource Executive*, issued a special report in 1992 called "Benchmarking HR: Measuring Up to the Leaders." The criteria they used to judge best practices are:

1. Ability to support the overall needs of the business
2. Creative and innovative approach
3. Application of quality management principles
4. Ability to enhance the relationship between the employee and the company[4]

Five winners were selected in each of seven categories: (1) work and family, (2) work force diversity, (3) health, (4) relocation, (5) recruitment, (6) training and development, and (7) pay for performance. The last three reflect some of the key arenas described in this book. Highlights of winners focusing on quality-related business initiatives follow:

Recruitment

DIAMOND STAR MOTORS: NORMAL, ILLINOIS. Diamond Star began to identify the need for high-quality, team-oriented staff in 1985 when it started a plant using Japanese work concepts. A five-stage screening process was developed using third-party assistance to locate the type of people who would fit the new workplace environment. The result was a stable and motivated work force, successfully operating in a team-based system.

Training and Development

Four companies were identified as having best-practice training and development efforts related to quality and customer service. The fifth winner, Walt Disney, was cited for an innovative program that was not related to quality and customer service initiatives, but Disney's record in that realm stood the test of time long before 1992. Here are brief descriptions of the other winners:

FEDERAL EXPRESS: MEMPHIS. Training reinforces both the company culture and Total Quality objectives. Managers are required to take two courses, Quality Advantage, and Quality Action Teams; several other courses relating to quality principles are also offered. The company's 90,000 employees go through an average of forty hours of training per year in areas like technical skills and customer service. New employees have extensive initial training, e.g., a new customer service agent may attend up to six weeks of training before even picking up a telephone. Programs are also used to communicate the company's philosophy on quality and familiarize employees with service quality indicators used to measure performance on a daily basis.

MOTOROLA: SCHAUMBURG, ILLINOIS. Motorola has been noted for some time as a leader in training and development and even has its own "university" that offers classes to employees, customers, and suppliers. All 103,000 employees receive five days of training a year. Training is geared to the needs of the people at different levels and at different places in the organization. Strategic sessions are held with executives to outline current worldwide business initiatives, and various sectors of the company customize training to their own business needs. For example, the government electronics sector is currently working toward improving its teams' understanding of sociotechnical design.

USAA: SAN ANTONIO. Customer service is seen as a competitive weapon in this financial institution, and frontline employees go through ten weeks of training before working with the public. Some training is nuts and bolts, but each employee's training plan is self-led based on his/ her needs. Empowerment is a current focus for managers, who learn how to move more decision making to the front line.

BC TELEPHONE: VANCOUVER, BRITISH COLUMBIA. In a newly competitive environment, managers are being trained in skills that were never a priority before. Responsiveness and empowerment are current topics emphasized by this ex-monopoly as the pyramid has been turned upside down and the customer placed at the top. BC Telephone has also developed a new selection process for its managers in the new environment; while not specifically cited for excellence, it might also be worth benchmarking.

Pay for Performance

In the area of pay for performance, three of the five winners cited productivity and quality business objectives as driving forces in forging new compensation programs. They are:

HERMAN MILLER: ZEELAND, MICHIGAN. This is not the first time that Herman Miller, an office furniture manufacturer, has been showcased for excellence in quality initiatives, implying that its HR practices have supported its business objectives for some time. As long ago as 1950, this company was using gain sharing as a means to link pay to performance. Bonuses are tied to several different criteria, among them customer service and product quality indicators and savings realized from employee suggestions. (Seeking continual cost savings is a way of life at Herman Miller.) Its program does not pay out to individuals, but rather to the entire organization by a predetermined formula in order to support the principle that it usually takes a team to implement a suggestion from start to finish.

C & S WHOLESALE GROCERS: BRATTLEBORO, VERMONT. The self-managed work team environment has caused this wholesaler to reduce product damage by 50 percent, and productivity averages stand at twice the industry average as a result of new pay programs. These program payouts are based on productivity and quality of the work team's efforts. Of the 1,000 employees, seventy-five percent are paid on an incentive basis that corresponds to standards set by the employees themselves.

CHARLES SCHWAB & COMPANY: SAN FRANCISCO. Simply put, quality of customer service is the main criteria for both managers and representatives based on internal and external customer feedback. The pay-for-performance program is driven by the belief that organizational results and the rewards of the top performers are critically linked to sustainable long-term advantage.[5]

Saratoga Institute Best Practices

One of the more renowned organizations that have been measuring best practices in HR for several years is the Saratoga Institute. In 1991, it cited nine characteristics that are common threads in the tapestry of the exceptional HR function. None have to do with technical excellence because that is expected of all companies. Instead, they have to do with values such as "to be the drivers of change, to excel, to have vision, to have extensive personal relationships, and to have business reasons for the persuasive case presented." These values and beliefs are what motivate the best HR departments or functions to practice their field differently from the norm. The nine best practices are:

1. *Communications.* Going to great lengths to communicate with the work force and putting significant effort into stimulating and supporting upward communications characterize world-class HR organizations. Ingenuity in methods was found, but the key to best-practice HR functions' communications was the effort made to make communications a daily, primary duty of the entire staff.

2. *Interdependence.* Best-practice HR functions realize that the work of one HR area affects the work of others. The territoriality of some human resources groups is counterproductive. In world-class HR functions, there are ongoing and regular formal and informal meetings across the subgroups to review the interdependent effects of one group's work on another.

3. *Strategy and planning.* Best-practice HR departments actually work from a strategy and then prepare operating plans, specific objectives, and actions that lead the HR effort. Evidence and testimony suggest that this unusual capability stems from having a well-considered, clearly articulated, and thoroughly disseminated vision of the role of HR within the enterprise. Strategy is defined broadly to include role, relationships, and contributions to corporate imperatives.

4. *Commitment.* "Staying the course" is common TQM jargon for long-term commitment by top management. Best-practice HR departments are showcases of commitment to a vision of constant improvement. Not bound by methodology, these staffs develop programs and processes that lead to the vision, and the methodologies used depend on what the vision needs to be realized. Flexibility, dynamism, and creativity are part of these HR cultures.

5. *Customer-focused.* All HR departments claim to be customer-focused. All companies do too. But the best-practice HR functions are proactive in their quest to go to their customers and ask what they are trying to achieve. This focus on the customer's objectives is the guiding light for assessing what types of HR problems or opportunities exist. Only in response to this feedback do the best-practice HR staffs return to the customer with recommendations that will assist them. Diagnosing customer needs as they relate to human issues is a way of life.

6. *Never satisfied.* We often hear that customers are never satisfied and that once a need is filled, there is always another need or want. That is what "the customer as a moving target" means. So, too, with best-practice HR departments. They are never satisfied. Even though the best-practice departments in the Saratoga Institute report were considered in the ninety-fifth percentile of over 500 HR functions studied, none of them were satisfied with their results! No matter what exceptional results were achieved, they had an idea or plan to make it better.

7. *Risk taking.* Total reorganizations, restructuring of job descriptions and titles, dropping of services, and reallocating resources to more value-added products are all examples of things best-practice HR groups have done. While these types of actions are generally risky, world-class organizations are willing to experiment to be the best.

8. *Culture consciousness.* Best-practice people believe that culture is critical in designing systems that one hopes will change behaviors. It goes something like this: Culture drives systems, systems drive behavior, behavior drives results. This is not meant to imply that cultures do not change. Rather, it implies that congruence with the culture is important, and the HR professional's role is to support some aspects of the culture as well as help change it where necessary.

9. *Relationships.* Best-practice people described over and over how they had worked with key individuals to obtain their support. They acknowledged that all the technical human resources knowledge in the world would not have made the difference. The key to success was the relations built and traded upon when needed.[6]

The 1992 Saratoga Institute winners of general excellence were not yet named at the time of this writing, but Barbara Jack, Saratoga's manager of information services, shared new trends that were inching their way to the forefront in the current best-practices research. These include:

• *Optimizing HRIS systems.* Useful information is now being provided, not just data. For example, total costs for an HR category, such as total compensation, can be provided on an ongoing basis by best-practice HR information systems functions.

• *Giving ownership to line management.* There is an emerging trend that may lead to a best-practice category of true partnership with the line. For example, some companies now have safety and workers compensation training and cost monitoring as a line responsibility. Another example is transitioning ownership (i.e., responsibility) for scheduling nurses to the line when mandated HR policies did not work.

• *Increasing priority of internal placement.* Innovative methods of increasing communications and encouragement for internal bidding for jobs is an emerging trend. E-mail, voice mail, and job hot lines now supplement the job posting bulletin board in best-practice organizations.

• *Adding value for employees.* Best-practice HR departments are distributing detailed statements of benefits to employees, not just with health care information, but with even 401(k) data. This increasing education is not only valued by the employee customer, but it is also reducing costs to the organization because employees' increased understanding leads to increased carefulness in their use of benefits.

Depending on the criteria used, there are many examples of human resources excellence. Over the next few years, new critical factors will obviously be sorting themselves out. For the time being, it is good to know that there are many arenas of HR excellence in many industries of many sizes. This synopsis of several best-practice sources is meant to share the increasing interest in identifying the benchmarks in human resources as professionals attempt to improve their own services across the country. They offer concrete examples of those who are leading the way and pique the imagination of those who are never satisfied.

Why Care About Best Practices?

This may seem like one of those "dumb" questions. But in TQM, no question is a dumb question, and neither is this one. If the HR team is not influential, none of the knowledge put forth in this book can help the HR Total Quality champion to succeed in continuing to expand his/her current effort to create the support necessary for having TQM become a corporate strategic imperative. Citing characteristics of best-practice HR functions can provide keys to help unlock the doors of power and influence to aid in following the roadmap of Total Quality organizational change.

These descriptions are also provided to assist HR executives and their staffs in building a continuously improving vision of the future of HR in their companies. However, in order to truly develop toward world-class levels, more research must be conducted globally. In 1992, Randall S. Schuler of New York University began to study the situation globally. Schuler says that the highest-ranking HR goals globally are:

1. Productivity/quality/customer satisfaction
2. Linkage of HR to the business
3. Attraction/retention[7]

Schuler addresses these challenges specifically by outlining the activities and practices of the globally competitive, world-class human resources function. They are:

1. Ensuring that HR is aligned with the needs of the business through human resources planning
2. Preparing to ensure future work force capability through training and development
3. Managing current productivity through quality and innovation, performance management, and compensation
4. Managing employee involvement through personnel research and communications

5. Managing quality of work life issues through EEO, work/family, and diversity programs
6. Managing relationships with external constituencies through customers and suppliers[8]

Robert Galvin, former CEO of Motorola and champion of HR as a strategic player, has said time and time again in many ways that "the HR manager and department is being offered the opportunity to be transformed from a functional, specialist department to a management team member who will be called upon to think and act like line managers to address people-related business issues as they relate to competitive advantage."[9]

In order to provide a final motivation for HR professionals, the following "best case scenario" may instill a concrete, tangible picture of HR as a Total Quality champion in a world-class organization.

The Class One Corporation: HR Leads the Way

In a little town called Uplifting, Washington, the Class One Corporation is the bulwark of the community. For more than 100 years, the principles of its founders, George and Mabel Visionary, have pervaded the organization's culture, and employees cannot say enough about these two people. Their overarching principle, "People Make the Quality Difference," has served the company well.

H. R. Motivation is the Visionarys' daughter. Her value system and desire to excel matches her parents'. H. R., who recently retired, began her career by setting out to develop the best human resources function in the world. As the company grew, she kept pace with the leading HR practices in corporate America. As she neared retirement, she sent her protégé, I.M. International, to Germany, Sweden, Japan, and beyond to harness the best from what H. R. considered at that time to be upcoming nations. By then, Class One had long established itself as a world leader in industry. When H. R.'s retirement arrived, she looked with pride at her legacy—a thriving business with an HR function second to none. "People Make the Quality Difference" was standing the test of time. With her retirement, I. M. International replaced H. R. on the board of directors.

Bob Peoples was the head of HR and one of those being groomed for the presidency of Class One. HR staff members sat on all major strategy teams and were integral players in the company's operations, often wielding influence well beyond their actual authority.

Total Quality had not even been heard of when the Visionarys started Class One, but Total Quality was a way of life for them. By the time their daughter, H. R., retired, the company had been a mature, self-directing organization for years. There were no barriers to communications, and everyone accepted their interdependence on everyone else in the enterprise. Although the company had grown tremendously, it still felt like a family, and a strong sense of purpose lingered in the halls.

Outsiders were amazed at how knowledgeable every employee was about the current business strategy and how clearly aligned all areas of the company were with the vision. People were open to change and felt secure in Class One's future no matter what competitive challenges they faced.

The human resources systems were constantly being improved, just like the products and services, and employees were intimately involved in all improvement processes. All employees owned stock in the company, and financial reports were commonly seen at various workplaces.

While there were other organizations in town, most of the residents of Uplifting wanted to be hired by Class One. In fact, Class One was often contacted by outsiders because of its reputation as a great place to work. Sometimes, one or another lucky person was added to the team at Class One, since diversity and fresh ideas were respected and rewarded. Turnover was historically less than 5 percent, so most vacancies were a result of growing needs.

Continuous learning was also a way of life at Class One, and employees with years of tenure often had held various responsibilities depending on their own and the organization's needs at the time. Individual career development had been a part of the human resources strategy from the onset of H. R.'s days, since she believed the future and the growth of Class One and its people were related. The strategy behind any recruitment effort was to hire the best for today and tomorrow, instilling the criterion of individual long-term potential in every hiring decision.

There had never been a formal appraisal system in place at Class One. People were always giving everyone positive feedback about their performance. The view on positive feedback at Class One was "any praise that can be showered should be, and any constructive advice should be viewed as a gift and an indication that someone else cares about you." The compensation strategy had always been to pay for the skills and experience of the people, to pay slightly above the rest of the local market, and to share the profits of the company with the employees on a quarterly basis. Stock was often a bonus for special performance at any level. It is rumored that there are some wealthy technicians and laborers, not just wealthy managers, at Class One.

In fact, there are no real titles in the organization. Those who need to assume a title for some external purpose usually put the word "leader" in it, since all people lead the way in their jobs at this company, taking responsibility and accountability for the success of their deliverable, whatever it is. Power is defined as empowerment of all and seen as an ever-expanding concentric circle with the vision of the organization in the center.

The Future Is What You Make It

As we look into the future, it may seem strange to consider this fantasy a potential reality. But it is. Those HR professionals who have the especially fortunate opportunity to work in young, fledgling companies could create a workplace of the future like Class One's. Maybe the scenario I imagine might actually be in place somewhere *today*. Whether it is or not does not mean that it can't be, and many of the principles of Total Quality would support a place like Class One.

Total Quality Management is not likely the answer in itself. But it is a solid road on the highway of change that should be traveled by most organizations in the United States. It is the beginning of tomorrow for many companies that need something of major proportion to revitalize and transform their organizations. Revitalization and transformation are powerful concepts. TQM is the reflection of these concepts in action. Can there be any better driving force for human resources professionals than to revitalize and transform the potential of the people and their organization? I think not. Hopefully, this book has cemented your resolve and given you a banner to uphold.

The human resources profession has a history it can be very proud of. It also has a boundless future. TQM is the human resources imperative of today. Maybe the Class One Corporation is the vision of tomorrow.

Notes

Chapter 1

1. Stephenie Overman, "Engineering HR at TRW," *HRMagazine*, August 1992, p. 68.
2. "Motorola Chief: Tap World Markets," *The Arizona Republic*, February 5, 1993, p. E1.
3. "The Value of Implementing Quality," *Quality Progress*, July 1991, pp. 70–71.
4. Edward E. Lawler III, Gerald E. Ledford, Jr., and Susan Albers Mohrman, *Employee Involvement in America: A Study of Contemporary Practice* (Houston: American Productivity & Quality Center, 1989), p. 14.

Chapter 2

1. "What Motivates Center Members?" *APQC Consensus* 1, no. 4, July 1988, p. 1.
2. *The First National Bank of Chicago: Pleasing Customers by Banking on Quality*, Case Study 77 (Houston: American Productivity & Quality Center, August 1990), pp. 5–6.
3. "McDonald's McMotivates Employees," *APQC Letter* 8, no. 5, November 1988, pp. 2, 7.

Chapter 3

1. Edward E. Lawler III, Gerald E. Ledford, Jr., and Susan Albers Mohrman, *Employee Involvement in America: A Study of Contemporary Practice* (Houston: American Productivity & Quality Center, 1989), pp. 12–14.
2. Richard J. Schonberger, *Building a Chain of Customers* (New York: The Free Press, 1990), p. 232.
3. "Roger Milliken Outlines Baldrige-Winning Philosophy," *APQC Letter* 10, no. 6, December 1990, p. 6.
4. *The First National Bank of Chicago: Pleasing Customers by Banking on Quality*, Case Study 77 (Houston: American Productivity & Quality Center, August 1990), pp. 4–5.
5. *Be Bold and Be Right: The Wallace Co., Inc. Wins 1990 Baldrige Award*, Case

Study 80 (Houston: American Productivity & Quality Center, February 1991), pp. 2–3.

6. James R. Houghton, *Leadership and Total Quality* (New York: The Conference Board, 1990), pp. 21–23.

7. "Training, Gain Sharing, Teams Produce Quality Results at Vickers," *APQC Letter* 10, no. 5, November 1990, pp. 1, 7.

8. Ira Moskowitz, "The Human Factor: Keeping Teams on Track," paper presented at Super Teams Conference (Denver: Manufacturing Institute of the Institute for International Research, January 1991).

9. "Self-Managed Work Teams Score for Insurance Company," *National Productivity Report* 19, no. 2, January 1990, pp. 1–3.

10. Richard C. Wagner, "Shenandoah Life Insurance Company: Improving Productivity and Service Through Self-Managed Work Teams," *Quality and Productivity Management* 7, no. 3, 1989, pp. 33–35.

11. Gaye E. Gilbert, *Framework for Success: Sociotechnical Systems at Lake Superior Paper Industries*. Case Study 71 (Houston: American Productivity & Quality Center, July 1989), pp. 1–2.

12. Ibid., p. 3.

Chapter 4

1. "What Motivates Center Members?" *APQC Consensus* 1, no. 4, July 1988, pp. 1–2.

2. Bonnie Donovan, *Rx: Ownership + Involvement + Incentives: It's Keeping Katy Medical Center and Its Parent Well*, Case Study 74 (Houston: American Productivity & Quality Center, March 1990), pp. 6–7.

3. " 'Baybankers' Are Motivated to Superior Service," *APQC Letter* 8, no. 5, November 1988, p. 4.

4. "Training, Gain Sharing, Teams Produce Quality Results at Vickers," *APQC Letter* 10, no. 5, November 1990, p. 7.

5. Ibid.

Chapter 6

1. Carla O'Dell, *People, Performance, and Pay* (Houston: American Productivity & Quality Center and American Compensation Association, 1987), p. 8.

2. Ibid., pp. 13–14.

3. *Variable Pay: New Performance Rewards* (New York: The Conference Board, 1990), p. 6.

4. Jerry L. McAdams and Elizabeth J. Hawk, *Summary Report: Capitalizing on Human Assets* (Scottsdale, Ariz.: American Compensation Association, 1992), pp. 8–14.

5. William E. Buhl, "Incentives for Nonexempt Employees: Keep Them Simple," *APQC Manager's Notebook Series* 4, no. 6, 1988, pp. 1–5.

6. *The Lincoln Electric Company*, Case Study 48 (Houston: American Productivity & Quality Center, October 1985), pp. 1–4.
7. *Variable Pay*, p. 9.
8. Ibid., p. 11.
9. Timothy L. Ross and Ruth Ann Ross, "Productivity Gainsharing: Resolving Some of the Measurement Issues," *National Productivity Review* 3, no. 4, Autumn 1984, p. 384.
10. John G. Belcher, *Reward Systems: Time for Change*, Brief 74 (Houston: American Productivity & Quality Center, November 1989), pp. 7–8.
11. John G. Belcher, *The Family of Measures*, Brief 85 (Houston: American Productivity & Quality Center, October 1991), p. 2.
12. "Training, Gain Sharing, Teams Produce Quality Results at Vickers," *AQPC Letter* 10, no. 5, November 1990, p. 6.
13. "St. Luke's Hospital: Gain Sharing in a Not-for-Profit Environment," *The Productivity Letter* 6, no. 7, January 1987, pp. 1, 6–7.
14. *Trans-Matic Manufacturing Company*, Case Study 19 (Houston: American Productivity & Quality Center, 1980), pp. 1–5.
15. *McDonnell Douglas Electronics: Gain Sharing Just One Road to the Future of St. Charles, Missouri, Firm*, Case Study 57 (Houston: American Productivity & Quality Center, April 1987), pp. 3–5.
16. Richard L. Bunning, "Skill-Based Pay: Restoring Incentives to the Workplace," *Personnel Administrator*, June 1989, pp. 67–70.

Chapter 7

1. Gordon Lippitt and Ronald Lippitt, *The Consulting Process in Action*, 2nd ed. (San Diego: Pfeiffer & Company, 1986), pp. 170–172. Used with permission.
2. Peter Block, *Flawless Consulting: A Guide to Getting Your Expertise Used* (San Diego: University Associates, 1981), p. 23.
3. Ibid., pp. 46–52.
4. Lippitt and Lippitt, *The Consulting Process*, pp. 12–35.

Chapter 8

1. Stephen Carroll and Craig Schneier, *Performance Appraisal and Review Systems: The Identification, Measurement and Development of Performance in Organizations* (Glenview, Ill.: Scott, Foresman, 1982), p. 54.
2. Mark R. Edwards and Ann Ewen, *Leadership Development with Multi-source 360 Degree Feedback* (Tempe, Ariz.: TEAMS, 1993), p. 3.
3. Mark R. Edwards, "Innovations in HRD Information: Building Effective and Legally Safeguarded Systems that Work for Career Development," paper presented at Performance Appraisal and Talent Assessment Workshop (Phoenix: TEAMS, May 1987).

4. Peter R. Scholtes, *An Elaboration on Deming's Teachings on Performance Appraisal* (Madison, Wis.: Joiner Associates, 1987), pp. 1–13.

5. Ibid., p. 16.

6. Thomas A. Kochan and Paul Osterman, "Human Resource Development and Utilization: Is There Too Little in the U.S.?" (Boston: Massachusetts Institute of Technology, Sloan School of Management, February 1991), p. 67.

7. C. Jackson Grayson, "Selected Comparative Data" (Houston: American Productivity & Quality Center, October 9, 1992), pp. 11, 100.

8. Norman Sklarewitz, "Rewarding for Quality?" *Human Resource Executive*, April 1992, p. 40.

Chapter 9

1. Gaye E. Gilbert, *Framework for Success: Sociotechnical Systems at Lake Superior Paper Industries*, Case Study 11 (Houston: American Productivity & Quality Center, July 1989), p. 2.

2. Patricia Aburdene and John Naisbitt, *Megatrends for Women* (New York: Villard Books, 1992), p. 90.

3. Beverly L. Kaye, *Up Is Not the Only Way* (Englewood Cliffs, N.J.: Prentice-Hall, 1982), p. 2.

4. Ibid., pp. 6–12.

Chapter 10

1. D. J. Paternoster, "Getting Started," paper presented at Communicating Quality Conference (Baltimore: International Association of Business Communicators, American Productivity & Quality Center, Maryland Center for Quality and Productivity, 1991).

2. Vin Hoey, "Communicating Globally," paper presented at Communicating Quality Symposium (Denver: International Association of Business Communicators, American Productivity & Quality Center, 1992).

3. Cathy Clark, "Fitting In—Integrated Quality Communications," paper presented at Communicating Quality Conference (Baltimore: International Association of Business Communicators, American Productivity & Quality Center, Maryland Center for Quality and Productivity, 1991).

4. "Texas Instruments' Internal Communications Reinforces Quality Message," *APQC Letter* 11, no. 12, August 1991, p. 2.

5. Clark, "Fitting In."

6. Ed Robertson, "Measurement: Doing Right Things Right," paper presented at Communicating Quality Symposium (Denver: International Association of Business Communicators, American Productivity & Quality Center, 1992).

7. Ibid.

Chapter 11

1. Karen Lambourne et al., *Guidelines for Implementing Labor-Management Problem Solving Teams in Manufacturing* (Ann Arbor, Mich.: Industrial Technology Institute, 1992), pp. 38–40.
2. Bob Ralston, Dearld Tibbe, and Hans E. Picard, "Implementation of a Joint Union-Management Work Measurement/Problem Solving Program in Electric Power Generation Maintenance at J. M. Stuart Station, Dayton Power and Light Company," paper presented at Ecology of Work Conference (Cincinnati: June 1989).
3. Bob Landsman, "Labor-Management Cooperation: 1989 State-of-the-Art Symposium" (Washington, D.C.: U.S. Department of Labor, Bureau of Labor-Management Relations and Cooperative Programs, 1989), p. 8.
4. David R. Reece and Carla C. Carter, "Total Participation: The Bridge to Total Quality," paper presented at Association for Quality and Participation National Conference (Seattle: 1992).
5. "Cadillac—The Quality Story," paper presented at Customer Satisfaction and Quality Measurement Conference (New York: American Management Association, American Society for Quality Control, 1992).
6. Landsman, "Labor-Management Cooperation," p. 6.
7. John Persico, Jr., Betty L. Bednarczyk, and David P. Negus, "Three Routes to the Same Destination: TQM," *Quality Progress*, January 1990, p. 30.

Chapter 13

1. Jac Fitz-enz, *Human Value Management* (San Francisco: Jossey-Bass, 1991), pp. 4–7.
2. Jac Fitz-enz, *How to Measure Human Resources Management* (New York: McGraw-Hill, 1984), p. 38.
3. Ibid., p. 125.
4. Fitz-enz, *Human Value Management*, p. 331.
5. Carla C. Carter, "Seven Basic Quality Tools," *HRMagazine*, January 1992, pp. 81–83.

Chapter 14

1. "Gallup/ASQC Poll Finds More Talk than Action on Quality," *APQC Letter* 10, no. 6, December 1990, p. 7.
2. Ceel Pasternak, "Editorial Column," *HRMagazine*, August 1992, p. 27.
3. Jennifer Laabs, "Optimas Winners Chart New Frontiers in HR," *Personnel Journal*, January 1993, pp. 50–51.
4. David Shadovitz, "Benchmarking HR: Measuring Up to the Leaders," *Human Resource Executive*, June 1992, p. 23.

5. Ibid., pp. 26–34.
6. *1991 Best Practices Report* (Saratoga, Calif.: Saratoga Institute, 1991), pp. 6–16.
7. Randall S. Schuler, "World Class HR Departments: Six Critical Issues, report prepared for IBM (New York: New York University, 1992), p. 14.
8. Ibid., pp. 111–112.
9. Ibid., p. 45.

Index